11/02

The Lazarus Case

The Lazarus Case

Life-and-Death Issues in
Neonatal Intensive Care

JOHN D. LANTOS, M.D.

The Johns Hopkins University Press
BALTIMORE AND LONDON

The Johns Hopkins University Press
2715 North Charles Street
Baltimore, Maryland 21218-4363
www.press.jhu.edu

Library of Congress Cataloging-in-Publication Data
Lantos, John D.
The Lazarus case : life-and-death issues in neonatal intensive
care / John D. Lantos.
p.   cm. — (Medicine and culture)
Includes bibliographical references and index.
ISBN 0-8018-6762-2 (hardcover : alk. paper)
1. Neonatal intensive care—Moral and ethical aspects.
2. Physicians—Malpractice.
[DNLM: 1. Intensive Care, Neonatal—legislation &
jurisprudence—United States. 2. Ethics, Medical—United States.
3. Life Support Care—legislation & jurisprudence—United
States. 4. Malpractice—United States.   WS 33 AA1 L296t 2001]
I. Title.   II. Medicine & culture.
RJ253.5 .L36 2001
174'.2—dc21   2001001327

A catalog record for this book is available from the
British Library.

For Bill Meadow,
neonatologist, coach, friend,
colleague, companion, mensch

Back of the bread is the flour,
And back of the flour is the mill,
And back of the mill is the wind and the rain
And the Father's will.

—*Methodist hymn*

CONTENTS

I can remember watching a birth for the first time, as a medical student. The woman was moaning, panting, screaming with pain. We could see the head appear at the vaginal opening, looking impossibly large. Then, with one last big scream and push, the impossible happened. I felt, along with everybody in the delivery room, an extraordinary sense of relief, wonder, awe, and gratitude. The cord was cut, and the pink, yowling infant was dried off, wrapped in a blanket, and handed to the mother for a hug.

Each birth is an everyday miracle, the miraculousness of it coming not from its being an event outside of nature but instead from its being so very natural, so very common. Not all births go so smoothly, of course. Every year 53,000 babies are born prematurely in the United States alone. Thirty years ago most of these babies died as a result of the medical complications of prematurity, but today most premature babies survive. Neonatal intensive care is one of the extraordinary success stories of modern medicine.

It has also created ethical dilemmas. Survival rates have improved, but not all survivors do well. Some babies are left with blindness, seizures, chronic lung disease, neurological damage, and other severe chronic ailments. Sometimes decisions have to be made about whether to provide or to withhold medical treatment. Withholding treatment in these circumstances usually means death.

When things go badly, when there is suffering or loss, the human tendency is to look for somebody to blame. In the United States that search for guilt, accountability, punishment, and recompense often takes the form of litigation. Lawsuits are our public morality plays.

This book grew out of my experiences as an expert witness throughout the 1990s in a number of lawsuits involving decisions about the medical care of newborns. As an expert in ethics, I was often asked to determine whether the decisions had been appropriate, ethical, or within the standard of care. My role was always somewhat ambiguous; determining what is legal or illegal is not always the same as determining what is ethical or unethical. The very notion of applying legal standards to ethical judgments raises interesting and complex questions about the proper or necessary relationship between contentious issues of law and morality.

Each of the cases involved a very specific set of facts and circumstances.

Furthermore, in every case the lawyers for each side developed a very specific strategy. The individuals involved in the events that led to each case and those involved in the prosecution were unique; the circumstances of each event were unusual; and the decisions that people made are difficult to reconstruct from memories. Together, these cases describe an area of controversy, namely, decisions made by doctors and parents for critically ill newborns in the delivery room. Each could be the subject of a book.

This book describes a deposition taken in a lawsuit about a decision made for an extremely premature baby. The story presented here represents an idealized paradigmatic case based upon many of the real cases with which I have been involved in the last decade. Thus, what follows is both fact and fiction, real and imagined.

I chose this method to examine the issues that arise in such cases for a number of reasons. First, each of the real cases is peculiar in the ways that real cases are always peculiar. The details are important parts of the cases, but what is important here is the patterns that the cases create. I felt that the patterns and themes might be easier to elucidate in a case that avoided some of these details. Furthermore, the truth about the actual cases is itself unknowable in many ways. The legal system has ways of deciding which facts are pertinent or "admissible" and which are not. Questions must be asked in a certain way. Some answers to those curiously formed questions are impermissible. Questions are asked, and answers given, over and over again in slightly different ways. At the end of all the questioning, uncertainty remains about what really happened or who said what or did what to whom. The "cases" thus become their own sort of fictional reconstruction of events. In addition, many of the cases were settled out of court, and the records sealed, so they are not available for public scrutiny. What we know of these cases and what we are permitted to talk about are thus removed from the facts in multiple ways— by the distortions of memory, by the legal construction of the facts into a "case," by the selective reporting of the facts in the public record, and by the deliberate sealing of that record. Thus, we never know all that we might want to know, though we know many details from many cases.

In certain cases, parents sued doctors or hospitals for resuscitating babies when the parents had requested "no heroic measures." Thus, in *Hospital Corporation of America v Miller,* a case recently decided in the Fourteenth Court of Appeals in Texas, the parents of a tiny premature baby alleged that they had requested nontreatment and that the baby had thus been treated without their consent. Further, they alleged that a policy of "mandatory treatment" for such babies abrogated the parents' right to give informed consent and thus constituted professional negligence in failing to properly seek informed consent. The trial court awarded the parents $50 million. The appeals court overturned this verdict, stating that "parents have no right to refuse urgently-needed life-sustaining medical treatment to their non-terminally ill children" (*Hospital Corporation of America v Miller,* 36 SW 3d 187 [2000]). Similar cases are currently working their way through the courts in Wisconsin and Mississippi. The parents of the baby in the Wisconsin case, Nancy Montalvo and Brian Vila, published an article describing their point of view in the *Journal of Perinatology* in 1999. In these cases the parents did not want treatment to be provided for their babies.

In two other cases the circumstances were closer to those described in this book. The case that bears the closest resemblance is *McDonald v Millville,* which went to trial in Wisconsin. In that case a doctor initiated resuscitation on a tiny "preemie," then discontinued resuscitation, and the baby survived. The case went to trial, and the doctor was found not guilty. In a similar case in Florida, *Hall v Desoto,* doctors attempted to resuscitate a full-term asphyxiated baby, discontinued their resuscitation, and the baby survived.

In each of these cases the baby survived with severe neurological damage. It is clear from these cases that doctors may face litigation whether they decide to treat or to withhold treatment from premature babies. In this book, I have created an "ideal" case that tries to crystallize the relevant issues in the ethics of neonatal intensive care. I do not provide an analysis of the facts, the legal issues, or the conclusions of any of these particular cases. Instead, I see these cases as constituting a sort of cultural locator, an indication of where and how our culture tries to understand and to frame the tough issues raised by the double-edged sword of neonatal intensive care and, by analogy, other innovative medical interventions. I hope this methodology illuminates, rather than obscures, the key issues.

ACKNOWLEDGMENTS

Books gestate over many years and owe their existence to many people. As I worked on this one, I benefited from discussions with many extraordinary people. My colleagues at the MacLean Center for Clinical Medical Ethics at the University of Chicago—Mark Siegler, Lainie Ross, Ann Dudley Goldblatt, Mary Mahowald, Kristina Orfali, Kyle Nash, Camille Renella, Bob Hsuing, and Carol Stocking—are a constant source of intellectual stimulation, emotional support, and delight. Mary Ann and Barry MacLean have faithfully supported the ethics center and encouraged my work there. Kwang Lee, the chief of neonatology at Chicago, has consistently encouraged all manner of inquiry into the difficult issues in neonatology.

Sander Gilman created the Medicine and Culture Workshop at the University of Chicago, where some of this material was originally presented. He encouraged me to pull these ideas together into a book.

William Meadow and I have worked together on the ideas in this book for so long and so collaboratively that I no longer know where his ideas, suggestions, and inspiration end and mine begin.

Joel Frader read an early version of the manuscript and made valuable comments. Lainie Ross offered constant conversation, critique, and insight. Lawrence Gartner and William Silverman, both pioneers in neonatology, gave the manuscript a careful read and corrected errors. Neil Ward, a lifelong friend and a great writer, offered a number of crucial insights and a few wonderful titles. Carl Elliott responded to an early draft with wit and insight. Martha Montello read earlier versions of the manuscript, made many insightful comments, and encouraged me to continue when this approach to these particular problems met with seemingly insurmountable conceptual obstacles. Richard Powers, whose fiction has been an inspiration to me, read a number of chapters and made excellent suggestions. Chris Feudtner, pediatrician, historian, and philosopher, helped sharpen the analysis. Jodi Halpern read, discussed, responded, and encouraged.

Maura Burnett and Joanne Allen, at the Johns Hopkins University Press, helped turn a rough manuscript into a coherent book.

William Stubing and the Greenwall Foundation supported me with two crucial grants, one to examine ethical issues in neonatal intensive care and a second to examine administrative and institutional ethics in an academic medical center. Both grants allowed work on the book to go forward.

Through the Robert Wood Johnson Clinical Scholars Program at the University of Chicago I had the opportunity to present portions of the work to colleagues and postdoctoral fellows. Their feedback has been invaluable.

My wife, Nancy Fritz, read more versions of the manuscript than I can remember and tried hard to keep me focused on the main issues in the book. My children, Hannah, Tess, and Emma, all read versions of chapters; more important, and more enjoyable, they accompanied me on many trips when I presented parts of the work. Their company, love, and energy sustain me.

The Lazarus Case

ONE

Somebody Will Pay

A baby who should have died did not die. Somebody was to blame. Clearly, somebody would have to take responsibility. Certain parties would pay a lot to find out why the baby had survived. They would figure out who was answerable. The culprit would roast.

This being America, there were also those who wanted to prove that nobody was to blame. No, they would argue, this terrible tragedy was not a tragedy, this apparent negligence was nothing like negligence. They would try to convince a judge and jury that such suffering was allocated randomly and chaotically, perhaps even unfairly. Bad things happen to good people all the time for no reason at all, your honor. There isn't a damn thing we can do about it.

Those people had hired me to help them.

An "expert witness," they called me, although I had not witnessed the events in question and did not claim any particular expertise at assigning blame for tragedies.

Well, I could use the money. I would do my best.

The deposition was to take place in the ornate offices of a successful downtown law firm. From the windows I could see the dramatic Chicago skyline. The three tallest buildings bespoke the three pillars of our society: the Sears Tower, temple of retailing, rising like a soaring bar graph above all the rest; the Amoco Building, built on energy, oil, and the antitrust laws that broke up the Rockefeller oil monopoly into competing cartels; and the John Hancock Building—insurance—a monument to our efforts to escape the tyranny of chance. The "premiums" we pay are our offerings against randomness, the regular sacrifices we make at the altar of the god of probabilistic predictability. Perhaps, we tell ourselves, if we make steady, regular offerings, we can truly insure ourselves against tragedy. Our offerings built the John Hancock Building and temples like it at the center of all the business centers in the center of all the great American cities.

Beyond the skyscrapers, I could see the sparkling waters of Lake Michigan, once a highway for iron ore coming to Chicago's booming steel mills. Now most of the mills are closed and the lake is dotted with hundreds of tiny white sails, the sails of pleasure boats, gliding and bobbing on the shimmering water. The sailors probably were not shipping magnates or steel barons but lawyers and doctors and dot-com instant millionaires. Times were pretty good.

I don't particularly like lawyers, but I love their offices. They always have a certain rich feel. The upholstery is lush, and the numbered lithographs on the walls, selected by the decorator at ArtExpo, are sort of modern, a cut above the framed prints one usually finds on the walls of doctors' offices. The big law firms always have their offices on upper floors of tall buildings, as if to suggest that elevation somehow correlates with moral stature, or at least litigious zeal. There seems to be a lot of money in guilt, blame, accountability, and punishment.

Somebody would pay, all right.

I don't often get called to be an expert witness. My area of so-called expertise, pediatric medical ethics, is generally too esoteric to be of much use to these practical men and women. They want people with a recognizable set of technical skills and an expertise based on scientific knowledge—neurologists, neonatologists, anesthesiologists, or radiologists—people who can give them the facts rather than the arcane ramblings of philosophers. But a rare case arises that is so unusual that even lawyers feel compelled to go beyond questions of what is legal or illegal, competent or incompetent, excellent or negligent, and try to figure out what is right or wrong and then assign a price to the wrongness. Such cases make them uneasy. When they arise, it is tough to know just how to play the jury. Our postmodern society chokes on the notion that there might be a "right" or "wrong" beyond the collective consensus of the law or the individual instincts of conscience. After all, who are we to judge? But judge we do, and if one side calls an ethicist to help with the task, the other side damn well better have an ethicist of its own to respond. It's my morals against yours, and may the better man win.

This was just that sort of case. The lawyer who first called me told me that it was a "Lazarus" case. I hadn't heard the term. "You know," he said. "Someone comes back from the dead." It sounded like they might need expertise that went well beyond ethics.

I liked the lawyers for my side. A man and a woman, both sounding earnest, both attractive with an easy television charm that highlighted, for me, the essentially dramatic aspects of litigation. They were, I suppose, on the side of good and right, defending the doctors, who, it seemed to me, had tried to do their best. Or perhaps we were all smugly on the wrong side, defending wealth and power even in the face of a tragedy that those with wealth and power had brought about, though inadvertently, in my opinion.

The lawyers had sent me nearly twenty pounds of records to review—the hospital records of the mother and the baby, the depositions of the doctors, nurses, physical therapists, experts on both sides, and the parents, the parents again, and the progress reports from the school. I started reading them at the dining-room table one night, after the kids had finished their homework and gone to bed. I couldn't stop. Although I had never seen the baby, I felt that I knew him. I could imagine what each session of physical therapy or speech therapy was like, the child's aching efforts to take a step, put on a shirt, hold a spoon, the parents' struggles to figure out a way to help him communicate.

I felt like I knew his suffering parents. Knowing how devastating it is to watch one's children struggle or suffer, my heart went out to them. I knew that they must have hoped that what the doctors had been trying to tell them for years was just wrong, hoped that their baby would be the one who might beat the odds. And I knew that eventually, gradually, they would come to realize that their dreams would not come true. Their life would be very different from the one they had imagined for themselves.

I knew how bad the doctors probably felt, unable to disentangle the pure tragedy from their own possible culpability. I am a pediatrician with a practice focused on the care of children with chronic disease. I take care of many kids with problems like this child's. I've seen parents ennobled by the experience of raising a child with such problems, but I've also seen parents hollowed out by the moral, emotional, and financial exhaustion of it.

The doctors inevitably wonder if they should have done something differently. Even if the peripartum events in the delivery room were unavoidable, and all that then followed almost inevitable, was there something they could learn from this case, something they could avoid next time? Were they to blame? Had they done all that they should for the parents in the weeks that followed? Why were the parents, who had seemed friendly and even grateful during the months in the neonatal intensive care unit (NICU), now trying to punish them?

This terrible, tragic case was every parent's nightmare.

What is the best way to summarize the facts of the case?

The first line of a story is important. For most sick babies, the first line of prose is the first line of the medical history. In this case it read, "Baby Boy

Jones is the 680g product of a 25 week gestation to a G1, P1, 25-year-old married woman." To translate: This extremely premature baby, weighing just over a pound, is this young couple's first baby, resulting from their first pregnancy.

Most of us, born in hospitals, were first described in some such way. Our first role in life was as patients, even if we were perfectly healthy. It doesn't have to be that way. We don't *need* to be born in hospitals. We could be born at home in bed or underwater in a hot tub. We don't need to start life as a patient.

There is an ongoing, often bitter scholarly and cultural debate about whether it should be that way, about the morality, the ethics, and the gender politics of childbirth. Arguments are carried on in the learned journals and on op-ed pages about informed consent, about which approaches are best for the satisfaction and safety of mothers and for the outcomes for babies, about whether some styles of obstetrical care lead to the objectification of women. Some outcomes are more measurable then others. Arguments focus on the use of forceps, C-sections, episiotomies, intrauterine monitors, midwives, doulas, or perineal massage.[1]

At the center of the childbirth controversy one point seems to be widely agreed upon but is usually unstated: doctors are a locus of accountability. If things go badly, the doctors are to blame. If things are going to change, doctors have to be the leaders. In this role doctors, like insurance companies, become the embodiment of our belief that we are not helpless against the randomness of the world. If we don't like the way things turn out, we can hold the doctors responsible. We can punish them. Surely this is one of the implicit reassurances in that first line of prose and all it represents, the beginning of the story that most of us tell about childbirth and our newborn babes, locating them in the precise prose of patienthood.

Of course, the story might begin another way:

"A baby was born at one o'clock in the morning in a small Catholic hospital in an economically depressed midwestern city."

"In the still hours of the morning a very tiny baby was born ..."

"An extremely premature baby was born ..."

"A moral dilemma was recognized when an extremely premature baby was born ..."

"A baby came to us but had not come to stay ..."

"A miscarriage occurred ..."

"A tragedy happened ..."

But why focus on the baby? Perhaps he should not be the central character in the story. Perhaps our storytelling should focus on the mother. It might go something like this:

A 25-year-old woman who had just recently married developed problems when she was six months into a much-desired pregnancy. But here, we begin a slide toward fiction. Was the pregnancy much desired? Perhaps she was ambivalent. Perhaps it was an accident. Who knows, maybe she'd had an affair and her husband wasn't the father. Interestingly, even after the baby had spent months in an NICU and years in rehabilitation, even after the baby's mother and her husband had filed a lawsuit, even after numerous experts had been expertly deposed by both sides, we still wouldn't know much about the parents, their marriage, their hopes and dreams, and we certainly wouldn't know much about the circumstances of the baby's conception. Nobody ever asked. It wasn't considered important to the "case." That information probably would have been seen as forbidden, irrelevant, not germane. The story we tell here is a partial story and can be shaped both by what is allowed in and by what is left out, never asked, stricken from the record.

Okay, so first there were the events. Then there was a case. And now there is a story. The three are related but not identical. The "case" is like a raft, floating on the current of different narrative streams. Its journey can be followed from either shore as it floats downstream, but sometimes it disappears into the mist, gets caught in the brambles, is swamped by a steamboat, or floats past the town where the rafters wanted to put up. We can start over:

A 25-year-old woman was six months into a medically uncomplicated pregnancy when, one night, while she was watching television, she began to feel contractions. Her water broke. She called her doctor, who told her to get to the hospital right away. The local community hospital, where her obstetrician had admitting privileges, was unequipped to handle an extremely premature baby, so the emergency room doctors quickly, desperately, called for a transport helicopter. The 25-year-old woman, who had only been in an airplane once in her life, was whisked by chopper to a referral center forty miles away, where she was now in the hands of strangers. They were experts but strangers nevertheless. Perhaps her terror as the helicopter lifted off the helipad or the strangeness of the new place and the new doctors contributed to the events that followed.

The American health-care system institutionalizes such strangeness. The sicker we are, the less likely we are to be cared for by the doctors we know and trust or in the places in which we feel most comfortable and familiar. We've chosen to prioritize objective expertise and technical sophistication over emotional connection and the comforts of familiarity. This likely has some effects on health outcomes, but these aren't ever studied. The system itself is not held accountable for the things it precipitates. The larger and more pervasive the system, the less it can be questioned. Systems are not sued. They just create the background against which the individuals are forced to act. Sometimes they create situations in which strangers face each other in the night and realize that there is no right action, only a range of lesser wrongs. It was within that systemic grid that Dr. Miller, the neonatologist, made his decisions about the tiny baby born in the still hours of the early morning in a small Catholic hospital in an unremarkable small midwestern town somewhere on the cold, windswept prairie.

What does the story look like if we focus on the doctor?

Dr. Miller, a middle-aged neonatologist, was on his last night on call for the month. It had been a difficult month. A number of extremely premature babies had died after prolonged stays in the hospital. He'd been in the NICU most nights that month, trying to rescue them. He hadn't been able to spend much time with his wife or teenage sons. Dinner at the Miller house that night had been a sullen affair, the resentment palpable in the air. One son had asked him why he seemed to care so much more about those "damn preemies"—"Watch your mouth!" his mother said—than about his own family. When Dr. Miller hesitated before answering, the boy went on to conjecture that he was mindlessly driven by a technological imperative, and when his father still didn't answer, he announced with all of the certainty of his fifteen years that he would never be a doctor when he grew up. Then sullenly, with a politeness that violated the very spirit of etiquette, he asked to be excused. His father wondered where the boy had learned the term *technological imperative.*

Dr. Miller, exhausted, was brushing his teeth, about to crawl into what he feared would be a loveless bed, when he got a call summoning him back to the hospital to attend the birth of a high-risk neonate. No, not one of his patients. Nobody they knew. The woman had just arrived by helicopter, twenty-five weeks. A baby at the borderline of viability. An extremely premature baby . . .

Dr. Miller rushed to the hospital, where he was met by the whole health-care team—the obstetricians, the nurses from the delivery room and from the NICU, the anesthesiologist. They were all poised and ready, waiting for their cue. The gestational age of the baby was reported to be approximately twenty-five weeks, based on the dates of the mother's last menstrual period and an ultrasound examination. But prenatal estimates can be wrong. Miller would be prepared for anything.

It was a difficult labor, with a double-footling breech presentation. When the mother had arrived at the hospital two tiny, bluish feet were protruding from her vagina. (Here we have to be careful with our language. She's not a "mother" until her baby is born. Should we call her a "pregnant woman"? a "woman in labor"? a "patient"? a "pregnant health care consumer"?) The choice of words colors the case; no word is morally neutral. Each swirls the current, nudges the raft.

The obstetrician handed the tiny, pale blue baby to Dr. Miller, who listened to the chest. There was a faint heartbeat but no pulse. The baby's little heart seemed to be quivering, churning, like an engine on a cold morning that coughs and sputters but won't quite turn over. The baby did not move his arms or legs. He did not grimace or cry. He did not gasp or breathe. He just lay there.

What should be done for him? What would he have wanted them to do for him? Perhaps he would have wanted to be dried off and wrapped in a warm blanket, to have a lullaby sung to him, to have a heartfelt prayer said for him. Perhaps he would have wanted to be enveloped in his mother's arms, held against her swelling breasts. (Now, cruelly, she was a mother, she would always be a mother, even though she might never have her baby. But she might have a moment here, a special moment. Like most mothers, she would stroke his head, count his little fingers and toes, caress him and love him. Then she could bury him.) That is what has been done for such babies from the beginning of time. Until now.

We could have done that. But that is not what we do now. That didn't even seem like one of the choices. We have broken with all of biological destiny, with history and tradition, with well-understood cultural norms, with ancient and time-honored understandings of families and the obligations within them and between them and the rest of our culture. In a sense, Dr. Miller stood poised between past certainties and an unknown future. Tradition would have called for prayers, for tears, for acceptance of death. But that is no longer our way. Dr. Miller's whole professional life represented a protest against that tradition. He could not just accept.

The neonatologist placed a plastic tube in the baby's windpipe. The tube was only one-twentieth of an inch in diameter, wide enough to pump some air into the baby's lungs, wide enough to give the baby a dose of adrenaline to try to stimulate his heart. The air filled his lungs and the adrenaline diffused into his bloodstream, but still the baby did not respond. His heart rate didn't increase. It remained slow, faint, distant. Dr. Miller squeezed the baby's tiny chest, holding the whole birdlike body between his thumb and forefingers. He squeezed the tiny chest a hundred times per minute, just a half-inch deep with each squeeze, and the nurse squeezed the airbag to inflate the lungs. After ten minutes Miller paused. The baby still was not breathing spontaneously. The monitor still showed a heartbeat, but Miller couldn't feel a pulse in the neck, the arms, or the legs.

Was this life?

Dr. Miller decided that it was not. He stopped. Perhaps he decided that to continue was meaningless, cruel, nonsensical, ethically inappropriate, futile. Perhaps he decided that to continue wasn't doing the baby a favor. Perhaps he worried that even if the baby survived, the likely outcomes were unacceptable. Perhaps he'd been taught that ten minutes was enough.

Or perhaps he was thinking less of the baby than of the parents. Perhaps he assessed the young parents and decided that in the end they would be better off with a single incredibly painful moment of terrible tragedy than with a lifetime of caring for a baby who in all likelihood would not do well even if he beat the incredible odds and survived, who in all likelihood would never walk or talk or eat table food, who might be plagued by seizures and chronic lung disease and cerebral palsy. (*Assessed* is a loaded word. What could lead to such an assessment? A brief glance at the father, gowned and masked, sitting by the head of his wife's bed, a terrified, lost, lonely look in his eyes?) There is too much that we don't know—can't know—when we are in such a story or when we try to reconstruct it. But doctors know that they don't know, and they also know they must act immediately. Continue or discontinue? Either choice might be terribly wrong, but a choice had to be made.

Regretfully, Dr. Miller ceased his ministrations. (Regretfully? That's another editorial comment, sympathetic to the doctor. Perhaps he felt no regret at all at the time. Perhaps he was relieved. Perhaps he'd been worried that the baby would survive and that then he would be in the NICU all night trying to save the baby when he really wanted to be home in bed. Perhaps, while he was brushing his teeth, he'd been anticipating getting into bed, thinking that perhaps tonight, for the first time in weeks, he would make love to his wife and that she would welcome him, that it would be nice the way it used to be nice. Perhaps this fantasy was interrupted by the ringing of the phone, and perhaps he still clung to it, even though he knew that it wasn't likely before and was less likely now. Or perhaps it was nothing so spicy. Perhaps he wanted to prove to his son that he wasn't driven by a technological imperative. Maybe he was just exhausted from recent political struggles in the hospital, battles over capitation payments for the NICU under the new managed-care contract the administration was proposing. Perhaps he was thinking that it was about time to retire, that medicine was no longer fun. Perhaps he was just eager to get back home.)

We don't know what Dr. Miller was thinking. In his deposition he stuck to the medical facts: The heart rate was 60, then 30. The Apgar scores, a measure of the body's condition, were very low—1 out of 10 at one minute, still 1 at five minutes. The baby's head was quite bruised from the delivery.

Dr. Miller carried the baby to the parents. Much later, under oath, he said that he had given the baby to them because he thought they should be allowed to hold their son for a few moments before he died. He murmured something to them about "doing everything we could, too small to survive, I'm sorry." He paused for a few moments, watched them cry, and then, feeling awkward and excluded from the terrible privacy of their grief, he walked away. He went to the doctors' lounge, had a cup of decaf coffee, and stared out the window at the dark night sky.

The father later testified that Dr. Miller had just given them the baby and left. The father didn't remember any conversation. He remembered being handed the baby, tiny and blue, as he sat sobbing next to his wife's bed in his gown and mask.

A few minutes later the baby began to gasp. The parents anxiously called the nurse, who sympathetically assured them that these were only "agonal" respirations, a sort of death rattle (*ag o nal,* adj., defined by the *Merriam Webster Dictionary* as "associated with or relating to great pain, especially the agony of death"). She sat with them for a few minutes and observed the baby, who gasped a few more times, and then she left. More minutes passed. The baby's gasps become more frequent. The baby let out a faint cry. The parents again summoned the nurse, who checked the baby's heart rate. It was 125 beats per minute. Shocked, she summoned the doctor, who, also shocked, reintubated the baby and arranged for his admission to the NICU.

The baby's neonatal course was a nightmare. He had nearly every complication a premature baby could have—jaundice, sepsis, patent ductus arteriosus, intracranial hemorrhage, feeding difficulties, apnea, bradycardia, bronchopulmonary dysplasia, seizures. But each got better. Throughout the neonatal course neither the doctors nor the parents ever discussed discontinuation of treatment. They didn't talk much about prognosis either. Those moments after birth must have been much on everybody's mind, but they were never mentioned. Instead, memories of them would lurk in the background, hovering over each doctor and nurse as he or she drew blood, suctioned a tracheal tube, or inserted a chest tube, hovering over the parents as they taped their pictures to the inside of the bassinet, as they placed tiny teddy bears in the corners, out of the way of the cardiac monitor wires or the intravenous catheters. Perhaps fear of those memories made everyone avoid discussions of prognosis or of the wisdom of continuing intensive-care treatment. Start one of those discussions and somebody might wonder, "What if . . ." Throughout the hospital stay and the months that followed the baby's parents were cooperative, friendly, even docile. They seemed to like the doctors, nurses, and therapists who were working with them, and the doctors, nurses, and therapists liked them. They were all working together. The baby had many problems, but each problem seemed to be self-limited, and no problem seemed sufficiently severe to warrant a decision to allow the baby to die. Everyone took things a day at a time, a decision at a time.

The baby was discharged from the hospital at nearly six months of age. He still had some difficulty breathing but did not require supplemental oxygen. His cognitive development appeared to be moderately delayed. His ultimate neurologic prognosis, though not good, was still uncertain. He took a number of medications—digoxin and Lasix for his heart, albuterol and prednisone for his lungs, phenobarbital and phenytoin for his seizures. His total hospital bill was over a million dollars.

The case manager arranged for the baby's enrollment in an "early intervention" program for children with developmental delays. His mother dutifully took him to weekly sessions of occupational therapy, speech therapy, physical therapy, and infant development programs. She subscribed to newsletters from the Zero-to-Three program and read them religiously. She carefully calibrated the Pediasure formula that supplied most of his nutrition through his gastrostomy tube.

Three years later his parents sued the neonatologist and the hospital. They alleged that the decision to discontinue resuscitation after ten minutes constituted malpractice, that the baby had been without oxygen between the time when resuscitative efforts were inappropriately discontinued and the time when they were reinitiated, and that this time without oxygen had caused his neurologic problems. They asked for 35 million dollars.

Somebody was to blame, and we were sitting on soft leather chairs in a conference room paneled in dark wood on the forty-second floor, overlooking the city that Carl Sandburg had called the "hog-butcher of the world," to decide who that somebody was and how much would have to be paid.

The lawyer for the plaintiffs was a tall, gray-haired man with a courtly appearance. Before the deposition started, he and I chatted amiably, sizing each other up. I'd heard that he was a physician who, after twenty years in practice, had gone to law school. Now he tried four or five malpractice cases each year. If he won just one big case like this one every two or three years, he would make much more money than he ever could have made practicing medicine. He worked for one of the bigger personal-injury firms in town. He looked like a television doctor from the sixties, Ben Casey or Marcus Welby. His manner was reassuring and paternal.

We settled in. The court reporter set up her arcane and complex set of recording devices, and after being sworn in (without a Bible), I stated my name and recounted my education. Undergraduate school, medical school, internship, residency, a fellowship in medical ethics. Then, surprisingly, the lawyer for the plaintiffs cut right to the chase.

"Since you completed a fellowship in medical ethics, do you consider yourself a moral expert?"

"Well I'm not sure what that means," I said self-deprecatingly. "I've read much of what has been written over the last two decades about issues in medical ethics, particularly those related to pediatrics and neonatology. I try to synthesize that knowledge to help doctors and patients understand the issues that they should at least consider when they are faced with difficult decisions in these areas."

"Can studying philosophy tell you whether what a doctor does in a particular case is right or wrong?"

The straightforwardness of the question caught me by surprise. It almost seemed to call for a yes or no answer. Reframed, though, as a question about whether anything or anybody could judge what was right or wrong in particular situations like this one, it was the central question of my life. Would a lawsuit such as this one determine that a doctor's actions were right or wrong? It seemed unlikely. But it seemed just as unlikely that definitive guidance would come from philosophy, sociology, religious doctrine, or any other single source.

The story of this case mirrors, in a small way, the much larger story of the moral dilemmas associated with all attempts to save the lives of critically ill premature babies. As we face these moral dilemmas, we look for guidance to prayer, meditation, introspection, psychoanalysis, economics, philosophy, theology, or fictional exploration. There have been many attempts over the years to tell the story of neonatal intensive care in ways that would allow an answer to the lawyer's question. I wanted to answer truthfully, but I also wanted to tell "the whole truth." To even approach it, I would have to tell him more stories about neonatal intensive care than he wanted to hear. Over the years, the morals to be derived from these stories and their conclusions about what is right and wrong have changed rather strikingly.

One such story begins almost like a fairy tale. Once upon a time, doctors in France invented an "incubator" to help in the care of premature babies. The incubator was most likely invented in the 1880s by a doctor named Alexandre Lion, of Nice. Lion was a philanthropic physician who established the Baby Infant Charity in Paris and other cities around France. The charities were supported by "admission fees" charged to those who visited and watched the preemies being cared for.[2] In 1896 two French physicians, Pierre Budin and Etienne Stephane Tarnier, had developed a similar invention to the point where it was ready to be displayed to the world. Like Lion, they called their invention an "incubator." The incubator was designed to keep premature babies warm. In this, it was similar to the devices designed for warming eggs until they hatched. The premature babies behaved much like eggs—when they were kept warm, their survival rates improved dramatically.

Martin Couney displayed actual premature babies in incubators at the Berlin World's Fair in 1896. Many visitors to the fair were fascinated by the exhibit. While the preemie exhibit was popular, nobody knew quite what to make of it. It was seen more as a curiosity than as a medical breakthrough. For the next few decades nobody seemed to know how to incorporate this curious innovation into everyday life. No interpretive cultural framework helped make sense of the project of keeping premature babies alive. Caring for preemies didn't really seem like medical care. At the time, most doctors were not particularly interested in saving the lives of older children, much less those of premature babies. Infant mortality was regarded as inevitable. Effort or expenditure by governments, doctors, or parents to reduce infant mortality didn't make much sense. William Silverman, one of the founders of modern American neonatology and a historian of the field, has shown that there was no great demand from parents for this sort of technology.[3] Often, after Budin and Tarnier saved preemies, their parents didn't even want to take them home. Incubators for premature babies were thus a technical and scientific curiosity looking for a market. They did not create the sense of personal or societal moral obligation to care for each and every premature baby that would come later.

Instead of being adopted by hospitals, the Budin-Tarnier incubator was first widely used by Martin Couney, who recognized that the fascinating spectacle of tiny premature babies could be quite lucrative. Couney developed "exhibits" of premature babies to be viewed at various fairs and amusement parks around the world.[4] At Coney Island, long lines of vacationers would pay 25¢ to enter Couney's pavilion and gape at the preemies, along with the bearded ladies, dwarves, and contortionists. That parents and society allowed the use of preemies in such "freak" shows illustrates just how drastically moral sensitivities have changed over the past decades. Less than a century ago nobody seemed particularly concerned with the moral rights of the babies, the moral obligations of their parents or society, or the moral complicity of the viewers in what now appears blatantly outrageous and offensive. But there is some continuity as well between that time and now. Efforts to save premature babies could only take place if someone could profit from them. Moral responses took shape within the infrastructure of economic arrangements. This suggests that answers to questions about right and wrong could evolve fairly rapidly if social and economic structures changed. Many of these premature babies did not live happily ever after. And like Budin and Tarnier, Couney found that many parents were not thrilled that he had decided to intervene.

In addition to being carnival attractions, preemies began to attract the attention of doctors. In 1898 Joseph Bolivar DeLee, at the Chicago Lying In Hospital, began using Lion incubators to care for preemies. In 1914 Julius Hess established a unit for premature babies at the Sarah Morris Hospital in Chicago. This unit was so successful that in 1922 he expanded it and converted it into a regional referral unit. In 1923 the world's first hospital-based nursery for premature babies opened at the Sarah Morris Hospital. (The hospital itself became almost a parable about American medicine as it shifted its identity over the years and became the Michael Reese Hospital of the Jewish Federation of Chicago, then Humana Hospital, then Columbia/HCA. With each change it lost a little of its identity, a little of its mission, and a little of its soul.) The mainstay of the care of premature babies in the Sarah Morris special unit was to carefully regulate their temperatures using incubators. In addition, the doctors would provide supplemental oxygen in some cases. Highly skilled nurses at Sarah Morris also refined the special feeding techniques that the French had invented. In short, neonatal intensive care began with the two impulses any parent might have, to keep the babies warm and to keep them well fed.

More importantly, the "Chicago model" of concentrating highly skilled experts and technology in one referral center became the basis for developing specialized perinatal-care centers that would serve a whole region. In some ways, this administrative innovation in the organization of health-care delivery was as important as the minor technological innovations that were taking place within the special-care nursery and much more radical. The creation of a special unit led to the creation of a specialized staff with a specialized ethos and mission. The gothic fairy tale of preemies as carnival exhibits became the parable of medical progress that NICUs represent.[5]

By the 1940s, doctors understood that warmth and feeding alone could help babies who were born a few weeks short of term, but these techniques couldn't save the tinier, more premature babies, who would still die as a result of breathing difficulties. The "respiratory distress syndrome," or RDS, of the newborn caused premature babies to struggle and gasp for breath as they used all of their energy trying to breathe. Most tiny preemies would eventually tire out, stop breathing, and die. The focus of research in neonatology became an effort to understand RDS and develop treatments for it. Many treatments were tried, and many failed. The need to carefully evaluate treatments led to the creation of a network of clinical researchers who developed new paradigms to meet the needs of the new clinical situations they sought to evaluate.

Interestingly, even in the absence of specific treatments for RDS infant mortality decreased dramatically over these years. Between 1900 and 1960 the infant mortality rate in the United States dropped from 122 per 1,000 to 26 per 1,000. The decline was due in part to better maternal nutrition, in part to better prevention of infectious diseases through immunizations and treatment of infectious diseases with antibiotics, and in part to the better medical care given to newborns.

The successes of hospital-based neonatal care led many to believe that even more success would be possible. More success, however, would only come with more money. The early 1960s saw the first calls for federal funding to further develop neonatal intensive care in order to lower infant mortality. The federal government responded by funding the Premature Infant Research Center at Stanford University Hospital in 1962. At Stanford and other places, trials of mechanical ventilation for premature babies were begun.

In 1963 First Lady Jacqueline Kennedy gave birth to a premature baby who died within hours of birth at Boston Children's Hospital. At that time the treatments available for premature babies were not much more effective than those used at Sarah Morris in the 1930s. The Kennedy baby was given highly concentrated, "hyperbaric" oxygen. It didn't help. This highly publicized death highlighted the need for more research into diseases of premature babies. At the same time, the development of new vaccines for whooping cough and polio led to dramatic decreases in deaths from these infectious diseases. Tellingly, in the mid-1960s the March of Dimes changed its focus from polio to premature births.

By the late 1960s two technical developments revolutionized the care of premature babies. One was the refinement and standardization of machinery and techniques to provide positive-pressure mechanical ventilation to premature babies. This was the first effective treatment for RDS in newborns. For many babies, a few days of mechanical ventilation allowed their lungs to mature to the point where they could breathe on their own.[6] Had the Kennedy baby been born just five years later, he would almost surely have survived. The other important development was the use of total parenteral nutrition (TPN), a method for providing babies with all the nutrients they needed intravenously.[7] Before TPN, it was difficult for premature babies to get enough nutrition. TPN made it possible to keep the more premature babies alive and strong enough to fight off infections and to eventually breathe on their own.

Between 1960 and 1974 the U.S. infant mortality rate halved again, to 12.3 per 1,000. More interestingly, for the first time, most of the decrease was due to a drop in neonatal mortality (i.e., deaths in the first 28 days of life), as opposed to postneonatal infant mortality (deaths between 28 days and 1 year of age). During this time the mortality rate for babies at every birthweight was slowly and steadily dropping.[8] Both these facts suggested that the decline during these years was due to better neonatal care. Neonatology became the fastest growing field in pediatrics. Board certification in neonatology began in the 1970s, and by 1999 there were twice as many board-certified neonatologists (3,708) as there were board-certified pediatricians in any other specialty (cardiology, with 1,609, and hematology-oncology, with 1,602, were next).[9] Neonatology seemed to be a phenomenal success story. Looking only at this part of the story, I might have answered the lawyer's question by saying that history teaches us how new and better ways of responding to premature babies changed the way we view our ethical obligations to those babies. One moral of this story was that Dr. Miller had been wrong to give up because, in a way, he had betrayed the narrative of progress that was central to the story of neonatal care.

But that wouldn't have been the whole truth. Alongside this tale of a seemingly inexorable march of progress was a parallel story about growing moral concerns with technology run amok. William Silverman was one of the first doctors to call attention to the fact that not all neonatal interventions were benign. He highlighted cases in which the indiscriminate use of oxygen for premature babies led to blindness. Silverman called for cautious, careful, and rigorous study of all new interventions, with particular attention to possible side effects, before their widespread introduction.[10]

In 1973 Raymond Duff and Arthur Campbell published a groundbreak-
ing article describing the moral and ethical dilemmas raised by neonatal intensive care. In particular, they focused on the problems they faced when
technology allowed them to prolong the life of a tiny premature baby even
though it appeared unlikely that the baby would survive for more than a few
weeks or months. They wondered whether it was appropriate to continue
treatment that might only prolong pain and suffering, whether it would be
more appropriate to discontinue treatment even though that would inevitably
lead to the infant's death. Their controversial article suggested just how dramatically societal attitudes had changed in the fifty years since Couney's
Coney Island shows. Duff and Campbell worried about whether their decisions to discontinue life-sustaining treatment might be illegal. They concluded with the suggestion that neonatal technology had outpaced the law
and that if what they were proposing was in fact against the law, then the
law needed to be changed. The paper presaged a decade of legal and moral
controversy about NICU practices.[11]

Norman Fost, a pediatrician, and John Robertson, a lawyer, responded
quickly, describing just how many laws they thought Duff and Campbell
might have broken. They suggested that decisions by parents and doctors to
withdraw life-sustaining mechanical-ventilator support from nonconsenting
babies might be construed as various crimes, ranging from neglect or child
abuse to manslaughter or conspiracy. In what reads like a direct warning to
neonatologists, they wrote: "If existing legal policy is inappropriate, it should
be changed through open discussion and not subverted through private
action."[12]

Around the same time that Duff and Campbell were writing, the theologian James Gustafson analyzed a case in which the parents of a newborn baby
who had Down syndrome and a congenital intestinal obstruction elected not
to allow surgery.[13] In his paper he tried to find a basis for deciding whether
such a decision was appropriate. He concluded that the decision not to operate was inappropriate because it violated the biblical obligation to love one's
neighbor as oneself. He said that this obligation required that we not focus
on the parents but instead try to identify with the babies and to figure out
what they themselves would want if they could express their wants.
Gustafson's baby-centered focus shifted the framework of moral decision
making. Before Gustafson, the focus had been on the parents' desires and
needs, with those of the babies seen as secondary, almost instrumental. Parents had been seen as having the right to do what was best for themselves and
to consider the needs and interests of their other children. After Gustafson,

it became more difficult to allow parental needs, intrafamilial utilitarianism, or consideration of societal interests to dominate the moral calculus. In a curious sense, by conceptualizing parents and their babies as biblical "neighbors" or fellow citizens, rather than family members, he changed the way we think about these relationships and elevated the moral status of the newborn. By this subtle shift of focus, Gustafson showed how family privacy might be detrimental rather than protective.

In a series of articles about the tension between those who focus on the sanctity of life and those who focus on the quality of life the theologian Richard McCormick also tackled the spiritual implications of "playing God." McCormick refused to see the matter in such simply dichotomous terms. Instead, he focused on the qualities that any life must have if it is have ongoing, meaningful spiritual aspirations. For him, the key factor was whether a life "contains some potentiality for human relationships." "If that potential is simply nonexistent or would be utterly submerged and undeveloped in the mere struggle to survive," he wrote, "that life has achieved its potential."[14] The implication was that prolonging such a life was not morally obligatory.

I could have answered the lawyer's question by summarizing these papers and shown that many learned scholars would respect and defend Dr. Miller's decision. Each of these arguments was interesting in itself. Even more compelling, in some ways, was the fact that such a discussion was taking place. The public discussion of very private decisions broke a taboo. The papers by Duff and Campbell, Fost and Robertson, and Gustafson led to unprecedented public interest in medicine, neonatology, and the moral dilemmas of medicine and neonatology. Prior to this, these issues had rarely been acknowledged or discussed publicly. With public discussion came public scrutiny through press reports, books, and symposia, and judicial involvement.

A series of court cases in the 1970s and 1980s examined decisions about the treatment or nontreatment of critically ill babies, including a pair of conjoined twins in Illinois, a baby with multiple congenital anomalies in Maine, and a baby with congenital heart disease in California.[15] All of these babies became the focus of judicial deliberations. In each case the parents didn't want to authorize treatment and the doctors weren't sure what to do. In many similar cases, no doubt, a private decision was reached to let babies die. In these cases, however, doctors judged the decision not to provide treatment problematic and requested a court review. Sometimes the judges authorized treatment, sometimes they didn't, but each case became part of the ongoing public discussion about what was the right or wrong thing to do.

A national conference about these ethical issues in Sonoma, California, in 1975 led to a set of proposed guidelines for deciding whether treatment should be provided. In a crucial paragraph the report stated: "In the context of certain irremediable life conditions, intensive care therapy appears harmful. These conditions are ... inability to survive infancy, inability to live without severe pain, and inability to participate, at least minimally, in the human condition."[16] It was difficult to know just what to do with such statements. Did the opinions of a self-selected group of concerned citizens meeting among the vineyards of California carry much weight? What were ordinary doctors and nurses doing?

In the late 1970s I. David Todres, a pediatric anesthesiologist and critical-care physician, surveyed pediatricians in Massachusetts, and Anthony Shaw, a pediatric surgeon, surveyed all program directors in pediatric medicine and pediatric surgery in the United States about their responses to moral dilemmas.[17] Both asked doctors whether they thought the treatment of newborn babies was obligatory, optional, or clearly wrong in a number of clinical circumstances. The responses to the two surveys were similar. Most pediatricians felt that parents had the right to refuse surgery for their newborns with Down syndrome or myelomeningocele (spina bifida), a congenital malformation of the spinal cord. Only a small minority would have pursued a court order to force such surgery if the parents refused permission. However, about 25 percent of doctors clearly would have pursued a court order and saw nontreatment as a form of medical neglect or child abuse.

It was clear from these surveys that doctors themselves were divided. There was no clear professional consensus about whether treatment should or should not be provided in particular circumstances. Todres repeated his survey every 10 years. In 1988 he found that there had been a slow and steady shift in attitudes.[18] More pediatricians were willing to override parental refusals of treatment. By 1998, however, attitudes seemed to have stabilized. The biggest changes between 1988 and 1998 were not in the treatment decisions for newborns but in the demographic makeup of the pediatricians in Massachusetts: there were many more women in 1998 than in 1978, but their attitudes were similar to those of their male colleagues.[19]

Such surveys do not make explicit moral arguments or lead to unambiguous conclusions. Instead, they rely on a sort of democratic approach to ethics. They tell us what percentage of doctors think or feel a certain way about a particular dilemma. Though public-opinion polls are not moral arguments, they clearly show that attitudes change over time. They also illustrate the importance of the way questions are asked and of whom.

In addition to the surveys, articles began to appear that showed that most doctors who didn't work in NICUs weren't very aware of recent progress in neonatal intensive care. Out of touch with current survival statistics, they didn't have the expertise to participate meaningfully in decisions about treatment versus nontreatment. For example, Steven Morse and his colleagues showed that "both obstetricians and pediatricians underestimated survival rates from 24 through 35 weeks of gestation and freedom from serious handicap from 23 through 36 weeks of gestation. Obstetricians who underestimated neonatal survival would less often administer antenatal corticosteroids, perform a cesarean section for fetal distress, and transfer a mother to a tertiary center. Pediatricians who underestimated neonatal survival would less often use mechanical ventilation, cardiopulmonary resuscitation, inotropes [medications to stimulate the heart], intravenous fluids, thermal support, and oxygen supplementation."[20]

One of the unique sociological aspects of neonatal intensive care that began with the Sarah Morris special care unit was its reliance on a small core of highly trained and professionally isolated specialists. In a sense, the NICUs set themselves apart from the society and developed their own particular mores. Neonatologists' attitudes may differ from the attitudes of other doctors or professionals. The difference may in part reflect more accurate knowledge of the capabilities of neonatal intensive care. It may also reflect other factors, such as the values of a particular professional subculture, economic or academic conflicts of interest, or simple naïveté about the long-term implications of certain decisions. Expertise in treating babies does not necessarily correlate with the ability or the authority to decide which babies should be treated.

Who should participate in such decisions? If only neonatologists had accurate, up-to-date knowledge about what was really going on in NICUs and even other pediatricians and obstetricians were out of touch with recent developments, then it seemed unlikely that parents could understand the complexities. The decisions being made by the small group of experts who understood what was going on had important implications that went far beyond the NICU walls. Not everyone was comfortable with the decisions that those experts were making. Scrutiny shifted from the philosophical basis for the decisions to the sociological milieu of the decision makers. The focus of moral inquiry shifted from the principles of the decisions to the sociology and cognitive psychology of the decision makers. Who were those experts, how had they been trained, how did they work, how did they think, and how should they think?

The sociologists Jeanne Guillemin and Lynda Holmstrom, who studied

two NICUs in the 1980s, wrote that "the focus of our research is on the complex organizational imperatives that have directed the growth of newborn intensive care." In their view the moral dilemmas of neonatal care were inextricably intertwined with the organizational structures of such care, even to
the point where "the bureaucratic dynamic in newborn intensive care generally overrides the individual physician's or nurse's authority, just as it has
undermined the guardianship role of the parents." They noted that the professional organization of NICUs is so rigid and specialized that even tasks
such as talking to parents are delegated to particular professional groups,
namely, nurses and social workers. This role specificity extends even to the
point of discussing death with parents whose babies are dying: "Physicians are
not usually educated to deal with death (except as an indication that they
have failed) or with distraught parents."[21] According to Guillemin and Holmstrom, the social organization of NICUs is designed to impose a certain morality upon all the individuals within it rather than to create a space within which
individuals can struggle with and act upon their own moral reflections.

Renee Anspach also writes about NICUs from "a sociologic point of
view," and she too tends to see decisions as collective, not individual, acts. "I
argue that matters of the heart and crises of conscience are social activities
anchored in a social context. . . . Much of what is wrong with life-and-death
decision is not the fault of the individuals who make them, but rather rests
with the broader social context." Anspach, like Guillemin and Holmstrom,
sees people's decisions as arising more out of their locations in the social
structure than out of their individual moral reasoning or moral convictions.
She challenges the view that such decisions are, in any meaningful sense, a
personal matter.

Nevertheless, Anspach notes some role for moral principle. "In both
intensive-care nurseries I studied," she writes, "a broad consensus around a
principle had emerged. If practitioners were reasonably convinced an infant
was unable to survive or would survive with serious neurological defects (e.g.,
severe mental retardation or cerebral palsy), then it was considered appropriate to withhold life-sustaining treatment from that infant." She goes on
to note that it was easier to articulate the principle than it was to opera-
tionalize it. "Even when practitioners could agree on the principle involved
in a life-and-death decision, they often could not agree on the prognosis of
the infant whose fate was in question."

The overall message of both these sociological studies is that individuals
may have less moral freedom than they think and that the social context creates external forces that shape decisions. "Decisions are shaped by the social

context in which they are made," writes Anspach. "Life and death decisions within the nursery are affected, in ways that are far from self-evident, by the allocation of resources in the society at large."[22]

The studies were carefully done, and their conclusions are persuasive. However, they take one in quite a different direction than do the theologians' reflections or the judges' opinions in particular cases. Before both God and the law individuals are held accountable for their actions. In the world of social scientists individual choice seems to be an illusion.

So I might say to the lawyer that any judgment about Dr. Miller's actions would need to consider both views, to see him as both a freely choosing moral agent and a man helplessly trapped within a complex sociological prison. It seemed incoherent to hold both views at the same time. But it seemed inadequate not to consider the implications of both as we tried to understand whether people's actions in NICUs were helping or hurting babies, parents, or society.

Much intellectual probing and sincere soul-searching has been brought to bear on these questions over the last decades. It may not have answered the questions, but it does constitute a sort of expertise. No obvious, straightforward response has emerged, but that does not necessarily indicate failure. Instead, it pinpoints the areas of the most difficult dilemmas. In struggling with our concerns in these areas, we need to seriously study the great texts of moral philosophy. Careful self-examination through meditation, prayer, or psychoanalysis is needed. We could seek more clinical training, experience, and research in hopes of finding technological solutions to some of the moral dilemmas. Careful analysis of human behavior and the values that underlie it might lead to a better understanding of what we are about. This, in turn, might lead to better choices by individual doctors caring for patients, ministers counseling parents, judges rendering legal decisions, and parents trying to decide what is best for their children.

Because the elements of good decision making are so broad, and because all sorts of people have to make decisions, it is not clear just what sort of arguments or what sort of knowledge best informs the decisions. Clearly, the education of an ethicist should be broad and multidisciplinary. Ethicists, like poets, must know a little about a lot of things. They must know something about philosophy, law, theology, history, sociology, economics, psychology, literature, and clinical medicine. This ideal seems to be reflected in proposals about the composition of ethics committees, which recommend that they include doctors, nurses, clergy, philosophers, social scientists, lawyers, and "members of the public."[23]

The desire implicit in this multidisciplinary ideal is that moral expertise be inclusive and synthetic. The disturbingly postmodern implication is that there really is no particular core knowledge or central discipline that constitutes ethical expertise. There is no ultimate answer, no final authority to whom we might turn. Somehow, the answers, if there were any, would come from a discussion that incorporated philosophy, theology, law, medicine, sociology, and common sense in a strange and new amalgam. The ethicist might mix a little Kant, Mill, and Rawls, a little Anglo-American case law, some Christian, Muslim, and Jewish moral theology, a little quantitative sociology, a little ethnography, the results from a public-opinion poll, a little clinical experience, and some self-reflection. This solution, while often practically useful, is theoretically unsatisfying.

Many of the pioneers of bioethics came to the field from more traditional and formally grounded fields of intellectual inquiry. Gustafson was disillusioned by the development of bioethics as a separate discipline. He found the field to be distorted by an encroaching "legalism" that cheapened rather than deepened the field. In his own work he moved away from the moral problems of medicine to broader moral concerns. Similarly, the sociologists Renee Fox and Judith Swazy, two pioneers in bioethics, announced in 1992 that they were leaving the field of bioethics, in part because they felt that it had not really become a "field" and did not have the methodological rigor of the social sciences.[24]

George Annas, a lawyer, and Leon Kass, a philosopher, have both taken their bioethics colleagues to task for a vagueness and a lack of direction. Kass thinks that bioethics has become all about talk, rather than action, and thus has failed to have a discernible impact on the day-to-day practice of medicine. Annas finds ethics committees to be temporarily useful as a way of articulating and examining principles and perhaps even shaping them into policy. But the committees themselves should have no standing function because they have no particular expertise. Instead, he suggests, they either perform risk-management functions or else simply dilute and disguise individual responsibility for tough decisions.[25]

Much of this disgruntlement arises, I believe, from a failure to appreciate just how morally tenuous the basis of much medical practice is. Until recently, doctors themselves supplied the values and moral norms that shaped the practice of medicine. Moral codes were written by doctors for doctors. Then something happened, something that was largely unremarked, unrecognized or ill defined, and it became clear that doctors were no longer perceived as adequate, sufficient, or trustworthy enough to perform this task on their own. Outside scrutiny was essential, but it was also risky. After all, any ethical theory in medicine must begin with the assumption that most practitioners themselves are, or at least aspire to be, moral. Conversely, the modern insistence upon the need for outside scrutiny does not encourage doctors to be the final moral arbiters of their own practices.

Perhaps the "something" that happened was grounded in the twentieth century's remarkable advances in the biological and medical sciences. These were the years when medicine developed knowledge, understanding, and tools that went far beyond what had ever been available before. Biochemistry, molecular biology, pharmacology, and physiology all began to create models, techniques, and paradigms that would change the way we think about health and disease. These discoveries allowed doctors to develop new ways of diagnosing and treating illnesses that changed the way we think about who doctors are and what they should be doing.

Bioethics can be seen as a response to these scientific developments and an attempt to remind doctors, who may be tempted to believe that medicine was invented with the discovery of antibiotics, that their moral roots go back farther than the early twentieth century. New developments must be understood and utilized within older ethical frameworks. Perhaps the growth of a separate field of bioethics reflects a belief that doctors, seduced by the glitz and glamour of the new technologies, can no longer be counted upon to remember these ancient roots when they try to think and act ethically, that they have become such technical specialists that they now need specialists in ethics to guide them. That was certainly the sort of concern that initially led nonphysicians to scrutinize the policies, procedures, and practices of neonatal intensive care. Tentatively stepping across the professional boundaries that had long insulated and isolated doctors, they began to ask whether neonatologists should be doing the things that they were doing.

However the field of bioethics is defined, it is a fence-straddling field. Its very existence as an independent field suggests some deficiencies in the traditional systems of medical education. But it is not clear whether bioethics per se is an adequate response or whether studying philosophy, theology, sociology, or survey methodology can help us decide whether what a particular doctor does in a particular situation is right or wrong.

.   .   .

The various stories about neonatal intensive care—of the carnival side-show, of our social obligation to children, of biblical obligations, of our sociologic enslavement to a technological imperative—and about the tenuous successes and glaring failures of bioethics are all true in their way. Studying them would not make someone more moral, but not studying them would make it difficult to understand the history, presumptions, culture, and constraints that Dr. Miller took into the delivery room that night. Not recognizing the dense web or appreciating the conflicting forces acting upon them would be disrespectful to him and to the collective moral wisdom of many thoughtful people who have struggled with these issues over the last few decades. Familiarity with each set of stories would seem to be necessary, but not sufficient, to make a judgment about the actions of a particular doctor caring for a particular baby on a particular night in a particular hospital in America in the 1990s.

But to explain all this would take more than a yes or no answer to the lawyer's straightforward question. The court reporter was looking at me expectantly, hands poised to capture my every word on that strange paper tape court reporters use. (Why, I wondered, don't they just audiotape or videotape the depositions? How was a transcript more or less useful or accurate than a recording? How much of the whole truth were they really after?)

"Well," I replied, "we study some philosophy, some theology, some law, sociology, economics, anthropology, and public policy. Each of these disciplines sheds a different sort of light. We try to understand the forces at work in modern secular pluralist democratic societies that make it easier or harder for people to live a good life. We read what other people have written about their own struggles to understand what is right and wrong. But it is difficult to determine what, exactly, determines the boundaries. Each case, including this one, is part of the process."

The lawyer made a few notes, shuffled through his papers, and nodded his head with a little smile to himself. Then he slowly looked back at me.

"Doctor," he said, "This case involves the care of a premature baby. Have you ever taken care of a premature baby?"

To tell the truth, which I had sworn to do, it had been quite a while since I had taken care of a premature baby. But yes, I had. The question stirred up some memories.

Passing Out in the NICU

I nearly passed out during my first visit to an NICU. I was in my fourth year of medical school. I wasn't assigned to the NICU—no medical students were. It wasn't considered an appropriate place for medical students or other outsiders. (Even today the NICU at the University of Chicago Hospitals is tucked away in a back corner, and the hallway leading to it has warning signs directed at all but "authorized" people.) I had gone to visit my girlfriend, who was a first-year pediatrics resident at a big children's hospital. That month she was assigned to the NICU. She was just one year ahead of me in training, but, owing to the mysteries of medical training, I was not invited to the NICU and she was the doctor primarily responsible for eight tiny, critically ill preemies. She was very proud of her work. She had invited me to come see what she was doing, hoping to persuade me to join her there the next year.

When I arrived at the NICU the medical-care team had already started making their morning rounds. I joined their large group—the attending physician, a postdoctoral fellow, a few pediatric residents, two respiratory therapists, a nutritionist, a couple of nurses—and we moved herdlike from patient to patient, bassinet to bassinet, Isolette to Isolette. At each stop there was a little plastic mechanical box wired to all sorts of devices, and in each box was a tiny premature baby.

Some of the babies were pink, others a little grayish. Some were in diapers and seemed to be looking around. Some were blindfolded, lying totally naked under banks of fluorescent lights like the tanning booth patrons at a health club. The bassinets of some of the babies were wrapped in cellophane. All were connected to a variety of machines and monitors—mechanical ventilators, cardiac monitors, intravenous infusion pumps, intraarterial pressure gauges, temperature sensors. Officious nurses hovered over the bassinets, occasionally picking up or turning the babies but mostly, it seemed, watching the monitors, keeping the buzzers from buzzing and the beepers from beeping, measuring medications in tiny syringes and injecting the needles, not into the babies, but into the tubes connected to the babies, then calmly documenting each hour's events on the graphs and grids of their thick notebooks.

The babies themselves did not seem quite real, or at least they did not seem central, except in a mechanical way, to whatever dramas were being enacted there. They were a crucial part of some vastly complex loop, the energy source to which all else was connected. They were clearly the place where the tubes and wires and catheters came together. But they were clearly not the place where the eyes of the professionals focused. Instead, the professionals focused on the machines and the monitors, listening to the rhythm of the beeps, watching the flickering digits on the ventilators and the infusion pumps and the mysterious tracings across the amber oscilloscope screens representing the electrical activity of the babies' hearts. (Oscilloscopes! What a mental image! Just two decades ago those oscilloscopes were state-of-the-art. They would now date a photograph of the NICU like a Studebaker or a hula hoop. Today there are only flat-screen graphics displays. There was no Internet then, nor were there desktop computers or cell phones. The technology has changed in so many ways, some more subtle than others.) Some of the tracings were reassuringly repetitive. Others were anxiously erratic. These patterns and numbers were, in a way, both a representation and a reification of the babies. The numbers and the patterns became the essence of some entity that might be called the "health" or "sickness" of the babies. The caring professionals cared for the babies by caring for that entity. If they cared well, the numbers would be good and the patterns regular, and they would preserve the baby's health. If they could not make the numbers right or the patterns regular, then the baby's health would slowly wane away, and the baby could not survive.

The doctors, nurses, and respiratory therapists talked to one another easily. They understood one another. Their language was the mysterious argot of abbreviations, jargon, and numbers that technicians everywhere use. They'd casually say things like, "This 26 weeker has RDS and a PDA, he's on a rate of 30, PEEP of 5, 35 percent O_2. Neuro: an ultrasound yesterday showed a Grade II. Nutrition, he's down 300 grams since birth, we're starting TPN today. Heme, he's had 3 cc's out and we're replacing it. Social, parents haven't been in." Right. Next baby. Sometimes the attending physician would ask a question or two; at other times that would be it, and we'd shuffle en masse to the next hub, just a few steps away. Of course they didn't talk to the babies, and the parents had been asked to leave the unit during rounds, so they talked around and about and through the babies in a way that made my head spin. Like a visitor to a foreign country who had studied the language once, a long time ago, I caught wisps and snippets and thought perhaps I understood what they were saying but wanted them to slow down, to translate a phrase here and there, to allow me to participate. Of course they didn't. I was a tourist, and they had work to do.

We moved from one Isolette to another, from one 700-gram elf to another, from miracle to tragedy and on to another miracle. At first I felt like a guest or a visitor, honored to be there, a little unsure of the etiquette. After a while, though, I began to feel like an intruder, an outsider, an alien. The things that were going on here were so very bizarre, and everybody involved seemed determined to pretend that they were normal. I had no voice. I couldn't even begin to frame my questions about what was happening, and I could hardly understand what was being said or done. I began to feel a certain desperation. Was this where I was going to have to work when I was a pediatric resident? Was this what pediatrics was all about? I knew that pediatric residents spent months and months in the NICU, more time than in the clinic with its healthy babies unknowingly waiting for their immunizations, more time than in the emergency department with its hoarse and croupy toddlers and their desperate, sleepless parents, more time than in the adolescent-medicine clinic with its emotional problems and sexually transmitted diseases, more time than they spent experiencing the pathos and triumph of the cancer ward or the visceral drama of the operating room. I knew that just like these preemies, I would be here for months on end, wired in to the nerve center of the children's hospital. We would be there together.

I wondered how the babies felt, their underdeveloped brains overwhelmed by the otherworldliness of it all. I had an image of myself, tiny, in a bassinet, surrounded by giants who poked and prodded me, stuck tubes in my every orifice and in some places where there were no orifices, and hovered around me but never really looked at me, never really saw me.

I wondered what it would feel like to be the parent of one of these babies, to hover close by but helpless, walled off by the Plexiglas Isolette and the professional barriers.

I began to feel a churning in my stomach. I thought I might vomit. It is not quite accurate to say that the room began to spin, but the reality of the room became more and more distant. The voices became fuzzier and hard to understand, as if they were coming from far away. I could feel my heart pounding, feel the blood rushing through the arteries in my neck to my face.

My palms became sweaty. I silently excused myself from rounds and went to sit on a sofa in the parents' waiting room, hanging my head between my knees like an exhausted athlete.

One can imagine many reasons why a fourth-year medical student might pass out during his first visit to the NICU. I was young, and I was in love with one of the interns who was working there. I was full of admiration and jealous of her competence and magic. I knew that if I joined her there the next year, we would have to work together. She would know more than I could ever hope to learn. That threatening thought may have been too much. In addition, we had had a lot to drink the night before while discussing whether I should join her and work in that hospital the next year—a conversation that was really about whether to get married and have children of our own. So, mixed with the concerns about work must have been some tiny recognition of the risks, embodied in the NICU babies, of what that sort of commitment might mean, what chances we'd be taking, what challenges might lie ahead. So it may be overstating the case to say that the NICU alone made me dizzy.

But the feeling hadn't hit me that morning when I'd walked through the emergency room or when I'd walked down the medical wards full of children with cancer or heart disease, which are not exactly peaceful, pleasant, or reassuring places. No, it had only hit me in the NICU, a strong, strange, powerful place.

There is probably no eerier place in a hospital than the NICU. One enters thinking that one is prepared to see tiny babies. But the babies are unimaginably tiny. They are magical. They look something like the strange *Life* magazine pictures of babies inside the womb. The babies seem almost, but not quite, human, almost, but not quite, fetal. In their chimerical, half-human, half-machine state they seem not only helpless and pitiful but also exotic, threatening, futuristic, feral, untamed, barbarous. They evoke a strange mixture of sympathy and disgust. Their vulnerability calls out to us, and we want to help them, but there is also something repulsively buglike about them that makes us want to obliterate them. They shouldn't be there, so vulnerable and so dependent on the machinery and technology of medicine.

The babies in the NICU make a claim on our humanity but also challenge the limits of it. We want to respond, but we also want to be free to reject the claim that they make upon us, to imagine them not as our babies, whom we must care for, but as something other, different, unrelated. In their terrible dependency aren't they asking too much? Perhaps more than we can give? This, perhaps, is the feeling that sometimes leads parents to give up, to insist that treatment be discontinued, to stop visiting the NICU. Today, just as in the days of Budin and Couney, parents sometimes do not seem grateful for what we are doing or eager to take home the babies we have saved for them.

As I watched the doctors and nurses, I felt ambivalence about them and their work. They seemed heroic and compassionate but also sadistic and bizarre. There is something inhuman and inhumane about this particular way of starting life, and the doctors and nurses are unavoidably implicated in the inhumanity. It is troubling that they become as intuitively comfortable with endotracheal tubes, umbilical-artery catheters, and phototherapy lights as ordinary parents are with breast milk, bibs, and diapers. There is something dazzlingly and disturbingly ultramodern about the whole scene. It is as ambiguously beautiful as a space shuttle coasting gently to a landing on a five-mile-long runway, as a Stealth fighter jet swooping secretly through the sky ahead of its sound wave and without a radar image, as the Manhattan Project. And there is something ambivalently wrong with these analogies, which, while apt, seem curiously inappropriate. The NICU isn't about war or destruction or space exploration. It isn't a project that is in any way vital to the national interest. These are just babies. Their lives are, or should be, about nurturing and caring, burping and snuggling.

Perhaps it was this sense of irreconcilable symbolic dichotomy, of inextricably mixed metaphors, that overwhelmed me when I first walked into the NICU and nearly lost consciousness. There was something about the *über*-consciousness of the NICU itself that clashed with my ordinary citizen consciousness, as if we couldn't exist together.

In the world of NICUs many of the doctors, almost all the nurses, and most of the clerks, physical therapists, and nutritionists are women. That seems right—women taking care of babies. But NICU femininity is strange. In some ways the NICU seems like a male fantasy of a womb as the sort of thing you'd build with Tinkertoys, little electric lights, and an erector set. Each baby is wired to and violated by a tangle of tubes and catheters, probes and monitor leads. Digital readouts show, in real time, the baby's oxygen level, temperature, heart rate, carbon-dioxide level, cardiac electrical activity. In a Tinkertoy way it's really cool. Except that the babies should be baby dolls, Barbies who turn blue if they don't get enough oxygen and wet their diapers when given the right amount of intravenous fluid. But they aren't. They are real little people, and this spaceship, this high-tech roller coaster, this cyberwomb, is their introduction to life on earth.

Maybe it was the gender confusion that made me swoon. A whole hospital ward seemed to be crossdressing, nurses pretending to be mothers playing like boys with Tinkertoy babies. For me, becoming a doctor was a process of growing up, of becoming a man. Pediatrics offered a masculine role that was gentle and nurturing. I loved children, and I wanted to take care of them and help them grow. What I saw in the NICU was not quite what I had in mind. Something, it seemed, was out of kilter.

Passing out is not uncommon among medical students. It probably occurs most frequently in the operating room. The first view of internal organs, of the pulsating heart, the glistening liver, the suction catheters siphoning off the leaking blood, and the smell of burnt flesh as the surgeons cauterize leaking vessels often generate an overwhelming physiologic response in the neophytes.

But I didn't pass out in the operating room. For me, the rituals and rhythms of the surgical suite worked. In the operating room everybody acknowledges the dehumanization of the surgical patient in explicit and protective ways. The patients to be operated upon are carefully draped so that only a small part of their bodies are visible. They are shaved and then scrubbed with an antiseptic solution that changes the color of their skin. They are anesthetized so that their consciousness is erased. The surgeons are also dehumanized, having ritually scrubbed, robed themselves in sacred green, and covered their hands with plastic, their mouth and nose with a mask, their eyes with a shield. There is no sense of human contact between surgeon and patient. All these symbolic barriers create distance. Those glistening organs seem like anything but the inside of a human being.

Surgery is the most masculine of medical disciplines, taking knives and penetrating the body to find disease and destroy it. It is a war game in which cold and shiny stainless steel is pitted against the unseen, sinister but discoverable and conquerable enemy. Pediatrics is in many ways the most feminine of medical disciplines, with its focus on small children, preventive care, nurturing. In terms of gender, neonatology seems to be somewhere in between.

I had made it through surgery just fine, but that morning in the NICU I remembered the one other time during my medical training when I had almost passed out. It was the first time I saw a pelvic examination. It was during the summer after my first year of medical school. A friend of mine who was a primary-care doctor in a public-health clinic had invited me to tag along as medical students often do. Put on a white coat, pretend to be a doctor, watch what I do. My friend saw a lot of sexually transmitted diseases and did a lot of gynecology, a lot of Pap smears.

Pelvic exams are, on the one hand, routine preventive medicine. Women are encouraged to have them every year. They are screening tests, generally designed to find asymptomatic disease, so most women who undergo them are not really sick or suffering. Unlike many screening tests, however, they involve the most personal of bodily invasions. The rooms in which gynecological exams are performed are usually sterile to a fault. The stirrups at the end of the examination table are of cold steel. A large operating-theater spotlight illuminates the table. The patient is undressed, but carefully covered with a medical garment, and the doctor wears a white coat and latex gloves. The speculum is made of either shiny stainless steel or disposable clear plastic. The culture plates are at hand, waiting to be smeared with the precious cervical secretions and whisked off to the bacteriology lab, the microscope slides to the cytopathology lab.

My friend prepared to examine a patient. He went through the usual patter to put his patient at ease. She climbed on the table, positioned herself with her genitalia exposed to us, and lay back to endure the indignity. The speculum went in.

"There," he said. "Come look at the cervix." And I peered through the open speculum at a glistening, rounded thing that looked vaguely genital but not quite like anything I'd ever seen, a little like buttocks, a little like a nipple. It was all shiny and wet and seemed to be deep inside and far away. I suddenly felt faint, as if the world were starting to fade away. I stepped back and took deep breaths. Sweat beaded on my forehead. My friend looked at me and was concerned.

"You better go sit down," he said, and I did, and I soon felt a little better. But by then the patient had gone, and we didn't talk about it any more, and I didn't watch any more pelvic exams that day or that summer. The next year, when I was a second-year student, I learned how to do pelvic exams and didn't have any problems. It was just that first view of the cervix, the womb, the secret entryway to life, that somehow nearly blew my consciousness away.

I wonder what the connection was between those two events—the first pelvic exam and the first visit to the NICU. They were the two times during my training when I just couldn't take it. There was something terrifying to me about the experiences and the practices of doctors in the gynecology clinic and the NICU.

Pelvic exams and Pap smears are about female sexuality and about the strange prerogatives of doctors to touch their patients' genitalia, to trespass in the most taboo and private of places. The examinations are dehumanizing in a complexly downplayed sort of way. The patient and the doctor meet as equals and converse with each other. The patient climbs onto the examination table, places her feet in the stirrups, spreads her legs, and exposes her genitalia to the doctor, who calmly and casually chats about the weather, or the president—anything but what is happening. This profoundly abnormal experience is normalized in an implicit and unacknowledged way, just as the NICU experiences normalizes the bizarre. In both cases, I, like the patients, was supposed to behave as if these situations were normal.

Since then I have seen many teenagers coming for their first pelvic examination. They are frightened, offended, aghast at what is happening to them. Often, their mothers have explained to them that this is part of what it means to be a woman, that they will have many such exams, that they need to get used to them, that it's not really so bad. But they don't believe it. They know that something very weird and unusual is happening, but they are gradually conditioned to accept the view that it normal.

In some ways, both my faintness as I witnessed my first pelvic examination and my dizziness when I first visited an NICU seemed to be a deep neural recognition that something very unusual was happening. Because there was no way to express that in the context of the complex but implicit dramas of normality that were being played out, something very unusual happened to me. Perhaps it was the way both related to my own process of becoming a doctor, itself a sort of crossing of barriers. In any case, both experiences triggered some concatenation of physiologic events that reached through the protective wall of emotional neutrality and reserve, grabbed hold of my very consciousness, and tried to obliterate it.

The psychosexual and political and cultural forces at work in gynecology range from the competition between midwives and gynecologists for professional control over the circumstances of childbirth to the women's-health movement of the sixties, with its messages of empowerment, to the latest battles over funding for breast-cancer research.[1] The larger issues surrounding women's health and disease have been in play for the entire twentieth century.[2] These same issues arise in neonatal care, but they have not been examined as extensively. Compared with women, premature babies are difficult to conceptualize as a sociopolitical entity. The "children's rights" movement exists but has been much less coherent or powerful than the women's-rights movement, and the complex history of neonatology in the twentieth century suggests the tensions and conflicts we feel as we respond collectively to babies, their needs, and their rights.

Part of the reason for the confusion or contradictions in our responses to children is that the claims they make upon us are not straightforward or traditional. Furthermore, their claims must inevitably be articulated and interpreted by someone else. The claims of preemies are not the usual claims that newborns make upon their parents or caregivers. As we interpret the claims and translate the messages, we decide what it is that we hear and what we are willing to do. Translating the unarticulated, inchoate message these babies send transforms us. As we discern and then articulate their message, we can no longer see either them or ourselves in the same way. Meaning, interpretation, understanding, and obligation flow freely and feed back upon one another. Older patterns of consciousness are obliterated, and we wake up to find our moral perceptions rearranged.

Over time, neonatal intensive care has rearranged the consciousness of us all. It has changed the way we think about what babies demand from us and about what we owe them. Being in the NICU, holding a tiny preemie in the palm of your hand, seeing one survive and another die, witnessing the mundane horror of a long, drawn-out death for a baby whose entire inner being is an impenetrable mystery—such events cannot but change the consciousness of the individuals involved. It also changes the consciousness (if you can call it that) of the institutions involved and of society as a whole.

In response, we have developed new technology, new law, new morality, new professional hierarchies, and new sociological arrangements, all coalesced into the professional specialty of neonatology, the administrative structure of NICUs, and the unique consciousness and morality of the people who work there. NICUs represent one of the most successful developments in pediatrics in the last thirty years. They have revolutionized the way we think about newborns and their diseases. The existence of NICUs and the knowledge we have gained through them has enabled us to dramatically lower both overall and birthweight-specific neonatal mortality rates.

Whatever else can or should be said about neonatologists and NICUs, one fact stands out: NICUs save lives. Each year thousands of babies who otherwise would have died not only survive but survive in excellent health. The challenge of incorporating the phenomenal success of neonatology into our understanding of what babyhood is all about, into our understanding of what it means to care for the most vulnerable among us, has changed the way pediatricians think about themselves, their specialty, their profession, their mission. It has changed the structure of pediatric medical education and of child-health policy. It has changed the way our society thinks about moral obligations between parents and children. It has goaded us to construct new legal and regulatory guidelines for enacting and enforcing those new moral obligations. It has created new economic challenges as we try to understand what these commitments cost and whether the cost is worth it. Without the technological achievements of neonatology a case such as Dr. Miller's would be unimaginable. In most societies in the world today it would be inconceivable.

It was shrewd of the lawyer to ask whether I'd ever taken care of preemies, but I wanted to throw the question back at him. Could anybody who hadn't spent time in the strange world of the NICU really understand what went on there? Had he ever taken care of a preemie? What about the people who would sit on the jury and pass judgment? After all, we were here together, these lawyers and I, to participate in a process that might change the way anybody and everybody facing situations like the one Dr. Miller faced would be called upon to respond. We were preparing to pass judgments. Abstract ideas about preemies were one thing, the visceral realities something else again. As we set out to struggle to a verdict in the case before us, we were also about to make broader policy for neonatal care. We would define the moral parameters within which anybody working in the NICU must behave.

Of course, we were required to pretend that what we were doing was about something else altogether. According to the script, we were there only to determine whether Dr. Miller had been negligent in his care of Baby Boy Jones. To do that, we would painstakingly reconstruct the "facts" of the case and then decide whether those facts created a picture of appropriate care or malpractice.

"I used to care for preemies many years ago when I was in residency training," I answered.

"But you don't take care of them now?"

"Well, I still see patients. Many of the patients I care for are survivors of the NICU. But no, my clinical work now is not in neonatal care units."

No indeed, I thought. Those long months, those long nights, had given me more than my fill of experiences in the NICU. There had been some good times, but there had also been some very bad times.

THREE

Learning about Death and Dying

Marcus Welby, retired doctor, now attorney at law, was leafing through my résumé.

"You were a resident back in the early 1980s?"

"Yes, 1981–84."

"How many premature babies did you care for?"

"Oh, we used to cover a 40-bed neonatal intensive care unit. I would be responsible for 10 or 12 babies on my own, and would cross-cover the others at night. We did that for six months during the three years of residency. So, over the years, I cared for at least a couple hundred babies. Not by myself, of course. There was always an attending physician supervising me."

"And during that time, did you ever have occasion to witness the deaths of any babies?"

"Many times." Almost every month at least a few of the babies would die. Some died blessedly quickly, others only after weeks or months of lingering in the strange twilight zone between premature birth and premature death.

"Were decisions ever made to withhold or to withdraw life-sustaining treatment?"

"Certainly."

"Did you participate in those decisions?"

"Well, sort of. But they were mostly made by the attending physicians."

"But, as a resident, were you taught the proper way to go about making those decisions?"

Oh, I see where he's going now. "Proper?" Now, that certainly gave him away. He was laying the groundwork to build up a completely idealized view of medical education. He would move on to a completely idealized view of what the process for making decisions about life-sustaining treatment should look like. Then he'd try to show that Dr. Miller's behavior in the real world didn't match the fictional ideal, and bingo, millions of dollars.

"Well, it wasn't quite like that. Some of the things that we learned as residents were things that we were taught. Others were things that we observed. In still other cases, we had to figure things out for ourselves." That statement, I thought, pretty much summed up the surprisingly haphazard process of medical education.

"What do you mean, exactly, when you say that you had to figure things out for yourself?"

Now, there was a good question. Medical education is a strange combination of lessons taught, lessons learned, trial and error, positive and negative role modeling, and pure chance.

I learned many lessons about both life and death during internship, and I learned a lot about myself as I faced life and death. It was while I was working in the NICU that I first achieved that dream of doctors everywhere, to actually save a patient's life. This happens a lot on TV but not so often in real life. Most of medicine is much more mundane—colds, rashes, vague aches and pains that can't be diagnosed, can't be cured, and don't go away. But every once in a while it's not like that. The first time I saved a patient's life was when I was on call as a second-year resident, and the patient was a 600-gram preemie.

The obstetricians called the NICU to warn us that a woman was in labor at twenty-five weeks. I called the neonatology fellow, assuming that he would be there to take over. Alas, he was at home, forty-five minutes away. Don't worry, he said, he'd get in as soon as he could. In the meantime I was to do my best.

Forty-five minutes! Do my best—was he kidding? I was just a resident covering at night. I wasn't ready to solo. I panicked. Then I became angry. I felt like I'd been abandoned. I didn't want to do this, didn't want to be there. It was a cold November night nearly two years after the day when I'd nearly passed out in the NICU. Since then I'd spent months caring for preemies. I'd gotten to know the strange, almost papery feel of their underdeveloped skin, to recognize the hairline wisps of blue just beneath it as tiny veins, tiny but not so tiny that we couldn't insert tiny intravenous catheters into them. I was in the middle of a thirty-six-hour work shift, tired and alone, holding the bag for the neonatal fellow, who was holding the bag for the neonatal attending physician. The attending physician too was no doubt holding the bag for somebody, but I was too preoccupied to wonder who that might be.

As residents we spent a lot of time in the NICU. Interestingly, this was not because anybody thought it was essential for our education as pediatricians to learn so much about neonatal intensive care. By this time, in the early

1980s, there was already a subspecialty board in neonatology. Any doctor who wanted to work in an NICU would have to do a three-year postresidency fellowship in neonatology in order to be certified by the sub-board. Most pediatric residents would never again work in an NICU, never again take care of 600-gram preemies, and probably never need the skills that we were so painstakingly learning and perfecting. But the NICU was the most labor-intensive unit in the hospital. Three or four professionals hovered over each bassinet at any one time. Because so many personnel were needed in the NICU, it claimed a disproportionate amount of the residents' time. The NICU needed us, and the hospital needed the NICU, so there we were, night after night, month after month.

My anxiety was gradually replaced by a seeping sense of vindictive euphoria. Fuck 'em all, I thought, I can do this, or at least I'll try. And in the end, nobody will really know or care how well I do because the task itself is so meaningless. In a moment they will hand me a baby who by all rights should just die, and I will run through the paces of a resuscitative routine that I've rehearsed and rehearsed and rehearsed until I could do it in my sleep. ABC—airway, breathing, circulation. Suction the trachea, intubate, check a pulse, start an umbilical intravenous line, give some fluid. If the heart rate is low, give some adrenaline. This wasn't magic, and it wasn't rocket science either. I made sure my hair was combed, put on a clean scrub suit, and strolled over to the delivery room to see how the mother was doing.

It was a quiet scene. Doctors and nurses were talking in whispers. I should go to the woman on the table, who was the quietest of all, introduce myself, and try to give the predelivery *schpiel*. "Very high risk, may not be viable, we won't know for sure until the baby is born, we'll do what we can, I'll let you know as soon as we know." This little speech seems to offer important information, but in reality it offers almost none. What it offers is a chance for doctor and patient to check each other out. Does she seem caring and concerned or strung out and indifferent? Is there a man in the picture? another woman? The grandma, perhaps? a friend? a lover? The words are placeholders, a vague recognition of shared humanity, a verbal handshake, valuable as vague gestures of caring rather than for what they mean.

Her eyes search mine quickly, then she turns away. What does she look for in the gowned, gloved, masked figure who presents himself at the precise moment of her life's most profound distress, at the moment when everything that was supposed to be good, beautiful, and life-affirming has become horrific, terrifying, mournful? At the moment when fear and dependency de-

fine her life as never before? She is certainly no health-care consumer negotiating a contract, purchasing health-care services, dispassionately evaluating the risks and benefits of this or that intervention. She is sizing me up,
not because she has a decision to make but just to see what hand she's been
dealt. Do I look experienced? trustworthy? Am I nervous? Do I know what
I'm doing? Will I be there for her? Can she talk to me?

What is she hoping for? That I will save her baby? Or that I will wisely
allow her baby to die, saving for her a life unburdened by an NICU cripple?
Or are her feelings even more vague—a primitive fear and a longing for
comfort and caring? Perhaps she only wants to be recognized as someone
who is suffering.

What sort of heroism is called for here? What sort of doctoring?

Based on our conversation, I might soon have to make some profound decisions about the baby about to be born. Should I have gone into more detail about the risks and benefits, the chances of intracranial bleeds or chronic
lung disease or cerebral palsy, or about the options for treatment or nontreatment? That sort of talk didn't seem appropriate to the powerful emotional tenor of the moment.

Thinking back, I realize that even this brief conversation, a conversation
that gave us so little time to cover so much ground and left so much unsaid,
was more than Dr. Miller had with the Jones family. He arrived as the baby
was being delivered. But even if he'd had time, he'd have been just one more
stranger at the end of the long helicopter ride. He would have faced the same
dilemma. There were big decisions to be made. In theory, we were supposed
to make them together. In fact, we all seemed to be part of some larger script,
and it wasn't clear that any of us had learned our lines well.

So, I introduce myself and make such explanations as I can. She doesn't
ask questions, which is just as well because I don't really want to answer her
questions. My mind is already focused on the technical tasks ahead of me, the
ones I may not be able to perform. And her questions would probably be
about matters of judgment, fears, and emotions, questions that only a doctor
who was ready to engage a patient at a deep level of shared humanity could
answer. I haven't really learned to be such a doctor yet. I am just the technically skilled bagman for the doctor, worrying about whether I'll be able to
get the tube into the trachea. It is not my province to make decisions or ask
why. I am just supposed to make sure that no one dies during my shift. To my
relief, she doesn't ask such questions. She lies silent and exhausted between
contractions and then moans with pain at every contraction, a low, mournful moan, not so much a moan of one in acute pain as a moan of one in a

sort of mourning. This is not where she wants to be. The contractions seem to be a sort of punishment.

She appears to be about my age. An older man sits beside the bed, holding her hand, saying little. I return to the baby warmer and get to work.

The nurses, as always, are solicitous of a rookie. They help me set out my equipment—a DeLee suction trap, a tiny laryngoscope to open the baby's airway and visualize the vocal cords, endotracheal tubes in the smallest sizes made, an umbilical catheter, a syringe with some saline flush. We turn on the heat on the warming table and ready the leads for the temperature monitor and the transcutaneous-oxygen monitor. The tension is like the tension before a ball game or before a showdown. I keep thinking that the neonatology fellow will arrive any minute to rescue me, that I am really a bit player, a stuntman, maybe even a stagehand, certainly not the star. We watch the huge clock on the delivery-room wall. It is a little after 2:00 A.M.

"Here it comes!" The obstetricians are doing their final shtick: "One little push, that-a-girl, here we go. OK, relax now. Ohhh. It's a girl! A pretty girl. Looking good. Just relax, now. Now we'll give her to the pediatricians. Lie back. There you go."

There you go! Check pulse—weak and thready, about 70. Respirations—an occasional gasp. Color—pale, blue. Give oxygen. Suction. Intubate. I get the laryngoscope. "Give me the 2.5 ET tube. There, I think that's in." Check breath sounds. With the puffs of the ambubag, her chest rises and falls. I'm amazed at my competence. Good. Heart rate? 100. "Can we get a BP?" "Its not reading." Pulse is still a little thready. "Want to start a line, doctor?" This is the nurse's gentle way of telling me what to do, handing me the umbilical catheter. I choose the larger umbilical vein rather than struggle with the tiny arteries. No time for subtlety here. It goes in easily, good blood return. Give a bolus, 10 cc/kg would be what, 6 cc. A teaspoon of saline. BP 40/20. OK, let's get her back to the NICU.

I wanted to go talk to the mother, to tell her what was happening. But I was needed at the bedside. I was the central technician. I beckoned to one of the nurses, "Go tell Mom that, so far, everything looks good." She looked at me with skepticism, but she went. As we rolled into the NICU, the neonatology fellow strolled through the door, calmly shed his street coat, and slipped into a sterile yellow gown. He took over effortlessly. The nurse read out the numbers to him, he listened briefly to the heart rate and breath sounds, shook his head slowly, and patted me on the back. "Nice job. The kid probably won't make it, but you did a nice job."

The baby died two days later, in spite of receiving all that neonatal intensive care could offer. There was no further discussion with the parents about whether to continue treatment. At the end there was a short, symbolic attempt at cardiopulmonary resuscitation. And the fellow was right: I had done a nice job. I had gotten all the tubes in place, the lines started, the right doses of the right drugs calculated, calibrated, and delivered. I felt good about all that but very bad about things that I couldn't quite name—the things that hadn't happened but perhaps should have, or the things that had happened but hadn't helped. We never talked about the case again. That was how we learned about death and dying.

That routine is the essence of neonatal care—a calm and orderly response, a sequence of interventions designed to address, with some semblance of reason and order, the cascade of life-threatening events that follow premature birth. Tiny preemies can't control their body temperature, can't breath, and can't maintain an appropriate blood pressure. They need to have their temperature, blood pressure, oxygen levels, and glucose levels constantly monitored and kept neither too high nor too low. If that works, and they make it through the first crucial hours, then they begin to have other needs. They need intravenous nutrition for weeks, sometimes months, before they can eat on their own. the functioning of their livers, kidneys, lungs, brains, and bowels has to be monitored. Their immune systems are underdeveloped, so they need a sterile environment, but they are still at high risk for overwhelming infections. What they really need is an artificial womb, so we try to build one with our medical Tinkertoys. The result is something that works much better than nothing at all but nowhere near as well as the real thing. Most preemies live and do well. Some die. Worst of all, some end up somewhere in between.

Are the efforts worth it? The years when I was in the NICU were the years when there were national controversies about decisions to withhold or withdraw life-sustaining treatment in both neonatal care and adult medicine. There were new journals devoted to bioethics, in which writers struggled with the questions. There were debates at national meetings, high-profile legal struggles, and policy statements by professional societies and other advocacy groups.

In one respect, the questions came down to one of perspective. Before one could answer whether it was worth it, one had to then ask, worth it to whom? And it was hard to frame an answer that was baby-centered. The babies couldn't tell us whether they wanted us to try to save their lives or would prefer that we let nature take its course. All we could do was try to reason by analogy, try to extrapolate somehow from our own experiences and per-

spectives or perhaps to incorporate the responses of some other more articulate group. But which group?

One analogous group is adults who have been in intensive-care units
(ICUs). What is it like for them, and what do they think afterwards? Are they
glad that they received treatment? Would they do it again? Many former patients have written about their experiences with various illnesses. Some of
these illnesses involved at least some time in intensive care. Interestingly, very
few books include actual memories of intensive care. That is usually skipped
over or described distantly and objectively, sometimes with a glorifying sense
of awe and gratitude. Those few works that do describe the subjective experience of being an ICU patient tell of a bizarre state of consciousness somewhere between a hallucinatory state and a nightmare.

Rachel MacKenzie's book *Risk* recounts her experiences in an ICU after
an experimental open-heart operation.[1] Her story is told entirely from the
patient's perspective, in the form of a journal, but one that includes images,
overheard conversations, and dreamlike sequences from the time when she
was thought to be unconscious in the ICU. Describing her experiences in
the third person, in disconnected, episodic recollections, MacKenzie writes:

She came whirling out of a long tunnel and knew at once she was in the Intensive
Care Unit. A wide board was jammed across her throat. It kept her from asking what
time it was, and it seemed important to know. There were people around her bed.
Someone was calling her first name loud. She was thirsty.

"Prick. This is your antibiotic," a woman's voice said.

"Prick. I'm giving you morphine."

Every time she opened her eyes, a nurse was bent over the bed doing something.
She wore a blue uniform. It was always the same nurse. (26)

A little black woman in a bandanna turban came to the side of the bed and fell on
her knees. "Oh Jesus, Jesus!" She rocked back and forth. The nurse kicked her hard.
"This is no place for praying," she said, "If you have to pray, find yourself some place
where you aren't in the way. Get out!"

Had the little black woman really been there? "Hallucination?" her mind offered. (28)

The doctors around the bed across from her were talking about Dr. Rudd. They were
angry. "He's requiring so much care for"—she heard her name—"he's endangering
the life of everyone else in this room," one of them said.

Dr. Rudd spoke up. "Please remember I'm the top man here," he said. "Any two-
bit surgeon who can do a valvulotomy can have a patient in this unit. My operations are the big ones. So long as I have a patient here who needs care, she's going to
get it." He was as calm as ever, but his voice was commanding. (30)

She heard her name from across the room. "———— may make it or she may not, but Dave Rudd will get a brilliant article out of this, either way." So that was his first name: David.

May make it? (33)

From this patient's perspective, the ICU is a place where one becomes almost disembodied, becomes a third person rather than a first person, where the "I" disappears, taking the active voice with it. Things happen—blood is drawn, tubes are placed. People talk about the patient as if she's not aware, or not human, or not conscious, and she herself is so disoriented that she doesn't know what is dream and what is real.

When MacKenzie awakens after days of such floating, she notices scars in places where she hadn't realized she was going to have incisions, stitches in places where there shouldn't have been scars, tubes and needles everywhere. Things had been done to her, said about her, and decisions had been made for her. She had even undergone a tracheotomy and now had a hole in her neck to which the ventilator was connected. She is in pain. She can't speak. She doesn't know what time it is, what day it is, or which among her memories was real and which was dreamed or imagined. She certainly does not recall participating in the decisions that were made about her care or wanting to. All she wants and begs for is a drink of water or to be positioned in a way that will not cause pain. She is entirely at the mercy of the staff. And they cannot even confirm for her whether what she had heard, experienced, or thought was real or imagined. In particular, she wonders whether the conversations she remembers in which some people suggested that she be allowed to die were real. So she asks.

Now that she had her voice, she told Dr. Rudd what she had heard in Intensive Care.

He sat down to talk. "It sounds to me like a bad trip," he said. "Anesthesia today is very sophisticated and you had a fever of a hundred and four and a lot of morphine those days." No one in the world would have said that kind of thing to you—it's unthinkable. It was hallucination."

"Some of it," she said, "I even thought that at the time. But I'd bet you on a good part of what I heard. My mind was in order." (42)

MacKenzie's experience does not seem unusual. Another book, *Raising Lazarus,* by Robert Pensack and Dwight Williams, tells the story of a psychiatrist with a congenital heart disease that eventually leads him to get a heart transplantation.[2] The book vividly conveys the bizarre reality of being a critically ill patient in the ICU. As in MacKenzie's book, the subjective experience is hallucinogenic, nightmarish.

During the first week of my stay in ICU there are no memories, only vague psychotic images. . . . The terror . . . of being trapped in a body I am certain is about to die slowly and miserably encompasses the knowledge that my mind is not my own, as it wanders aimlessly beyond the sympathetic boundaries that keep us all sane. The immaterial becomes material: agitation become a worm capriciously eating its way from ear to ear, a mad doctor, I am convinced, has transplanted my personality as if it were an organ. (263)

It is a private nightmare, a wilderness of mirrors. . . . All is out of control. Curious faces appear and vanish, the nurse's breath strikes my chest, paranoia rises up in me like a wave. (265)

What if I were to momentarily forget myself and blurt out that it's not worth it, that the pain and the terror were too great, that they stole my mind, took my heart, that the procedure itself is barbaric. (275)

Pensack's reflections and questions raise a crucial question. What if, he asks, he even momentarily allows himself to believe that it just isn't worth it? To do so, he hints, would be to "forget himself," but in another sense it would also be to represent his true self at that moment. Perhaps it really isn't worth it. In that moment he speaks for any and all ICU patients. His voice of doubt is like MacKenzie's questioning whether the voices she recalls hearing were real. Perhaps they were her own doubts incorporated into fantasy. In both cases the doubts themselves are quite real. Patients and caregivers both question the value of intensive care and the morality of the suffering that inevitably accompanies it. Pain is worth it if the benefit is commensurable, but what scale can accurately weigh and measure such things?

Poignantly, adults like Pensack and MacKenzie consented to the treatment they received. They passionately desired it for themselves. They nevertheless describe the experience of undergoing it in terms that liken medical care in modern ICUs to horrendous torture. After one of his hospital experiences Pensack developed post-traumatic stress disorder, the same psychiatric syndrome that afflicts soldiers in combat. Such modern hospital intensive-care treatments can take patients to the limits of human endurance of suffering. The consent of the patient seems necessary to justify such interventions.

If the patient is a newborn baby, and a premature baby at that, with a consciousness so rudimentary and unformed as to be almost unimaginable, the problem of deciding whether it is worth it to provide such treatments becomes even more difficult. It is hard to imagine a moral yardstick to evaluate the experiences of adults in the ICU, particularly since even the adults have difficulty remembering the experiences. The inner experiences of neonates are even farther beyond our imagination. These babies are the blankest of slates upon which we record whatever fantasies come to our minds. We can project upon them our fantasies of rescue or torture, of benevolence or malevolence, love or sadism, suffering or obliviousness or redemption.

In his book *A Personal Matter* Kenzaburo Oe tried to imagine what a critically ill baby might experience, "What did death mean to a baby like that? Or, for that matter, life? . . . Only a few hours on this earth, spent in crying, tongue fluttering in his stretched pearly-red mouth."[3] He concluded that the experience of such a baby was essentially unimaginable. Instead, the only anchor we have for our moral sentiments is our own responses and our own experiences as caregivers. We must hope that through our empathy our feelings somehow reflect the experiences of the babies themselves.

Lorrie Moore wrote about the experience of being a mother to a baby who undergoes major surgery and ends up in the ICU in her book *Birds of America*. Interestingly, like the other authors, she distances herself from the pain and resorts to the third person. Instead of naming herself or her child, she talks about the Baby and the Mother.

How can it be described? How can any of it be described? It is a horror and a miracle to see him. He is lying in his crib in his room, tubed up, splayed like a boy on a cross, his arms stiffened into cardboard "no-no's" so that he cannot yank out the tubes. There is the bladder catheter, the nasal-gastric tube, and the Hickman, which, beneath the skin, is plugged into his jugular, then popped out his chest wall and capped with a long plastic cap. There is a large bandage taped over his abdomen. Groggy, on a morphine drip, still he is able to look at her when, maneuvering through all the vinyl wiring, she leans to hold him, and when she does, he begins to cry, but cry silently, without motion or noise. She has never seen a baby cry without motion or noise. It is the crying of an old person: silent, beyond opinion, shattered. In someone so tiny, it is frightening and unnatural. She wants to pick up the Baby and run-out of there, out of there. She wants to whip out a gun. *No-no's, eh? This whole thing is what I call a no-no.* Don't you touch him! She wants to shout at the surgeons and the needle nurses. Not anymore! No more! No more! She would crawl up and lie beside him in the crib if she could. But instead, because of all his intricate wiring, she must lean and cuddle, sing to him, songs of peril and flight: "We gotta get out of this place, if it's the last thing we ever do."[4]

In Moore's account the experience of the caregiver is one of pity, anger, sorrow beyond words, and an overwhelming helplessness, all mixed with the strange sense of gratitude that comes from witnessing something miraculous. After all, without this he would be dead. With it there must be indescribable suffering.

Interestingly, perhaps surprisingly, most people who go through an ICU stay report that the experience was not so bad and that if they were similarly ill in the future, they would do it again.[5] Nobody has asked patients who were premature babies whether they would "do it again," but Saroj Saigal and her colleagues at McMaster University have asked former preemies about their preferences and valuations of different health states.[6] They found that both parents of preemies and adolescents who had been preemies were less pessimistic about the value of life with particular disabilities than were doctors or nurses. Nevertheless, many parents and former preemies, along with many health professionals, rated some health states, such as being blind, deaf, mute, or dependent upon another person for all activities of daily living, as being worse than death. Clearly, people judge the value of intensive care or any other medical care by the probable outcomes. Extraordinary levels of pain and suffering can be tolerated and even, apparently, forgotten if they lead to the desired outcome. Nowadays there are even drugs that can facilitate the forgetting, that seem to erase memories of the experiences.

One problem with using such studies to make judgments about intensive care is that they all inevitably share a common flaw: they only report responses from survivors. The studies miss a crucial subset of the population, those who underwent the same interventions but did not benefit and so might not have wanted to do it all again. Concerns about these patients show up in studies of end-of-life care, in which many family members of patients who died report that the patients were in severe pain and were suffering intensely during their last days. The moral, psychological, and economic cost of providing such treatments seem worth paying when the outcome is good. But what about when the patients don't make it, when they undergo the torture without the benefit and die in the ICU? How can we weigh the importance of the probability, at the time of treatment initiation, that the treatment will not be successful?

A few years ago, David Schiedermayer and I tried to characterize this particular "selection bias" by imagining how the group that was treated but not sampled might feel. With a flippancy that probably reflected our own anxieties as much as anything else, we called this group "the ungrateful dead." Schiedermayer and I somewhat playfully imagined asking not just those who survived but also those who died whether they were grateful, whether they would do it again. We suspected that their answers would be different.

It seems odd that studies should focus either on patients who survive or on patients who die, showing that one group is grateful and would do it again, while the other group can't speak for itself, but it's spokespeople express regret and remorse over what was done or not done. The real problem, however, is that in intensive care it is hard to tell for sure at the time when decisions must be made which patients are going to live and which are going to die. To be useful in the real time of clinical decision making, a clinical approach would have to be developed that didn't depend upon the outcome.

In a sense, this thought experiment is the basis of the modern hospice movement. As we imagine the "ungrateful dead," we come to the conclusion that they would not thank us for the intensive-care treatments that we provided in a desperate attempt to prolong their lives. Instead, they might have wished to die another way, in another place, with treatments directed toward another goal. For them, we begin to question the value of intensive care in a more profound way. We must begin to develop criteria for determining who should be treated and who should not, and we must imagine a moral, legal, and cultural framework that would allow the possibility for choices like Dr. Miller's to discontinue mechanical ventilation for Baby Boy Jones. Such choices will always be difficult, and sometimes they will seem wrong. The implications of wrong decisions are so enormous that the doctors and nurses who make them find ways of protecting themselves from even an awareness that they are making them.

Lorrie Moore's story of the cancer ward beautifully captures the odd complacency of the doctors and nurses. When, in answer to a question, the oncologist shrugs his shoulders, she thinks, "What casual gestures these doctors are permitted!" In that response she summarizes the galactic differences between the engagement of professionals, for whom critical or life-threatening illness is a day-in, day-out experience, and that of parents or patients, for whom it is a singularly intense, life-shattering moment of profound existential awareness.

There is a reason for the professional's complacency or casualness. Most patients in NICUs or pediatric hospitals do well. For most babies *no* life-and-death decisions have to be made. Surprisingly, the day-to-day experience of professionals in the NICU is not one of constant moral dilemmas. In one recent study examining outcomes for babies who weighed less than 1,500 grams at birth, 83 percent of infants survived, compared with 74 percent in 1988. Survival rates ranged from 49 percent for infants weighing 501–750 grams at birth to 95 percent for those weighing more than 1,000 grams.[7] The majority of deaths occurred soon after birth and did not involve agonizing moral decisions. Instead, the babies died in spite of the fact that everything that could be done was done.

Dr. Miller acted almost intuitively, and if he had been correct in his assessment, as most of the doctors are most of the time, Baby Boy Jones would have died and the case would have been sad but not agonizingly stressful, not the basis for ongoing controversy. The overall survival rate for even the tiniest babies who survive the first three days is close to 90 percent. In order to survive, these babies need supplemental oxygen, intravenous antibiotics, and intravenous nutrition, but these interventions work. Babies who surely would have died without the ministrations of the caregivers are cured and sent home with their grateful and uncomprehending parents. Run-of-the-mill miracles are common in the NICU. Lives are saved, tragedies averted. Oddly, however, such cases leave little emotional residue. As a resident in the NICU, I generally did not feel like a miracle worker. The miraculous cases quickly became almost boring, perhaps because they were the ones that took the least personal or emotional involvement. It didn't feel like I was the one who was saving lives. Instead, lives were saved by a collective of which I was a small part. The most successful cases were the ones in which the medical interventions all worked just as they were supposed to, with the result that it seemed simple, almost mindless, as if it could have all been done without me.

At the opposite extreme were disastrous cases. Some babies developed one complication after another and exemplified, in their short lives, whole textbooks of polysyllabic Latinate pathology. These were cases like the one involving Dr. Miller and Baby Boy Jones. They had intraventricular hemorrhage, patent ductus arteriosus, cholestatic jaundice, nephritis, uremia, septicemia, necrotizing enterocolitis, bronchopulmonary dysplasia, periventricular leukomalacia, spastic quadriplegia. These babies haunted me and all my colleagues. Even when it seemed that the babies could not possibly survive, and I longed to just let them die, somehow neither doctors nor parents could bring themselves to stop. The babies lived on, from one month to the next, and were passed from one intern to the next with sighs and averted eyes. Their parents would visit the NICU less and less. The nurses would try to avoid assignment to their care. The social workers would be called in to try to pull together the pieces of the families that had been torn apart by the emotional demands of a roller coaster with no brakes. And, of course, in the back of everybody's mind were the extraordinary hospital bills that we were generating and the nagging concern that this was not only money down the drain but money that could be spent much better elsewhere for children who would truly benefit from it.

There was something both terrible and arbitrary about the NICU. It was hard to tell which babies would live and which would die. Sometimes, against all the odds, these seemingly doomed babies would get better. Not just a little better but all better. They would begin to breathe, to pee, to eat, and to move. The light would come back into their eyes. Their parents would reappear. They would go home, swaddled in a blanket, and come back to the clinic looking for all the world like normal happy babies in normal happy families. And we would point to them and say, "See, that is why we keep going, that is the goal, that is the justification."

In other cases the endings were not so happy. The babies would remain on oxygen, remain on their ventilators. They would not be able to eat because their premature intestines, which had collapsed and died under the stress of living, had been surgically removed. The bleeding into their brains left the babies retarded, spastic, and epileptic. They would be on medications to help them breathe, medications to stop their seizures, medications to relax their muscles, dry their oral secretions, and supplement their inadequate parenteral diets. But early on we couldn't tell which babies would be which, and by the time we could tell, it wasn't clear whether it was morally right, legally permissible, or emotionally tolerable to stop treatment and let them die.

Sometimes they would die anyway. It was never clear what sort of response that demanded of interns. Death was seldom explicitly acknowledged. When it occurred, no allowance was made for its power or impact, no time or support was given for grieving. The implicit message, imparted through the design of our educational curriculum and the schedule of our responsibilities, was that we should take the deaths of our patients in stride and not let them affect us or our work. There were, after all, many more patients who needed us.

For most of the attending physicians the death of a baby was a personal defeat. Only one, Dr. Anne Fletcher, seemed to have gotten beyond this narrow view. She was willing to talk to parents of babies in the NICU about stopping treatment and allowing their babies to die. Some parents seemed receptive to such talk, and together the doctor and the parents would make a decision that it was time to discontinue life support. The baby would be moved to a quiet back corner of the NICU, the family would gather around the bassinet, and a nurse would remove the endotracheal tube, turn off the monitors, and sit with the family. Usually death came quickly. It was usually peaceful and almost anticlimactic after the drama of intensive care.

As interns we had mixed feelings about Dr. Fletcher. She was the only attending physician who seemed to have any sense of the perverse reality of what we were sometimes being called upon to do in the NICU and the only one who seemed to be willing to do something about it. Her willingness to acknowledge the limitations seemed so right in some ways. But there was also something a little frightening about it. What if she was wrong? What if some of the babies for whom she stopped life support would have survived? Was she just "into death" in some weird way? We made jokes about her and kept our distance. She had a different sort of power and mystique than the other doctors. It didn't seem to be something that she could teach or that we could learn even if we aspired to it. Her special power was something that she had earned, in ways that we could only imagine. She seemed to carry within her some secret, incommunicable grief that allowed her to talk to parents in a special way and gain their trust. Mostly, we were happy to be in the NICU during the months when she was the attending physician, though it was sometimes a little hard to tell whether that was because she was taking good care of the babies or because she was taking good care of us. And we needed care badly.

By February of my internship year the schedule was taking its toll on those of us in the trenches. The hospital was full to the brim, mostly with children who suffered from one chronic disease or another and had gotten diarrhea or the flu, which, in their already debilitated condition, they couldn't handle. Every night would bring six, eight, or ten new admissions and as many discharges. We were both treating and triaging, trying to allocate the scarce resource of a bed in the children's hospital by figuring out who really needed one and who could get along without one. Our care was all crisis intervention. We were not sensitive or holistic. We were technically pragmatic and ruthlessly competent. The emergency room was full and chaotic. The busier it got, the more exhausted we became. We were starting to catch all the viruses we were treating and beginning to wonder if we would to make it. We insisted on a staff meeting with our chief residents.

It started as a basic gripe session. Too much work, too little sleep, complaints about medical records. But then Ellie began to talk. Ellie had the toughest schedule of any intern. By the luck of the draw, she had gotten her vacation months early in the year and then had to work eight straight months on the wards. February was her sixth month in a row on call. She had gone from the NICU to the cancer ward to adolescent medicine and back to the NICU. At the beginning of the year Ellie had never been without a smile. Now her face was tense, her eyes hollow, and in her voice there was both a strange resignation and an unsoothable ache.

When she began to speak at this meeting, she didn't complain about all the things that everybody else was complaining about—the inadequate food when we were on call, the medical records that didn't show up when we needed them, the lack of sleep, the unfair call schedule. She seemed almost beyond those petty concerns. Instead, she started to talk about death, the topic that hovered all around us all that year like a faithful ghost but that we were all afraid to acknowledge.

Ellie described the recent death of one of her teenage patients. It was someone whom Ellie had met during her month on oncology and to whom she had gotten quite close. The girl had bone cancer. Her leg had been amputated, but the cancer had returned and metastasized and there was nothing more that we could offer. Her death was anticipated, inevitable. At that time there was no home hospice that would accept a teenager, and so she had been in and out of the hospital, receiving palliative care for the incurable and painful metastases to her liver and brain. On some admissions she would perk up a bit and even tell funny stories. She liked to adjust her own narcotics so that she would still be able to read, watch movies, and otherwise enjoy the little bit of life she had left. Her story was moving and tragic. We'd all gotten to know this patient over the course of the year, but Ellie had cared for her the most and gotten the closest. Her parents and younger sister were loving and devoted, as well as dejected and angry. They sometimes fought with one another or with us. Like all good advocates, they were not always easy to get along with.

When the end came, it was peaceful but also very sad. No matter how much a death is anticipated, it is always shockingly painful for those close to the patient. Ellie cried. The family cried. The nurses cried. The hospital room became transformed momentarily into something different, a surprisingly spiritual place. As deaths go, this was a good one. The grief that came with the inevitable end was not entirely unwelcome. It was a healing sort of pain.

Then, Ellie said, her beeper went off. It was the Emergency Room. She had two asthmatics to admit. Her beeper went off again. It was a nurse in the toddler unit saying that a patient's IV line had fallen out and asking Ellie to come and restart it. Her beeper went off again. Sitting next to the deathbed, she felt a deep moral obligation to stay connected. And she felt her own emotional need to grieve a little. At the same time, all the routine stuff of a pediatric intern's night on call was piling up. The two sets of demands seemed incommensurable, absurd, ultimately enraging. As she told this story to the hushed group of interns and chief residents, she began to cry, but she kept talking, tears rolling down her cheeks, her voice getting huskier with her determination to say what she had to say, to demand what she knew was her right to say and be heard. One by one, we all began to cry with her. How could we be expected to carry on like this? How could we be human when our education consisted in such institutionalized inhumanity? She was not asking for much, Ellie said. She could do eight months in a row of caring for sick and dying children. She could do it without sleeping every third night. She could cover the cancer patients and the preemies and those injured in motor-vehicle accidents and the child-abuse cases. She was pretty tough, she thought. But she also thought that when one of her patients died, she should be allowed a little time, just an hour or two, to sit with the family and grieve and to let herself feel something. Couldn't the educational system allow a little time for doctors to feel something now and again?

Our chief residents said they would see what could be done, but not much could be done. Doing anything would require some explicit acknowledgment that death happens and that some explicit planning for it was appropriate and humane. Such an acknowledgment was not part of the administrative mindset, the educational mindset, or the institutional culture. We were learning a lot about death and dying and about how doctors were supposed to respond to it.

In *The House of God* Samuel Shem tells of the suicide of a colleague during his internship year. All of the other interns wondered whether they should have seen it coming, whether they could have done anything about it, and whether it could also happen to them. They were sad and angry. They needed time to process the loss, time to try to understand it, time to grieve for their lost friend and colleague. Shem writes, "[The Chief] seemed upset, puzzled that one of his boys had killed himself. He talked about 'the pressures of the internship year' and about 'the waste of a great talent.' He reassured us that he wanted to give us some time off to mourn. However, he could not do this. In fact, we'd have to all work a little harder, to fill in."[8]

The psychological result of this sociological approach to death should come as no surprise. The lost emotions of grief became terrifying talismans of pain. Any situation that even begins to remind doctors of death becomes a situation to be avoided. The cycle is self-reinforcing. The longer it goes on, the harder it is to break. There was no attempt in the residency program described in *The House of God,* and no attempt in our residency program, to begin to acknowledge the sadness, the pain, and the grief that comes when a patient dies. There was no inkling that these feelings were not something to be avoided but something to be honored. We hurt because we care. If we could not allow ourselves to really feel the pain, even for an hour or two, then we would certainly not allow ourselves to continue to really care very much either. And any conversation that might trigger those feelings would become a dangerous conversation to be avoided. Discussions about death and dying would become discussions about the proper way to do cardiopulmonary resuscitation or the proper doses of drugs to give, about ventilator settings or, for the more touchy-feely, about new modalities of palliative care, about morphine drips, about living wills. Some of the things we needed to learn weren't in textbooks. The most important of these had nothing to do with helping patients survive. It had more to do with how we were going to survive.

It was strange, so strange, how thoughts of these scenes, these books, these memories, and these fears came to me unbidden as I sat in the law office years later and the lawyer, in his scabrous innocence, tried to gently and disingenuously establish the unreliability of any opinions I might later give. Thoughts of these scenes flitted through my mind as I struggled to answer the questions honestly but defensively. I didn't want to give away any more than I had to.

"Well, much of what we were learning was not really what we were being taught. It was almost in spite of what we were being taught. We were *being taught* to think rationally and carefully through problems in differential diagnosis or pathophysiology. And that was important. But what we were *learning* was how to make intuitive assessments of the health status of critically ill children, and how to leap into action in the middle of the night, cold and sleep-deprived and a little groggy, and how to intervene to avert crises." He seemed intrigued with my characterization of the process of medical education. I wondered whether he had similar memories of his own.

"Are you suggesting that doctors in training are doing things that they are not being taught to do by their professors?"

"Medical training, as you know, is set up like an apprenticeship. It is experiential. We learned some things from the professors and other things from the senior residents. Those were the real survival skills. In a teaching hospital, there are many things that everybody is doing that are so new that nobody really understands them. We learn together."

"Did you learn that doctors should use their skill and training to save the lives of patients who were in their care?"

"Objection. Leading question."

It was the woman lawyer. She was starting to sense that things were heating up. I wondered if she understood what was going on, how sneakily disingenuous this line of questioning was, coming from a physician. He knew the answers to these questions better than I did. He had done an internship decades before, when the supervision of interns was even more haphazard. But he also knew that nobody outside the medical profession really knew or wanted to know. There were layers upon layers of meanings here, the strange dichotomies between the patients' experiences of ICU care and their subsequent choices, the bizarre process of medical education, the learning how and when to save lives and sometimes how and when not to even try, the spiritual repercussions of those experiences of that strangely anticlimactic moment of death, the mystique of a Dr. Fletcher, the holiness of Ellie's suffering, all filtered through my own consciousness and brought to bear on the evaluation of another doctor, Dr. Miller, who himself must have suffered similarly and must have wanted to do something about the suffering. Was he a Dr. Fletcher? Was he an empathetic idealist or a burnt-out cynic? I didn't answer.

"I'll rephrase the question. Did you learn that preserving life is the central goal of the medical profession?"

"Same objection. You can answer."

"Well, I began to see that the decisions about treating or not treating premature babies were among the most difficult that any doctor, or any parent, could ever be faced with. It became clear that there were no easy answers. Different doctors had different approaches. Sometimes, we would do everything 'right' and the results would be horrific. Other times, we did things that seemed wrong or even made mistakes and the outcome was okay. The lessons I was learning from these experiences were not straightforward. But I became intrigued by the challenge of trying to figure out what it might mean to decide which decisions were the right ones in which circumstances. I was like a scientist who realized that there were many areas of medicine in which we didn't seem to understand the most basic things about a particular disease. In this case, though, it wasn't the scientific part of medical care that we were ignorant of but the moral part. So mostly what I learned was how much we didn't understand. And although I did not become a neonatologist, I did become committed to learning about and studying the issues surrounding these decisions."

He grimaced dourly, as if this answer left a sour taste in his mouth.

FOUR

Standards of Care

"Doctor, is it your understanding that in this case Dr. Miller thought the baby was going to die?"

"Yes, I think he did."

"But he was wrong . . ."

He paused.

I waited. After all, I was there to answer questions.

He waited too, looking at me. He seemed both sure of himself and also just a little puzzled. There was something heartrendingly simple about the way he was going about this. Right and wrong seemed to him to be straightforward and dichotomous.

" . . . wasn't he?"

"Yes, as it turned out, he was wrong."

"And do you thing that his mistaken assessment of the baby's prognosis was the basis of his decision to discontinue medical therapy for the baby?"

There he goes again, I thought, trying to set another of his little traps. If I say that Miller stopped treatment because he thought it was futile, then he clearly made a mistake. If he stopped for other reasons, then what were those reasons? Perhaps he considered the fact that even if the baby did survive, it would likely be with terrible neurological damage. But if so, then his decision would be characterized as one based upon the baby's anticipated "quality of life," and he could be accused of discriminating against the disabled. Miller would then be caricatured as someone who thought that some lives were not worth living, as little better than a Nazi. Tough choice. Is it better to be simply incompetent or to be downright evil? Got to be careful here. I glanced at "my" lawyers. They seemed complacent. The strange rhetorical game of malpractice testimony, with its formal rules of evidence, its theatricality, and its rhythm of move and countermove, seemed almost chesslike. In both there were rules for types of moves you were allowed to make. But chess, though complex, had a finite number of possibilities, and there was, it seemed, always a "best" move. Build a big enough and fast enough computer, and it could overcome even the best combination of imperfect calculation and excellent intuition. I wondered about the possibility of building a computer that could arrive at a good moral judgment. I guess I'd rather fight it out as a mistaken futility assessment than as a paternalistically imposed "quality of life" assessment.

"Well, I don't know what Dr. Miller's thought process was, exactly. But for most doctors in this situation, the extremely low likelihood of survival would have been the primary consideration."

"Doctor, it seems to me that when the decision is a matter of life and death, we should set very high standards for competence. Our tolerance for mistakes should be zero. Do you think it is *ever* acceptable for a doctor to discontinue life-sustaining treatment on a nonconsenting patient before he is certain that his patient will not survive?"

"That seems to be asking for more certainty than is possible. Doctors are often uncertain whether their patients are going to survive or die."

"Well, then, don't you think that the most ethical thing to do would be to continue treatment until they are certain?"

"Sometimes," I lamely suggested to the lawyer, "patients in ICUs don't want to be treated."

"Was there any evidence in this case that the patient did not want to be treated?"

"No, that doesn't apply to this case."

"Is there ever such evidence in neonatal cases?"

"No, obviously, the patients do not participate in such decisions."

"Well, then, shouldn't the doctors err on the side of life?"

"Generally, they should."

"Well, tell me this, then, doctor. Given that the patient could not participate in the decision, and given that the decision was based on a mistaken assessment that the baby could not survive, don't you think that Dr. Miller should have continued his resuscitative efforts until he was certain that they would not be successful?"

There's a nice, simple idea, I thought. A world without risk. Just continue treatment until we are certain. That way, obviously, we would only treat babies who would live, and we would not treat babies who were going to die. This seemingly simple solution to a complex problem quickly becomes a complex problem of its own with no simple solution. What does it mean to be "certain" when we are trying to predict the future? Prediction, prognostication, and prophecy have always been more a divine than a human prerogative, but we are getting better at these tasks, at least on some levels. We no longer rely on divine revelation. Instead, we rely on logistic regression. Clinical epidemiologists have developed statistically rigorous predictors of morbidity and mortality for many critically ill patients.

There is a certain irreducible level of ambiguity about each baby's chances for survival as well as each baby's subjective experience. How much do they suffer? This is an important but essentially metaphysical, rather than scientific, question. Would a baby in these circumstances want to be treated or allowed to die? In similar circumstances reasonable adults may disagree on the appropriateness of treatment. Those disagreements serve as a sort of metaphoric moral guideline to neonatal decisions, which seem to be irreducibly individualistic and imperfect. Perhaps the best we can do for babies is be equally idiosyncratic.

"I think Dr. Miller provided exemplary care," I said. "He did just what was appropriate, neither too little nor too much."

I felt partly heroic, partly ridiculous. Why should my opinion matter?

"I just want to be clear about this, now, doctor," Marcus Welby continued, in that tone of voice that says "watch out." "Is that merely your opinion as an ethics expert?"

"That is my opinion, yes."

"But Doctor, aren't there standards of care which tell us what should or shouldn't be done in particular cases?"

"Not always."

"But certainly in cases such as this, where the question is whether or not the doctor has properly performed cardiopulmonary resuscitation, the standards of the American Academy of Pediatrics or the American Heart Association would apply?"

"Not necessarily."

"Are you saying that *your* opinion as an *ethicist* about whether babies should be resuscitated is somehow better than the standards developed by clinical and scientific experts in physiology and pharmacology of cardiopulmonary resuscitation?" (I tried to judge whether the level of snideness in his voice peaked on *your* or on *ethicist*. It was a close call.)

"Not my standards, no. But there are different ways of determining what is or is not the 'standard of care.' Just because a committee or an expert says something is standard doesn't necessarily mean it is."

"Are there any books, articles, or guidelines about resuscitation that you consider authoritative?"

"No."

"Then one doctor's opinion is just as good as another's?"

I hate it when lawyers start talking about what is or is not the standard of care, as if it were a simple or straightforward concept. If it were so simple, there would be no need for expensive malpractice litigation. We'd simply turn to "the standard of care" manual, and it would say that for babies of this or that birthweight resuscitation must be continued for this or that length of time. The legal myth that energizes malpractice litigation is that there is a so-called standard of care out there somewhere, that it doesn't need to be created or defined but simply discovered and recognized. The cumbersome, arcane machinery of tort litigation is thought to identify that standard of care in a way that will allow the jury to determine whether a particular doctor adhered to or deviated from it. The "legal evidence" that will allow the jury to make that determination is imagined to be a sort of "truth," a set of facts about what was or was not *the* standard of care. It was that sort of truth that my questioner imagined (or pretended) we were in the process of illuminating.

The reality is completely different. Malpractice cases, and the lawyers, doctors, and juries involved in them, are doing something much more interesting and more complicated than uncovering an existing truth. They are listening to competing moral, scientific, and professional versions of the ideals of care and deciding which among them to authorize. In doing so, they are not merely identifying and applying existing standards; they are creating new ones. The real work of tort litigation is to identify situations in which there are no existing standards for behavior or areas in which the existing standards may be wrong and to use them as reference points in order to define new norms. Where there is a clear standard of care, it is usually pretty simple to determine whether it has been violated.

The process of defining the standard of care can take many forms. One is the method the lawyer suggested to me—looking to authoritative texts or other written documents. Another is to ask an expert what he or she thinks is the standard of care. A third is to study actual practices and empirically describe a standard. If the question was whether Dr. Miller was doing what other doctors would have done in similar circumstances, we could easily come up with an empirical answer. Good observational research shows that many doctors in fact do, and have done, exactly what Dr. Miller did. No, the real question was whether Dr. Miller and those other doctors should be allowed to continue doing what they have been doing. In other words, should we as a society permit doctors to discontinue the resuscitation of tiny premature babies after just ten minutes, or should we set a different standard? The process of litigation is a process of reification. In searching for a standard, the lawyers, doctors, judge, and jury will create one. If they do their job well, their newly created standard will become part of the next set of deliberations, and the process by which standards are validated and promulgated will continue.

Interestingly, the law is fairly clear and fairly uniform from state to state in telling lawyers, judges, and juries what they are about in such cases. In almost all jurisdictions a physician is obliged to use the "skill and care ordinarily used in similar circumstances." Negligence is defined as the failure to do so. Except in rare instances (e.g., leaving a sponge behind during an operation) lay juries are assumed to be unfamiliar with medical practice and so rely on the testimony of expert medical witnesses. These witnesses, in turn, are charged with describing the standard of medical care on the basis of their knowledge and experience.

But there is an inherent, well-recognized problem with this approach. Recollections of individual experience are inevitably flawed. Furthermore, they are consistently flawed in a nonrandom way. People asked about events in the past underestimate large numbers, overestimate small numbers, and skew responses in favor of outcomes deemed more "appropriate" or "desirable."[1] Experts are not immune to these all-too-human memory flaws. The net effect of this well-recognized psychological phenomenon upon malpractice testimony is predictable. Experts' opinions about the standard of care tend toward an ideal rather than a real description of clinical practice.

This tendency can have a real and important effect on the process of malpractice litigation. In order to show how this might occur, William Meadow and colleagues surveyed a number of pediatric experts regarding the following clinical scenario:

A 9-month-old boy presents to the Emergency Room with fever and irritability. The clinical personnel suspect meningitis. They perform a lumbar puncture, send spinal fluid to the lab, draw blood tests, start an intravenous line, and administer intravenous antibiotics.[2]

This is a common clinical scenario. The doctors surveyed would recently have participated in the care of children with suspected meningitis. These potential experts were practicing physicians in pediatric emergency medicine and pediatric infectious diseases. In answering, they might have been expected to draw on recent memories of actual cases. Meadow and his colleagues asked them to report their experiences regarding the median time from initial presentation in the emergency room until the administration of intravenous antibiotics to a child with suspected meningitis by answering one simple question:"How long does it take, from the time of presentation to the emergency department until the time of antibiotic administration, in your hospital?"

This survey, conducted in 1993, was motivated by a real malpractice case in which a child brought to the emergency room was eventually diagnosed as having meningitis and treated with appropriate antibiotics. He survived but ended up with a profound hearing loss. In a review of his records it was noted that there had been an initial delay of about two hours from the time he arrived in the emergency department until he got his first dose of antibiotics. His parents and their lawyers alleged that this delay had led to the hearing loss and that the doctors had been negligent to let so much time pass before the antibiotics were given. A number of "experts" who were regarded as leaders in the field of pediatric infectious diseases agreed that a two-hour delay was negligent. In their depositions they stated that it was the standard of care to administer antibiotics within thirty minutes to a child with suspected meningitis in the emergency department. Leading textbooks in pediatric infectious diseases and emergency medicine support this view.

Meadow and his colleagues then compared these "expert" opinions to reality. In order to do that, they reviewed medical records of all the children who had been diagnosed with meningitis over a two-year period in the emergency departments of two large children's hospitals. They noted exactly how long it took from the time when a child registered in the emergency department until the time when the antibiotics were given.

The opinions the experts offered about the standard of care generally differed significantly from the actual practices of doctors whose care might be thought to represent the "ordinary circumstances" imagined in the legal definition of the standard of care. Moreover, the experts' opinions were "wrong" in a predictable direction. They leaned toward the desirable outcome, that is, a shorter elapsed time. The emergency room physicians estimated that the time was 46 minutes, and infectious-disease physicians said 80 minutes. In actual practice the average elapsed time was 120 minutes.

So what is "the standard of care" when it comes to the amount of time that should elapse before a child suspected of having meningitis is given antibiotics in the emergency department? If, as defined in the law, the standard of care is what a reasonably prudent doctor would actually do in similar circumstances, then it would be 120 minutes. If, as often seems to be the case in malpractice litigation, it is whatever an expert who appears to be knowledgeable can convince the jury that doctors ought to do, then it might be 30 minutes, 46 minutes, or 80 minutes. It would be interesting to know whether experts say what they think doctors *actually* do or what they think doctors *ought* to do, that is, whether their standard of care is an empirical real or a moral ideal.

And this only scratches the surface of the controversy. In the above example, 30 minutes and 120 minutes represent single points of a value that is distributed across a range. Even if the *mean* is 30 minutes, the range could be 15 to 45 minutes. At exactly what point does a delay become negligence? At the 50th percentile of standard care? the 10th percentile? the 90th?

It is clearly possible to determine what doctors actually do in some circumstances. In the case of Baby Boy Jones the lawyers wanted to know whether doctors always initiate resuscitation for babies born at 600 grams or twenty-five weeks' gestation. The clearly provable empirical answer is that they do not. Numerous peer-reviewed studies published in mainstream medical journals in the United States, Canada, and Europe show that resuscitation is never even attempted for many babies born at this birthweight and gestational age.[3] However, in most guidelines for resuscitation of premature babies no absolute cutoff is given for the birthweight or the gestational age at which resuscitation should never be attempted or at which resuscitation should always be attempted. There is still room for a Dr. Fletcher or a Dr. Miller to exercise professional judgment, to take a personal moral position, that may be slightly different from that of his or her colleagues.

Because the existing guidelines constitute a necessarily incomplete indication of the standard of care, one might conclude that there is no standard of care, or no known standard of care, or a wide range of clinical decisions that fall within the standard of care. Or one might say that the standard of care leaves room for clinical judgment and individualized decision making. Or one might say that the standard of care is not determined by doctors alone. The conversation between a retired physician turned plaintiff's attorney and a pediatrician-ethicist called as an expert witness was part of the process of determining the standard of care to which doctors would be held in the future. The plaintiff's attorney was goading the ethicist to "clarify" something that both understood only too well. We were both pretending for the jury that doctors were more knowledgeable and precise, and that medicine was more scientific and orderly, than in fact is true. He and I were doing more to define the standard of care for neonatal resuscitation than all the neonatologists in practice in the world, or all the consensus panels, or all the scientific studies. If he could get a $35 million settlement for his tiny client, then the standard of care would certainly move toward mandatory resuscitation for all 25-week babies whether or not the scientific evidence supported it, experts endorsed it, or doctors in active practice thought it was medically or ethically appropriate.

Many scholars who have studied decision making in NICUs have noted that doctors seem driven by a technological imperative to push the limits, to develop new and better machines and techniques, to save sicker and sicker patients. In the late 1980s Jeanne Guillemin and Lynda Holmstrom undertook a sociological analysis of decision making in the NICU and concluded that "the most fundamental decision—whether or not to 'go all out'—was easily and routinely made, and the answer was in the affirmative. . . . the decision to be aggressive did not involve long discussion, reflection, or emotional agonizing. On the contrary, such decisions were virtually automatic."[4] They noted that physicians would rather err on the side of treating someone who would ultimately die than not treat someone who might ultimately have survived.

Guillemin and Holmstrom echo the common perception of neonatologists and other critical-care doctors as unreflective, more interested in their high-tech machines or their survival statistics than in the lives of their patients, callously imposing unwanted treatment on helpless babies and equally helpless parents. The doctors are seen as the driving force, while the parents are seen as passively succumbing to the doctors' mindless decisions. It may be, however, that the individual doctors are not nearly so powerful or autonomous. Dr. Miller tried to act autonomously. He made a difficult decision to resist the temptation of technologic determinism. As a result, he was being meticulously scrutinized and might be severely punished for it. Doctors seem to be just as passive as parents, not proactive but responsive, in complex ways, to powerful legal, moral, economic, and other social pressures.

In some ways, even the verdict in the case won't really matter. Dr. Miller is being punished whether he wins or loses. Cases like his are already part of every neonatologist's nightmares. It takes years for such cases to make their way through the courts.[5] Sometimes the cases are settled secretly, without a clear determination of what does or does not constitute negligence. Awards seem to bear little relationship to the egregiousness of the actions they are meant to punish.[6] After all, there will always be experts on both sides. What will the jury do when experts disagree? Clearly, juries may be swayed less by the facts of the case than by the charisma of the witnesses or the skill of the cross-examining attorneys. The result is that similar cases may not be decided similarly and that the decisions will reflect something other than a dispassionate determination of whether the standard of care was met. This violates a fundamental principle of jurisprudence, namely, that a judicial system of negligence determination should reach similar conclusions in similar cases. From the individual doctor's perspective, it is far better to do whatever it takes to avoid litigation, even if it doesn't seem to be the right thing to do, than to risk entanglement in this crazy system.

When calculating the effect of this case on doctors' behavior, it little matters that the system of malpractice litigation in the United States today is arbitrary, expensive, quite different from the systems in other countries, and often unjust. It little matters that cases of known negligence often do not lead to litigation or that litigation is often pursued in cases of no negligence.[7]

One fundamental reason for this failing is an inability or unwillingness to confront the implications of the observable difference between what doctors actually do, what they say they do, and opinions about what they ought to do. In the case involving antibiotics for meningitis, a review of what real doctors do in real situations showed that actual practices varied substantially from what experts in the field said that doctors actually do in this situation. Furthermore, the experts' opinions were closer to the standards advocated in medical textbooks, although they were not consistent with the actual data in the empirical scientific medical journals. These experts and textbook writers were trying, in a subtle and implicit way, to change what *is* in order to make it conform more closely with what they thought *ought* to be.

Dr. Miller's decision to discontinue resuscitation was at odds with some, but not all, expert recommendations. It was consistent with common practice in many hospitals around the country and throughout the industrialized world. But there were many experts who, for many reasons, thought that decisions such as that made by Dr. Miller should not be accepted or acceptable. They were ready and willing to testify that Dr. Miller's decision fell outside the standard of care, and they would be paid a lot of money to do so. And I was being paid a lot of money to testify that it did not fall outside that standard.

These pressures upon doctors often push them in opposing directions. Moral pressures can push them one way while the legal and economic pressures push them another way. Was Dr. Miller right to stop resuscitation? Philosophers, theologians, social scientists, and parents might all have an opinion, but the opinions of the jury, guided by these lawyers, would be the only opinion that was backed up by millions of dollars in punitive damages.

. . .

I answered the lawyer's question slowly.

"It is not that one doctor's opinion is as good as another's, or that there is no standard of care. It is just that in situations like this, practice is more complicated than theory. In this case, there may have been a violation of some theoretical standard of care. You will probably find plenty of experts who will testify that that is the case. But I don't think that the care given by Dr. Miller was in any way out of the ordinary. In fact, I think it conforms quite well with what many good doctors do, or would want to do, or wish they would have done in similar circumstances. In that sense, it is not merely my *opinion* that Dr. Miller did a good job. It is an empirical fact that he did his job the way most competent and caring doctors in his field would have done it. If that isn't the standard of care, then I don't know what is."

The lawyer looked back at me with a curious expression on his face. His eyes narrowed and seemed to harden a bit. I had the feeling that this contest was really just beginning. He scared me a bit. His real goal, in all this seemingly friendly conversation, was to destroy my ideas and my credibility. His technique was like some subtle martial-art form. He was trying to get me to destroy myself. He wasn't overpowering or dominating. Instead, he was subtle and insinuating.

The sky over the lake was still a brilliant blue. Oddly, although he scared me, I sort of liked him. I envied his certainty and his simplicity. We were far from the academy, where the play of ideas was simply sport. We were out in the tort jungle, where no holds were barred and the best argument was not necessarily the most elegant or subtle or even correct one but the one that could best persuade the good citizens on the jury. And although I was not the defendant, I was starting to feel that my ideas were on trial. I smiled and met his gaze.

Prognostication and Futility

"Doctor, you said a moment ago, did you not, that Dr. Miller thought the baby was going to die?" The tone of voice here was historical, matter-of-fact.

"Yes, I think that is what Dr. Miller thought."

"But the baby didn't die, did he?" A hint, just the faintest hint, of triumphant glee. He was like a boxer, dancing and jabbing, maneuvering for a knockout punch. He was warming up to it.

"No, the baby did not die."

"So, in your opinion as an ethics expert, would you say that Dr. Miller was wrong?"

"Yes, as it turned out, he was wrong."

"He made a mistake?"

"In a narrow, technical sense, he made a mistake, but I'm not sure that, in a larger sense, he made a mistake."

"Doctor"—his voice, now patient and condescending, was like that of a stern but loving parent gently guiding a naughty child to tell the truth about a bad thing the child had done—"Doctor, he thought the patient was going to die. Clearly the patient didn't die. It was a life-and-death decision. Does that seem like a 'narrow and technical' issue to you?"

"Decisions about death and dying are not so straightforward as they used to be."

"Shouldn't even a minimally competent doctor have the basic expertise to not pronounce his patient dead before the patient has died?"

What could I say? "Generally, yes."

"And as a moral issue, shouldn't a doctor who makes a mistake in this regard be held accountable for that mistake?" He was feeling pretty full of himself now. I had an image of a fisherman reeling in a big catch, a butterfly collector with his net poised, a big game hunter with a rhinoceros in his telescopic sight.

"Accountability is a complex concept. Miller should be held accountable in the sense that he has an obligation to care for his patient as best he can, but that doesn't necessarily mean he should be sued or punished."

"Doctor, I'm asking a yes or no question. Should a doctor who makes a mistake be held accountable for that mistake?"

"Generally, yes."

"Yes or no?"

"Sir, if you want to both ask and answer the questions, than you don't need me here, thank you."

"All right. Generally? Why not always?"

Why indeed? Right and wrong, good and bad, ethical and unethical, accountable and unaccountable, all seem to have become much less straightforward concepts in medicine than they used to be. He might as well have asked whether it would be suicide if an adult patient who didn't want to receive every available life-sustaining treatment were allowed to refuse treatment. He might have asked whether a doctor who agreed to withhold life-sustaining treatment for such a patient was assisting suicide or murdering his patient. He might as well have asked why people must make use of such complex procedural devices as living wills, advance directives, and hospice care in order to die as they wish to die. He might have asked why a field of inquiry that questions the moral presumptions of doctors and medicine has grown up in the late twentieth century and why one of its primary areas of interest has been the way we make decisions for critically ill and dying patients. But no, instead he was carrying on with his increasingly paradoxical line of thought. His questions suggested that doctors are, and should be, supremely reasonable and competent, that they follow orderly standards of care, and that they should be held to those standards. He imagined a medical profession that could and should hold itself to very high standards of perfection. Yet his whole field of professional activity was based upon antagonism toward the autonomy or professionalism of physicians. He tried to lock doctors into a set of standard procedures that would be defined from outside the profession. Of course, he pretended, perhaps naively, perhaps disingenuously, that he was not doing the defining, that he was merely uncovering, articulating, elucidating. But the structure of the inquiry was as much a part of the results as the substance. The legal reductionism and the oversimplification of the circumstances, the moral challenges, and the ultimate implications were not naive. This inquiry was as hostile as any inquisition. I wondered whether he took only cases involving babies, or only cases involving the withholding of life-sustaining treatment? Had he once allowed someone to die who might have lived, and did the regret still haunt him? Did he see himself as the last true moralist and this conversation with witnesses like me as an ultimate struggle for authenticity, for identity?

This sort of moral scrutiny of medical practices by nonphysicians, be they lawyers, philosophers, theologians, or social scientists, is interesting and new. The ethics of doctors and their medical practices have always been a focus of concern, but in the past, codes of ethics primarily addressed moral concerns that focused upon the unique and fragile relationship between doctors and their patients. Because patients were ill and vulnerable, the doctors could easily misuse their superior power and knowledge to take advantage of patients. The situation was one of inherent moral risk. Codes of ethics focused on issues such as confidentiality and trust, on prohibitions against the sexual exploitation of patients, and on reinforcing doctors' promise to be devoted loyally and single-mindedly to each individual patient. The codes tried to make explicit the implicit promises that each and every doctor was to offer to each and every patient.

The codes often prohibited certain types of medical activities. The Hippocratic oath, for example, specifically prohibits abortion, euthanasia, and surgery ("even for stone"). The prohibitions did not derive from the firm conviction that such procedures were intrinsically wrong or immoral. Instead, they grew out of a sense of professional purity. There was a specific philosophy of healing in the Hippocratic distinctions and prohibitions. Surgery may sometimes be healing, as may abortion, but both represent an attempt to work against the forces of nature rather than with them, and the Hippocratic approach opposes that sort of intervention. Thus, it might be right for a woman to have an abortion in certain circumstances, but it would be wrong for a Hippocratic physician to perform it. Surgery might be necessary in some instances, but it did not follow that the Hippocratic doctor should perform the surgery.

This focus on professional purity remains a part of medical ethics. It recently led a group of doctors to oppose active euthanasia by arguing that "doctors must not kill," suggesting, by omission, a more tolerant attitude toward nonphysicians who engaged in euthanasia.[1] It wasn't the euthanasia per se that was objectionable; it was the taint upon professional purity that participation in such an act would entail. It would violate the implicit promise of a particular type of physician, a Hippocratic one, to refrain from using his or her professional power and scientific knowledge to end life. Professional purity and professional limits were the primary issues addressed by ancient codes of medical ethics. They are not, however, the central concerns of modern bioethics.

Times have changed. Doctors were accountable then and remain accountable now, but in different ways and to somewhat different standards. Medicine is socially organized in a way that creates a new set of obligations. Doctors today serve society as well as individual patients. It is not clear whether we've made progress or fallen from grace, but things are clearly different.

Modern bioethics differs from all the medical ethics that came before in that it confronts a new type of moral ambiguity. It is no longer the case that doctors need only think about their psychological power and their character as it functions within the doctor-patient relationship. Unlike in bygone days, doctors cannot assume that if they forswear exploitation, conflicts of interest, and "impure" procedures, then their practice will be morally exemplary. The new moral problems are of a different type altogether. They arise in situations in which the doctors do everything right but the result is still wrong.

Modern bioethics confronts and tries to understand a new dualism that seems to be at the heart of modern medical practice. This dualism becomes evident when we recognize the moral problems that come from the successes rather than the failures of doctors and their interventions. When I expertly resuscitated that 600-gram baby only to have her die as predicted two days later, I did everything right, in a narrow sense, both medically and morally. As my teacher noted, I did a good job. The result was that I succeeded only in prolonging the baby's pain and suffering. I might ask whether I did the right thing. The answer should involve a careful calculation of the probabilities, a weighing of the risks and the benefits, a consideration of the costs, scrutiny of the decision-making process, or an attempt to understand the moral or spiritual status of a tiny premature baby. Modern bioethics focuses on those equations in which the sum of a series of right actions is an outcome that seems terribly wrong.

Although this sort of ethical dilemma is new for doctors, it is not new to technology in general. In a sense, it brings medicine into a debate involving new technologies that has been conducted for centuries. It is a debate familiar to American literature and philosophy. When Thoreau went to Walden Pond to live a simpler life, he bemoaned the encroachment of the railroad upon his pastoral retreat, recognizing, in a microcosmic way, the tradeoffs inherent in technological progress. Railroads, cars, nuclear power, and synthetic plastics have all raised issues such as this. Until recently, though, medicine has been largely exempt from this sort of questioning, primarily because the goals of medicine seemed so straightforward and supportable. That is no longer the case.

The new tension arose from the power of the new tools and techniques doctors had harnessed. In the Hippocratic past, doctors' most powerful tool was their healing persona, their charisma. The healer was the medicine. That the healer be with the patient was far more important than any particular treatment the healer might prescribe. Such healers suggested changes in diet and patterns of rest or prescribed pain-relieving drugs. These interventions seldom directly affected the underlying pathophysiological reality of the disease. Instead, they might alter people's perception of that reality. Doctors gave the suffering a meaning and a context. They could relieve the isolation that illness brings. Sometimes, because of their knowledge of different diseases, they could reassure patients that their disease was not fatal, and then the patients would get better. In other cases they could prepare patients for the possibility that they might not recover. These interventions were important. They created a moral framework for dealing with the limitations of being human, of getting sick, suffering, weakening, dying. But because the medicine itself was so relatively powerless, the patient was, in a sense, protected from technical mistakes the doctor might make. Instead, the main risk was of a moral or psychological error. Thus, these errors were the ones that the moral codes of ancient times addressed. The ethical issues that arose were the ethical issues of persona, charisma, and relationships. A helplessness in the face of human frailty and finitude was taken for granted; the question was how to affirm an idealism grounded in caring, compassion, and concern for another person who was suffering or dying.

Doctors today have a fundamentally new and different sort of power. By their interventions they can direct the course of an illness. They can actually cure some diseases at the physiological level without necessarily having any relationship with the patient. A surgeon can operate on a patient he has never met. An oncologist can diagnose a tumor based upon a pathological specimen and recommend an appropriate chemotherapeutic regimen without knowing anything about the patient's hopes, dreams, fears, or fantasies. Modern doctors can often influence the symptoms or the progression of diseases of patients who cannot be cured. They can diagnose and treat illnesses that cause no symptoms whatsoever, such as hypertension, or diseases that are only symptoms, accompanied by no measurable physiological abnormality, such as depression. The ancient safeguards are still necessary in the world of this new clinical reality, but they are no longer sufficient. The doctors' new power is not always benevolent or benign. Some interventions have terrible and un-foreseen consequences. The dilemma of ancient bioethics was how to care for one another in the face of the terrible and uncontrollable scourges that the world sent our way. The dilemma of modern bioethics is how not to create scourges of our own that are worse than the ones we are trying to alleviate.

The moral consequences of modern medical mistakes are different in sur-prising ways from the moral consequences of ancient medical mistakes. These modern mistakes can be of two types. One type is an unforeseen bad side effect of an intervention. This type of consequence is well known. For ex-ample, diethylstilbestrol (DES), an estrogen derivative that was widely used in the 1940s and 1950s to prevent premature labor in pregnant women, turned out to have terrible consequences for the daughters born to those women. Many had uterine abnormalities that caused infertility. A few developed vagi-nal cancers at a young age. Another example of an intervention with a bad side effect is the use of radiation therapy to treat acne, which caused cancers of the skin and of the thyroid gland. Others include thalidomide taken dur-ing pregnancy, which caused birth defects, and supplemental oxygen therapy, given to premature babies with breathing problems in the 1940s and 1950s, which caused many of them to develop a bizarre and previously unseen dis-ease of the retina that led to blindness.[2] Many other such stories can be told.

This type of terrible consequence raised concerns about the way new medical interventions were marketed. In response, the federal government tightened the process of drug testing and drug approval, expanded the man-date of the Food and Drug Administration, and developed more rigorous sta-tistical techniques for evaluating new drugs. These debacles and the responses of regulators and scientists represented one aspect of modern medicine's new ethical problems and suggested one type of solution. These sorts of prob-lems demanded careful attention and analysis. In many cases they led to im-portant corrective institutional or programmatic changes. But they did not really demand a fundamental moral reevaluation. Instead, they could be un-derstood as problems within the moral paradigm by which scientific progress entailed certain tradeoffs and certain injustices. The goal of those within and those overseeing the program of scientific progress was to minimize the costs, maximize the benefits, and try to ensure that the costs were fairly distributed. The paradigm itself did not need to be questioned. Instead, more careful ap-plication of well-accepted moral and scientific principles could correct these problems. They were internal problems. We could use them to learn more.

Another terrible consequence of medicine created an entirely different sort of challenge. As medicine became more successful, it became possible to keep people alive longer without necessarily being able to cure them of their underlying disease. These people became dependent upon medicine in a whole new way. They didn't go to the doctor, as people generally had in the past, episodically, only when they were sick. They began to live in a strange codependent partnership with their doctors, their diseases, and the pharmacological or technological interventions that kept them alive and functional.

In many cases this new relationship did not create a moral problem. People with diabetes take insulin, people with hypothyroidism take thyroid replacement therapy, people with cardiovascular disease take digoxin, and people with asthma use bronchodilators regularly and chronically. For all of these conditions, lifelong therapy for a chronic and incurable but controllable disease may be necessary. It is certainly effective in vastly improving both the quality and duration of a person's life.

However, some new therapies are not as simple as taking a pill or giving oneself an injection. With the development of renal dialysis, people with renal failure could be offered a long-term maintenance therapy that might keep them alive for decades, but the intervention was so expensive and so burdensome that many people chose to forgo treatment and die rather than continue.[3] In making that choice they seemed to be saying that the treatment was worse than the disease and that they'd rather die than live the life that modern medicine could offer them. Similarly, people with chronic respiratory failure might be saved through long-term mechanical ventilation, but such therapy was not for everyone.[4] Some people choose to discontinue life support rather than spend their life tethered to a machine. In these cases the "best" medical care seemed to result in more harm than good, not as an unforeseen and correctable side effect of treatment, as with DES, but as a direct and unavoidable result of the treatment itself.

Lewis Thomas, a physician, scientist, and essayist, called these interventions "half-way technologies."[5] They half worked and half didn't. He reflected on the medical treatment of polio and saw the iron lungs of the 1950s as a sort of halfway measure. He recognized the moral dilemmas of such technologies, how they created a sort of medical purgatory of patients confined to wards that seemed to be a form of long-term storage, how they left patients alive but not really living. For Thomas the solution was more science, more research, and ultimate faith that scientific creativity would allow the medical profession to ultimately develop better technologies that would alleviate the dilemmas created by halfway ones. In his polio example, the moral dilemmas created by the "half-way technology" of the iron lung became a stimulus to researchers, who eventually developed a more definitive and attractive technology, the polio vaccine. The vaccine was cheaper, more effective, and more scientifically elegant. Instead of ameliorating the side effects of polio, it eliminated the disease at its root. For Thomas, the parable of this response to polio was the parable of medical progress. It implied that scientists should seek and could find the equivalent of a polio vaccine for every disease for which we now have only the equivalent of iron lungs.

As it happens, however, we create "half-way technologies" at a much faster rate than we do the definitive technologies that could eliminate them. Thomas's dream of progress begins to seem unrealistic at best. Writers such as Rene Dubos in *The Mirage of Health,* Ivan Illych in *Medical Nemesis,* and Daniel Callahan in *False Hopes* question the underlying faith that our medical-care system can or will follow the polio paradigm, spinning off scientifically elegant preventive treatments that will make us healthier and healthier at lower and lower costs.[6] These writers note that medicine instead seems to develop more and more technologies that are only partly effective at best but that we don't have a framework for understanding the limitations and the unsustainability of a medicine that is both powerful and powerfully inadequate. Somewhere along this path medicine begins to seem more like part of the problem than like part of the solution. It makes us sicker rather than healthier. It begins to cause more pain than it can relieve. Dubos, Illych, and Callahan call attention to a destructive, diabolic impulse within medicine, an impulse frighteningly intertwined with the benevolent, divine impulse.

To the extent that ethical conundrums arise not from inadequate knowledge or unforeseen consequences but as an inseparable part of good medical practice, doctors who are not doing anything "wrong" or "immoral" or "unethical" may still be doing the wrong thing. They can be seen as exemplary participants in a system of medicine that seems to be somewhat off course, good soldiers fighting in a bad war. These new problems with medicine are not "side effects," not necessarily even mistakes, and will not be correctable by more and better science. Instead, they are problems so inextricably linked with medicine's mission that, paradoxically, they only become manifest at the moments of greatest success. They are results of modern medicine's working too well.

When modern bioethics first started addressing these issues, many doctors misunderstood the focus of the most scrutiny. Physicians argued that there was no need for outside scrutiny or oversight of their decisions, saying that they were uniquely qualified to make the sorts of decisions that they, and only they, made as part of their daily work.[7] By this argument, they did not need ethicists or ethics committees because they, as individuals, were themselves quite ethical. And the confusion was bilateral. Many ethics committees were uncertain of their role in addressing particular cases or particular physician decisions.[8]

One of the first times that such a problem was implicitly recognized was in 1958. That year a group of Catholic anesthesiologists went to Pope Pius XII. They were concerned about cases in which they had cared for patients who had undergone surgery but whose operations had not gone well. Routinely, patients who are about to be operated on are anesthetized to the point where they can no longer breathe on their own. They are kept alive by mechanical ventilators, a wonderful new technology that allows anesthesiologists to breathe for the patients. But sometimes, when the operations do not go well, it becomes clear that the patients are dying and that they are only being kept alive by the ventilators. The anesthesiologists' question to the pope was whether it would be morally permissible in those cases to discontinue a seemingly effective medical treatment by stopping the ventilator and allowing the patient to die.

This was one of the first situations in which doctors realized that medicine's new powers were creating a whole new class of moral dilemmas. The anesthesiologists' dilemma did not have to do with loyalty, trust, exploitation, or even the mission of medicine. It could not be solved by coming up with better ventilators, better anesthesia, new technology, or better scientific studies. In a sense, all those things would make the dilemma harder. And by going to a spiritual leader, rather than to a professional society, the anesthesiologists acknowledged that medicine needed help from outside, from religion or philosophy, to answer the questions they were facing. It was one of the first instances in which doctors realized the limits that the new medicine was challenging.

Even in this situation one can imagine a technical answer of sorts, and it would be the sort of technical answer that the lawyer was imagining as he questioned me. One might respond that it would be morally permissible to remove the ventilator only when the doctors were *certain* that the patient's death was imminent or that survival was impossible. Such certainty would require careful epidemiological studies in order to clarify the physiologic predictors of imminent death. This sort of response would be a variation on the "more research is needed" response. It would imagine that the problem was one of ignorance and that the solution was more data.

This was not the answer the pope gave. Instead, he described the problem as one of ultimate ends and moral obligations.[9] Our continued life on earth is not the ultimate end, he said. Instead, it is a means to a larger, spiritual end. Achievement of that spiritual end is not dependent upon good health or upon prolonged survival. But, the pope said, it can not be achieved by devoting all of our moral and spiritual resources to the development of extraordinary means of medical intervention. Therefore, extraordinary interventions, such as mechanical ventilators, should not be thought of as morally obligatory.

Both the epidemiological response and the spiritual one make distinctions. The former distinguishes prolonging dying from prolonging life; the latter distinguishes extraordinary measures to prolong life from ordinary measures. Both distinctions require that fine moral judgments be made on a case-by-case basis. Both can be phrased in technical terms. What does it mean, precisely, to "prolong dying"? How, precisely, do we define "extraordinary"? The ambiguities implicit in these terms highlight the fact that there is an ineradicable component of moral judgment that will never be avoided simply by developing more precise measurements, definitions, or principles.

Another recognition of the ways in which modern medicine was creating a new type of moral dilemma occurred about a decade later, when a group of physicians at Harvard proposed what was to become a new definition of death, *brain death*. One might think that the determination of death should involve criteria that are fairly immutable, time-honored, and unambiguous. Yet new developments in medicine seemed to require reexamination and revision of even this basic fact. Just as the anesthesiologists who petitioned the pope realized that technology was creating new challenges in the operating room, the Harvard committee realized that there were patients whose brains had "died" but for whom attentive ICU care allowed their bodies to be kept alive. They asked themselves and the rest of society whether those patients should be considered alive or dead.

In this case the answer involved morality, economics, law, and psychology. Arguments for classifying such patients as dead included considerations of the meaning of life, the meaning of personhood, the relationship between consciousness and selfhood or humanity, and the differences between humans without brains and other mammals with healthy brains. Arguments also considered the monetary cost of keeping such patients in ICUs on ventilators and the detrimental psychological effects that such care might have on family members, who could not get on with the grieving process. Questions about the definition of death went beyond purely medical concerns. If someone shot someone else in the head and the victim became brain dead but his heart kept beating, was the person who shot him a murderer? Finally, considerations of brain death were enmeshed in the development of new techniques for organ transplantation. If brain death were accepted as death, then organs could be taken from a patient who was brain dead before cardiorespiratory death caused organ failure. These were important considerations that, in some sense, overshadowed the central philosophical and biological questions about whether the patients were *really* dead.

The Harvard committee focused on the narrow technical question of how to determine whether there had been irreversible cessation of brain function. In a sense, they were laying the epidemiological foundation for a large new edifice of moral and legal doctrine, a new understanding of what we mean when we say that a person is dead. But they were also recognizing that medicine's powers might need to be curtailed in new and unprecedented ways. It was no longer enough to be a competent ICU doctor or a competent pulmonologist who could expertly manage air flow and gas exchange. Doctors could no longer simply use their technical expertise without considering the goals to which that expertise was directed. It was a brilliant intuitive leap to use the dramatic metaphor of "brain death" to liken irreversible cessation of brain function to the death of an organism as a whole. The power of the metaphor was in the way it highlighted and encapsulated the contradictions of medical technology that could be used to preserve the bodily functions of a patient who was, in some sense, morally equivalent to a dead person. The need for such expertise, such carefully nuanced reasoning, and such tentative but far-reaching conclusions also suggests that recognizing when a patient is dying or dead is far from simple.

These two moments, in 1958 and 1969, foreshadowed a series of court cases, national commissions, and agonizing dilemmas about what to do when medicine worked so well that bodies could be kept alive after the brain, or the spirit, or the soul had died. These were cases in which the dream of mechanical medicine became the nightmare of humanistic medicine, in which the machines were so effective that they began to do evil, in which an excess of reason led to ultimate irrationalities. As in fairy tales such as "The Sorcerer's Apprentice" or "The Pasta Pot," overcoming limits could create more problems than were involved in being bound by them. We still struggle with these dilemmas. We still cannot figure out the goals or limits of medicine in the hardest cases, those in which we have to decide whether to stop. In such cases, to err on the side of life sometimes means to mindlessly use technology. But not to err on the side of life can sometimes mean that a patient who might have been saved will die.

Such dilemmas become the central focus of bioethics and a source of ongoing concern and uncertainty for doctors. When Dr. Miller faced precisely this sort of dilemma on that fateful morning, he had to decide, in minutes, about matters that had puzzled philosophers for decades.

In neonatal intensive care these dilemmas have been particularly thorny because the consequences of neonatal intensive care can last a lifetime. Babies whose lives are saved but who are left with severe heart, lung, brain, or intestinal damage become hostages to technology, as do their parents. Doctors who pursue survival at any cost, who err on the side of life, can be seen as morally pure or as morally simplistic, as ultimately responsible to an appropriate goal of medicine or as profoundly irresponsible and insensitive to the needs of real human communities.

The internal morality of medicine dictates certain moral norms for doctors. They are obligated to try to preserve health, prolong life, and relieve pain and suffering. Sometimes these obligations conflict. When faced with deciding whether to discontinue life support, the simplest resolution of conflicting moral obligations dictates that doctors should do so only when death is inevitable. Over the past decade, clinical epidemiologists have struggled to refine the skills necessary to make precise predictions, to develop reliable and quantifiable scores of illness severity, to make objective judgments about medical futility. This has proven difficult.

The procedures for developing techniques of prognostication are straightforward. Patients who are critically ill are monitored continuously for physiological stability. The more unstable they are, the less likely it is that they will recover. The degree of instability can be quantified as an *illness severity score*. Illness severity scores attempt to mathematically combine precisely measured variables, such as electrolytes, oxygen saturation, and blood pressure, according to a statistically verifiable algorithm in order to predict which infants will live and which will die. Although many such scores have been developed, they have not been as accurate or as powerful as originally hoped. In general, they are about as good as the doctors' clinical intuitions. Studies comparing illness severity scores with clinical judgments in both adult ICUs and NICUs found very little difference.[10]

For extremely premature babies the best illness severity score is a simple one. The most accurate way for a doctor to predict the outcome is by accurately assessing how premature the baby is. The more premature the baby, the less likely it is that he or she will survive. Maturity and prematurity are expressed in terms of *gestational age,* usually measured in weeks, with a *full-term* baby being more than thirty-seven weeks of gestational age and the limits of viability being around twenty-two to twenty-three weeks of gestational age. Unfortunately, it is difficult to measure the gestational age precisely. It is always an estimate, based on the presumed date of conception, modified by measurements taken on prenatal ultrasound, and confirmed or contradicted by physical characteristics at birth. These sources of information are not always consistent with one another, so there is always a margin of error in estimates of gestational age that confounds its reliability as a predictor. By contrast, it is easy to measure a baby's weight at birth, and birthweight is roughly correlated with gestational age. As a result, birthweight often serves as a quick and reasonably accurate surrogate measure of gestational age and a fairly good predictor of survival or death. (Birthweight is not quite perfect since some babies are small for their gestational age, leading to underestimates of true maturity, while others are large, leading to overestimates.) Many statistics about outcomes for premature babies are given, then, as a function of birthweight. At 600 grams, which corresponds to about twenty-five weeks of gestational age, the tiny patient whom I resuscitated that February morning had predictably little chance for survival. The neonatology fellow's sardonically accurate prognostication was probably based on that alone, since at the moment when the fellow arrived in the NICU the baby was doing pretty well.

For the smallest babies, birthweight has an almost linear relationship to survival. Each increment in size leads to a corresponding increment in the likelihood of survival. But the simplicity of this geometry hides a few important subtleties. First, although birthweight is always highly correlated with survival rate, the percentage of babies who survive at any given birthweight has been increasing steadily over the past twenty years. In 1980 only 20 percent of babies who weighed 500–800 grams survived. This figure increased to 36 percent in 1985 and nearly 60 percent in 1995.[11] These trends have led many doctors to a belief in inexorable progress, a concomitant unwillingness to rely on past statistics in order to prognosticate for today's babies, and an unshakable sense of their obligation to just keep trying. "We shouldn't give up on 500-gram babies even though their survival rates are terrible," a neonatologist will say. "After all, where would we be today if we had given up on 800 gram babies 20 years ago?"

Other subtle factors that modify the accuracy of birthweight as a predictor of mortality are the race and gender of the baby. For reasons that nobody really understands, at any given birthweight tiny girls have a better chance of surviving than tiny boys, and African American babies have a better chance of surviving than do Caucasian babies having the same birthweight. Tyson precisely calculated the effects of these modulators upon survival rates. He showed that everything else being equal, being female is worth the equivalent of about 70 grams and being black is worth another 50 grams. Thus, a

650-gram black female has about the same chance for survival as a 770-gram white male.[12]

The other unusual thing about birthweight as a predictor of survival is that although it is quite accurate at the time of birth, it becomes much less useful or relevant after just a few days. More than half of the babies who are going to die do so in the first few days of life—35 percent on the first day, another 20 percent on the second.[13] The NICU is a brutal Darwinian universe. Only the strongest survive, and those who do survive are, by definition, strong. Short-term survival thus becomes a highly useful predictor of long-term survival. As a result, the chance that any particular baby will ultimately survive increases enormously with each day that they actually do survive.

This may seem intuitively obvious, but, interestingly, it is not the case in adult ICUs. There, the opposite phenomenon occurs. The healthiest adults get out of the ICU the most quickly. Thus, the longer any adult is in the ICU, the less likely he or she is to survive. To put it another way, the length of time that a preemie stays in the NICU is *positively* correlated with survival, while the length of time that an adult stays in an adult ICU is *negatively* correlated with survival.[14]

Furthermore, and this is crucial, for preemies this improvement in the chance of survival as a function of the length of survival is independent of birthweight. That is, even the tiniest babies who survive for three days have a fairly good prognosis for survival and discharge from the hospital. This contrasts with the adult ICUs, where the highest-risk patients, those who are oldest, have a far worse prognosis than younger patients. The combination of advanced age and prolonged length of stay in the ICU is additive. Patients who are over age 85 who have been in the ICU for three days have a nearly 90 percent chance of dying during that particular hospital stay. Any baby, regardless of birthweight, who has been in the NICU for three days and is still alive has a nearly 90 percent chance of survival. Thus, though birthweight is the most reliable predictor of survival at the time of birth, it quickly becomes less and less accurate. Babies born at 600 grams who have survived for four days have the same chances for long-term survival as babies born at 1,600 grams who live four days.

These empirically observed phenomena have some interesting implications for the way we think about death and dying and about the ethical dilemmas associated with the care of patients who might die in the NICU. Based on these phenomena, neonatologists can and do use "response to therapy" as a sort of diagnostic or prognostic test. Rather than making decisions at the time of birth about which babies to treat or not to treat, they generally initiate treatment on *all* tiny babies, knowing that the sickest babies will die anyway and that the ones who respond to treatment will be a self-selected group of babies with the best prognosis.

One result of this highly reasonable approach, however, is that many babies whose prognosis is dismal nevertheless undergo days of painful and useless interventions because of the uncertainty that the treatments are useless and impossibility of accurately predicting that they will not respond. We continue to provide treatment even if it seems futile and painful because we recognize the unreliability of our predictions. It seems rational, even morally correct in such circumstances to discount the baby's short-term suffering. Under the sway of this approach, doctors act as I did as a resident: they treat first and think or ask questions later. They allow the situation to clarify over the first few days. One benefit of this approach is its simplicity. Neonatologists don't really have to gather data, integrate it, and make a decision rapidly. Instead, they initiate treatment, a course of action that, because it is the default position, is conceptualized as passive, as not being a decision at all. The decision to discontinue treatment comes later, after more data are available. By contrast, a decision to withhold or withdraw treatment in the delivery room such as that taken by Dr. Miller is felt to be the active approach and thus the one that takes energy and would require justification.

Once treatment is initiated, the doctors wait for the babies to "declare themselves." They will become harder to ventilate or easier, will or will not have a big intracranial hemorrhage, will or will not develop an overwhelming infection. If bad things happen in the first day or two, then many doctors suggest that treatment be withdrawn and the baby be allowed to die. Data from the NICU at the University of Chicago and others suggest that the treatment of at least half of the babies who die in NICUs has been limited in some way. Some are not given vasopressor medication to support their blood pressure; some are taken off the ventilator and not given CPR when their hearts fail.[15]

By using this approach, doctors are able to conceptualize such events less as a moral decision to withhold or withdraw treatment and more as an epidemiological or physiologic assessment that further treatment would simply be futile. Thus, it is not that they decide to stop treatment. It is that the baby has declared himself or herself and further treatment would be ineffective. The language suggests that the baby, rather than the doctor, makes the decision.

Such "declarations" by the babies, however, are not totally unambiguous. There are many cases in which doctors and nurses are convinced both that babies have declared themselves and that they cannot survive and then the babies do, in fact, survive. Just like Dr. Miller's baby. In order to show that this is the case, Laura Frain and colleagues recently did a study in which they asked nurses, residents, fellows, and attending physicians for their opinions regarding the ultimate survival or nonsurvival of each infant in the NICU who was receiving mechanical ventilation.[16]

Every day for a year they asked each doctor or nurse working in the NICU to say whether they thought each patient would survive until discharge or die in the NICU. The survey focused upon patients who were on mechanical ventilation, as those were the sickest babies in the NICU. Over the course of the year there were 505 predictions by a doctor or a nurse that a particular baby would die. Of these, 304, or nearly two-thirds, were incorrect; that is, some doctor or nurse thought the patient would die before discharge, but the patient survived. Even rarer, and somewhat more accurate, were the 140 days (5%) on which every doctor and nurse caring for a baby predicted that the baby would die. Of these 140 group-consensus predictions 44 (31%) were wrong. The inescapable but disturbing conclusion seems to be that neither doctors nor nurses were very good at predicting which babies would die. Working together, they do a little better, but even then they are wrong a third of the time.

Waiting for the patient to "declare himself" seems sensible. It is, I think, the approach that most neonatologists implicitly take. It is the approach that I took when I saved the life of the 600-gram preemie, only to see her die two days later, as the neonatology fellow had predicted. Should the fellow's accurate prognostication that the baby would likely die have been enough to save the baby the pain and suffering of two days of intensive care? That pain would have been clearly justifiable if she had survived. Did her death somehow retroactively invalidate the moral justification for initiating treatment? It certainly made the decision to continue treatment seem wrong and even heartless. But the lawyer was suggesting that Dr. Miller's decision to rely on his assessment that survival was extremely unlikely was more heartless.

It seemed clear to me that some mistakes were unavoidable in this area and that there was no clearly right or clearly wrong approach to these dilemmas. Instead, it seemed that there was moral peril in both approaches—both in trusting clinical intuitions and in treating all babies until we were certain that further treatment was futile.

Doctors and nurses were good at some things, bad at others. One large group of babies whom everybody consistently predicted would live in fact did live. And a group whom everybody thought would die actually did die. There was a smaller group, about 10 percent of the babies, about whom the

prognoses were little better than chance. Some of these babies who were predicted to die lived. Others were predicted to live but died. This third group
of babies is the most complicated and controversial.

Frain and colleagues discovered one thing that was interesting and sur-
prising about these babies. For those who were predicted to die but who did
not die, the incidence of long-term neurodevelopmental problems was very
high. Nearly 90 percent of the babies who had been predicted to die but survived had major neurological problems, such as significant developmental
delay, severe cerebral palsy, or seizures. They concluded that clinical predictors of medical futility are not very accurate if futility refers only to survival.
However, if it refers to neurologically intact survival, the doctors and nurses
were very good at foreseeing the future. The babies for whom they foresaw
a bad outcome generally did not do well. In this sense, Dr. Miller may not
have made such a big mistake after all. He foresaw a bad outcome, and a bad
outcome occurred. His problem may have been less one of technical skill or
medical knowledge and more one of semantics. If, instead of saying that he
thought the baby would die, he had said that the baby's prognosis was dismal,
he might not have been on trial. But that semantic shift is also, of course, a
moral one, focusing on types or degrees of badness.

Neither doctors, nurses, nor statisticians are perfect. Theologians and
philosophers are not perfect either. All attempt to balance the harms of particular moral compromises with the harms of moral rigidity. If we treat every
baby until we are 100 percent certain that the baby will die, we may occasionally save a baby who otherwise would have died. There clearly are babies
like Baby Boy Jones, for whom the doctors predict imminent death but who
can and do survive. But treating every baby until we know they will die
would likely lead to more neonatal and parental pain and suffering. Alternatively, we could try to determine consistent thresholds for treatment and nontreatment decisions, knowing that these might not always be completely accurate. A system that demands decisions of doctors under conditions of
uncertainty cannot also demand perfection in those decisions. Mistakes are
the price of being human.

The lawyer had asked whether doctors and nurses who made a mistake
should be held accountable for that mistake. Thinking of Dr. Miller's
dilemma, I tried to answer simply.

"I think medical treatment sometimes does more harm than good," I said.
"There are cases where survival may not be the best outcome. The sort of
certainty that you are imagining when you say Dr. Miller should be held ac-

countable for his mistake would not necessarily be wonderful. And it would only be achievable at a great cost."

"Cost?" His eyes lit up! "What cost? Are you suggesting that we put a price on human life?"

"No, I'm trying to recognize the negative value of suffering. In order to insure that no mistakes like Dr. Miller's are ever made, we would need to make much bigger mistakes for many more babies that would cause tremendous suffering for the babies and for their families. Like most experienced and competent neonatologists, he surely knew that and took it into account. Given the irreducible level of uncertainty, his judgment was right and his action was right. It allowed for the small possibility of a bad outcome. Unfortunately, in this case the bad outcome happened. He should not be punished for that."

SIX

Consent, Communication, Shared Decision Making

"But Doctor, whose decision should that be? In this case, Dr. Miller made the decision to discontinue resuscitation all by himself. Don't you think he should have discussed that decision with the parents?"

"Objection. Two questions, vaguely worded, leading."

"I'll reword the question. Doctor, in your opinion, should Dr. Miller have discussed his decision to discontinue resuscitation with the parents?"

"Well, back up a little. I don't agree that he made the decision entirely by himself."

"How can you say that? He initiated the resuscitation, decided that it wasn't working, and stopped. He didn't discuss those decisions with anybody. In your opinion, doesn't that violate the doctrine of informed consent?"

"Objection. Same problem."

"Could you repeat the question? Actually, could we take a little break. I need to get a drink."

"Sure, break."

We stood up, stretched. The court reporter looked relieved. We hadn't been there that long, but it seemed like a long time. I was tired and starting to feel a little muddled. Things didn't seem to be going the way I'd hoped. I had thought this would be an easy case to defend. Now, I was starting to wonder if I had been wrong, or crazy.

I found my way to the bathroom. The defense lawyer followed me in. Even the bathroom had that lawyerly feel of pretentious wealth. The walls behind the toilets had marble facing. The fixtures were brass. It was oddly reassuring. If they were making this much money, they must be pretty good. It's the same with doctors, though it plays out in a somewhat different way. We always want new hospitals and the latest equipment, as if new and more expensive are always better. Those who have the latest and most expensive stuff are always the most successful, though not always the best. We stood beside each other, the lawyer and I, facing the brass fixtures and marble walls.

"How do you think it's going?" I asked.

"Oh good, good. You're doing fine. A little slow. But that's ok. He's good, but you're keeping up with him, I think." He sounded a little more tentative than I would have liked.

"Ever had a case like this one before?"

"Not like this, no. We defend hospitals and doctors a lot, but not too many baby cases. It's funny. If the babies die, they usually don't sue." He gave a little laugh. "Dead babies don't usually bring very big settlements. The ones who survive with brain injuries are the ones that are hardest to defend."

Back in the conference room, the plaintiff's lawyer was nowhere to be seen. The other defense lawyer was standing at the window, looking out at the lake. I wondered what these lawyers thought about as they sat watching and listening while "their" witness sparred with the defense. How did they go about constructing an adversarial drama as a way of resolving complex moral problems? They were obviously sizing me up. Would I be able to deliver my lines convincingly? Would I hold my own in front of the jury? Was I experienced? Did I look wise? Would I get flustered? How would my arguments play? I went over and stood beside the female defense lawyer. She looked at me with slightly raised eyebrows, slightly challenging, slightly questioning.

"Beautiful day," I smiled.

"Yeah, wish I were out there sailing."

"You have a boat?"

"A little one, 22-footer. I like to race but haven't gotten much time this summer."

"Too many cases?"

"Too many cases that drag on too long, cases that start out seeming straightforward and end up convoluted. I don't even know what I think about this case. Do you really think Dr. Miller was right?"

A thoughtful, sailing lawyer.

"Do you have trouble defending cases if you don't think the defendant did the right thing?"

"Oh, no, not really. It is usually fairly technical work. There's not a lot of personality or passion in it. It isn't much like TV, or O.J. We settle most cases eventually and never get to make those ringing closing arguments to the jury."

"Medicine isn't much like TV either. Even the NICU is fairly mundane most of the time."

"Yeah?" She looked a little surprised.

"You should come down and visit sometime. I'd be happy to take you on a tour. I don't see how you can do cases like this if you haven't actually been in an NICU."

That was somewhat true. On the one hand, it seemed like you just had to be there to understand and that those who hadn't been there were in no position to judge. On the other hand, things looked so much clearer from far away, where the events could become stories, the stories could become cases, and the cases led to decisions, precedents, rules, and regulations. Like a pointillist painting or a constellation, things might make more sense when seen from far away.

The plaintiff's attorney came strolling back in. We settled back into our leather chairs.

"Could you read back the last question?"

The court reporter looked at her little paper tape and read, "How can you say that? He initiated the resuscitation, decided that it wasn't working, and stopped. He didn't discuss those decisions with anybody. In your opinion, doesn't that violate the doctrine of informed consent?'"

"Doctor, did Dr. Miller make the decision to initiate the resuscitation?"

"Yes, I believe he did."

"And ten minutes later, he discontinued resuscitative efforts."

"Ten or eleven, yes."

"Is it your opinion that the parents gave their informed consent to discontinue resuscitation?"

Involuntarily, I let out an exasperated sigh.

Informed consent is probably the most revolutionary, the most rudimentary, the most misunderstood and misused term in all of health law and bioethics. Everybody talks about it. Everybody seems to mean something different by it. It is both sacrosanct and ludicrous, idealistic and cynical, central to modern medical practice and almost irrelevant, all at the same time. The "doctrine" of informed consent is the feature that, more than any other, makes contemporary American medical practice historically and morally unique.

The goal of informed consent is to make the patient and the doctor partners, to introduce an element of shared decision making into a process that is so often one of seemingly insurmountable differences in knowledge, power, and will.[1] The doctor is highly skilled, highly trained, specialized, and professional. The patient is sick, vulnerable, scared, untutored, and dependent.

In the past, the solution to this problem of power disparity was to create a form of professionalism that required the doctor to promise to use all of his knowledge and power only to protect the patient. The doctor would take an oath, swearing by whatever gods were sacred that he would act only for the good of the patient and that he would never use his superior power or knowledge to exploit or harm the patient. The details of professional oaths were elaborations of the meaning of this promise. Until quite recently it was widely inferred that it was the doctor's moral obligation to decide what was best for the patient. In fact, the doctor involved the patient in such decisions only to the extent that it was necessary to ensure the patient's cooperation. This might involve minor deceptions, such as the withholding of information that might be frightening. Sometimes it involved more straightforward lies about diagnosis or prognosis. Patients were generally not given detailed information about the risks and benefits of proposed treatments. Such deceptions were considered justifiable when they were incorporated into a larger project of trying to make the patient well. The widespread presumption, held so unquestioningly that it was unnecessary to state it explicitly, was that too much knowledge was bad for the patient, that patients could not emotionally handle or intellectually comprehend the decisions that had to be made.

Today, as a matter of legal and moral principle, there have been two important shifts. First, it is acknowledged that doctors have dual loyalties. They work for their patients but also, sometimes, for managed-care companies, corporations, drug companies, government-funded science consortia, law-enforcement agencies, and others. These conflicts of interest are seen as inevitable, in some sense even desirable, in that they allow doctors to fulfill multiple social roles and achieve many different societal goals. The health of the patient still comes first, but it is first among many of the doctors' goals. Second, doctors' traditional paternalistic medical discretion has been curtailed. We still want doctors to be bound by their professional oaths and obligations, but we also want them to be bound by morality and by law to ascertain and abide by the stated wishes and values of the patient. To a certain extent, we have diluted the internal morality of the medical profession and tried instead to compensate by amplifying the moral input of the patient. The substantive values that used to drive doctors have been partially replaced by procedural ones. To know what is right, it is no longer enough to know what would make the patient healthier. We also have to know what the patient means by "health" and, thus, what the patient would want us to do.

According to this view—which seemed to be the view the lawyer was now working toward—the real wrong in this case was not that a baby had been born so prematurely that he was barely viable, not that he had almost died, not that the doctor had negligently stopped CPR, and not that the baby had then survived with severe disabilities. It was that the decision about whether to continue or to stop treatment was not made by the properly empowered moral authority. The genuine tragedy that took place had receded in importance, and the story had been reimagined such that the key fact was that the parents had not been consulted. If they had been, and if they had authorized discontinuing resuscitative treatment, as Dr. Miller would have recommended, there would have been no legal wrong and no lawsuit even if the outcome for the baby had been the same. Alternatively, if the parents had decided that treatment should be continued and the baby had survived with the same major disabilities, or died after prolonged suffering, again there would have been no legal wrong. In a sense, through the informed-consent doctrine, we theorize the problem of tragedy as a problem of improperly constituted authority, of disempowerment, of exploitation.

This is a thoroughly democratic way of approaching these matters. By this approach there is no substantive justice, only procedural justice. There is no substantive concept of "the good," only procedural mechanisms like elections or consent forms for stumbling toward mutually agreed upon conceptions of what it might be. The individual or the public are the only authorities to whom we might turn for ideas of what is right or wrong.

Interestingly, if we focused on the nature of the conversation that took place, or ought to have taken place, between the doctor and the parents of his patient, we would find ourselves closer to the ancients than to the moderns. We would be focusing upon the sort of relationship doctors must strive to create, especially in cases involving the decision whether to withhold or withdraw life-sustaining treatment. By this line of argument, the primary focus should not be on the doctor's skill or knowledge but on the relationship between doctor and patient. The modern approach differs from ancient codes in imagining that the doctor has an obligation, not to the patient's health, but to the patient's desires.

There was something disconcerting about this shift in emphasis, as if suddenly our gaze were being redirected from something that had seemed to be at the moral center toward something that had seemed to be at the periphery. And the implication was that our notions of central and peripheral were all wrong. I was reminded of Camus's *The Stranger*. Toward the end of that novel the main character is on trial for murder. At the trial, however, very little is said about the murder itself. Instead, the prosecutor focuses almost entirely upon the relationship that the accused had with his mother. Why had he put her in a nursing home rather than caring for her himself? Why had he smoked a cigarette during his vigil with the coffin the night before the funeral? Why hadn't he cried at her funeral? How could he have gone out to a movie the next day, to a movie, and a frivolous comedy at that, with a girl that he'd just met. And how could he have slept with her that very night, or, in the Prosecutor's words, "indulge[d] in the most shameful of orgies on the day following his mother's death"? These events had nothing whatever to do with the crime for which he was on trial, but as they are brought up, one after another, the defendant "felt a sort of wave of indignation spreading through the courtroom. . . . For the first time I realized how all these people loathed me . . . and for the first time I understood that I was guilty."[2]

It seemed that the focus on parental informed consent in a case like Dr. Miller's could take us down a similar path. Though not a murder case per se, it was a case involving life-and-death decisions, a case in which the most serious moral issue would seem to be that one citizen had made a decision that might lead to the death of another citizen. (The twist in this case was that the "victim" did not die.) Yet the key issue could turn out not to be the actions that the defendant had taken but the talk that had or had not preceded the action, or that should or should not have. Those conversations, putative or real, brief, perhaps trivial, and only dimly remembered, were now seen as representing for us Dr. Miller's moral stance toward the world. Was he autocratic, dictatorial, and paternalistic? Or was he democratic, inclusive, and fraternal? Even if he wasn't technically negligent, he may still have been conversationally nihilistic, and that might be even worse.

According to this view, both he and the parents had a set of roles that they must play. It is interesting to examine the relationship between these expected roles and what we might call morality or medical ethics. At the time, it seems, neither doctor nor parents were prepared to play the roles that the master script of the informed-consent drama called upon them to play. Later, the parents were upset that they hadn't been given a chance to play that role, and the doctor was held accountable for precluding them from doing so.

In complex ways, it seems that an enactment of those particular roles, an improvisational reading of that script, maps onto the domain that we call ethics. But examining the particular questions does not help to elucidate the correspondence between morality and action. What, exactly, did Dr. Miller say or not say? What should he have said? What was his mood in that thirty-second meeting? Was he sympathetic or distant, paternalistic and directive or fraternal and inclusive? Did he strike the right attitude? These considerations, it suddenly and surprisingly seemed, could have more bearing on the

outcome than facts about infant survival rates or about the normative standards for a doctor's behavior in similar circumstances. The case could turn on
the power relationships between doctors and parents and whether Miller had
been duly deferential. I wondered if anybody would ask whether, when he
had gone to the doctors' lounge, Dr. Miller had callously and indifferently
smoked a cigarette.

Interestingly, to the extent that Miller should have sought the parents'
permission before discontinuing resuscitative efforts that he thought were futile, this was not the sort of patient empowerment that had been initially
imagined or sought by those who codified the doctrine of informed consent. Instead, the patient-empowerment movement had begun by focusing
on situations that were the precise opposite of this one, situations in which
doctors wanted to provide treatments that were too risky or had too little
chance of success and thus withheld from patients important but frightening information about the risks. At that time the concern was that doctors
would use their special knowledge to disempower patients by withholding
information that might allow patients to understand the truly risky nature of
medical procedures and thus refuse to undergo them. Judges seemed to believe that doctors were too enamored of the technological imperative and
that their interests in providing new and dangerous interventions were too
conflicted. Thus, they couldn't and shouldn't be empowered to unilaterally
make decisions in these difficult and trying situations. Patients needed to be
included in order to allow them to refuse, to resist, to forgo.

Competent patients were empowered by the legal requirement for informed
consent. Even incompetent patients could be empowered by using a *living will*
or a *durable power of attorney for health care,* which would be completed while
they were competent and would remain in force if they became incompetent.
These legal documents are forms of *advance directives.* They tell doctors, in unambiguous terms, that the patient would not want pointless and aggressive
care if the end of his or her life appeared to be at hand. The hope was that if
patients rather than doctors were empowered, different decisions would be
made. In particular, it was thought that patients who were fully informed of
the risks or the possibilities of bad outcomes would likely refuse many treatments that doctors recommended even if that meant that they would die.

It is hard to tell whether this approach has been successful. Although advance directives are widely available, many people don't use them. The percentage of adults who have an advance directive varies widely in different
populations and different settings. Recent studies from different locales and
among different social and economic groups report rates as varied as 9 per-

cent, 25 percent, 55 percent, and 85 percent.[3] Once the directives are used, their impact also varies widely. In some studies, the directives seemed to influence the actual treatment that patients received. In many other studies, however, the directives seemed to have very little influence on what was or was not done for patients. In spite of these mixed results, there remains a widespread belief that patients want less interventionist care at the end of life than their doctors do and that advance directives are a way of empowering patients to convince their doctors to treat them appropriately.[4]

At the same time, there is a countervailing view, articulated mostly by physicians, that many patients do not want to limit their treatment in any way. In fact, when asked, they often want and demand more aggressive and interventionist treatment than even the doctors are willing to provide. In this view, it is the doctors alone who recognize when further intervention will be futile, but patients often cannot be convinced.[5] This has led to the desire for "futility policies" allowing doctors to override patients' and families' wishes for continued treatment.[6] But once the doctrine of informed consent for particular procedures became enshrined in law, it was but a short step to seeing the validity of a need for informed refusal before treatments could be withheld.

It is not clear in the medical literature which problem is more common— overtreatment by doctors of patients who do not want to be treated or insistence by patients that their doctors provide them with futile treatment. Most of the cases involving NICUs and neonatologists that attract media attention involve the first type of case. They describe parents who want doctors to stop life-sustaining treatment. The conflict arises when, for one reason or another, the doctors are unwilling to do so. (The cases in which both doctors and parents are willing to stop life-sustaining treatment generally lead to a quiet decision to do so and do not make headlines.) The conflict in these cases is thus dramatized in the national media as one between, on the one hand, unsubtle and vitalist doctors who are insensitive to their own limitations or to the human suffering of babies and parents and, on the other hand, concerned, reasonable, humanist parents who are disinterestedly committed to their own philosophical or religious ideas of the good life rather than mindlessly wedded to an abstract and inhumane respect for the sanctity of mere biological activity. This generally makes very good theater. It is a morality tale that is simple to tell. It is easy to recognize who is the hero and who is the villain.

Among cases that come before the ethics committee at the University of Chicago Hospitals the overwhelmingly more common scenario is one in which doctors believe that further treatment is futile and the time has come to stop. The conflict arises when the parents do not agree or are not emotionally ready and therefore are unwilling to discuss, let alone authorize, the discontinuation of life-sustaining treatment for their baby. While there has been public discussion of such cases involving adults and even some involving older children,[7] public discussion of such cases involving neonates seems to be taboo. Doctors do not talk about them because, in the wake of the legal and political controversy about such decisions in the 1980s, the law remains unclear about when it is permissible to stop life-sustaining treatment for a neonate. Furthermore, doctors who advocated discontinuation of treatment in the 1980s were pilloried by the press, harassed by the government, and victimized by aggressive lawyers.[8] As a result, doctors who care for neonates do not feel culturally or socially sanctioned to raise these issues.

Furthermore, unilateral decisions by doctors to discontinue even futile treatment do not map easily onto our preexisting moral presumptions about the way things really are or should be in the ICU. We have a place in our cultural iconography for the doctor as a technology-crazed automaton, more eager to play with his high-tech toys than to realize the inherent limitations of his powers. Against this image, we are comfortable imagining parents as protectors of their children, spiritually enlightened, willing to accept death with equanimity. The proper partnership is thought to be between a value-neutral but technically proficient professional and an engaged, thoughtful, and morally reflective parent who should interpret the facts provided by the doctor in light of his or her values and arrive at the right decision. The cases that become high-profile cases do so precisely because they reinforce these images, because they "play well" to an audience happy to have its world-view validated.

The reality is much messier. Often, parents' sense of loss or overwhelming denial prevents them from seeing just how much their baby is suffering and just how hopeless the situation is. At other times, things happen so quickly that it is difficult for parents to take in the relevant details. For better or worse, doctors must act with limited input from overwhelmed parents. Many doctors are not technologically crazed automatons but think carefully and deeply about the moral dilemmas involved and try to develop a practice informed by moral values as much as by scientific knowledge. Many patients admire such doctors and look to them for guidance in difficult decisions. Doctors and patients often struggle together to figure out what is right. The tension in many of these cases is not really between the doctor and the patient (or parent) but between the doctor and the parents, on the one side, and the tragic choices that need to be made, on the other.

As part of an ongoing research project, a chaplain at the University of Chicago has interviewed scores of parents, nurses, and doctors who have been involved with babies who died in the University Hospital NICU.⁹ The stories they tell about the process of decision making for critically ill babies are complex and moving. Transcripts of two interviews with mothers whose babies died are printed below (names and certain details have been changed; *I* = Interviewer, *M* = Mother):

I: When did you first know that Faith had medical problems?

M: When they first told me, I was pretty groggy, from the medicine they were giving me—I wasn't really taking it all in. [*pause*] When I was first told and when I first knew are really two separate things. But I knew something was wrong when they rushed me so quickly out of my room. I guess I knew when they told me that her heart rate had stopped. It was kind of confusing. They had given me an epidural and she had some kind of thing on her head—I can't remember what that thing was called. There is too much stuff.

I: That's ok. Do you know what this thing did?

M: It was to monitor her. I just kept drifting off to sleep. But then suddenly they were saying her heart rate had stopped and that they had to get her out. And so they whisked me off for a Caesarian. It happened so fast. I remember them preparing me for the C-section. I felt them cut into me, but then I drifted off. I can't really remember anything else, until I came back to. I was in recovery at that point.

I: What do you remember about the time in recovery?

M: I remember that I asked about my baby—where my baby was.

I: Did you get an answer?

M: I don't remember being told anything, but I kept drifting off. I did remember hearing the words "code blue."

I: Code blue?

M: Yeah, while I was in recovery.

I: Was anyone with you in recovery?

M: I guess my family and friends were there, in and out a lot.

I: Do you remember anyone telling you anything about how Faith was doing?

M: The doctor came in and told me . . . hmmm, now what did he say? . . . he said she was in critical condition, and if she does live she will probably be [*starts to cry*] brain damaged. [*more tears*] That's all I remember the doctor saying. [*choking on her tears*] But I kept drifting off.

I: It sounds like the doctor was pretty straightforward about how sick Faith was. Do you remember what you thought or felt hearing this?

M: Just that I wanted to see my baby. I know I kept asking them when I could see her. I know what the doctor said, but I just didn't believe it. [*she laughs briefly*] I know... even though he told me, I just didn't think that anything bad was going to happen to my baby. Not my baby. Then they finally took me to a room upstairs. I kept asking to see her... they kept asking me if I could move my legs... I said I could, even though I couldn't [*she laughs*], but I just wanted to see her. They kept coming back to check on me. Finally they brought me down to see her. But I was just there for ten to fifteen minutes.

I: What can you tell me about your time at the bedside?

M: My husband was there. I was just talking to her, holding her hand, we took some pictures.

I: While you were there, did anyone tell you how they thought she was doing?

M: I don't think so, but I just wouldn't have heard it anyway. [*starts to cry*] I just wanted her to be ok. She had to be ok. I wouldn't let myself think otherwise. I mean everything had been ok my entire pregnancy, so I thought she would get through this, whatever it was.

This sort of situation, this sort of interaction, these sorts of conversations, common in neonatal units as well as other areas of hospitals, suggest some of the difficulties doctors face in the clinical world when they try to obtain fully informed consent for treatment decisions in critical situations. In the scenario above, the medical situation for the baby was dire. Important decisions needed to be made. The doctors were busy providing medical care and were also trying to stay in touch with the mother, but they had multiple goals. They wanted to offer her hope and emotional support, but they also wanted to give her realistic and honest information in order to allow her to participate, as best she could, in the decisions. She was eager to participate in the decision. She was willing to lie about her own condition in order to get to see her baby. By her own admission, she did not want to believe what the doctors were telling her. She just wasn't getting it, and what's more, she didn't want to get it. She even understood, both at the time and in retrospect, exactly how important it was for her *not* to understand what the doctors were trying to tell her.

Ultimately, decisions were taken without her participation. In a sense, she was disempowered. Her powerlessness was partly imposed upon her, but in a complex and not entirely conscious way she also chose it. She didn't want to play the role she had been assigned in the informed-consent drama—listening carefully to the facts and then making a decision based on her values. Perhaps she signaled her ambivalence. Certainly, the doctors would have needed to decide how much to tell her, how much to ask her, and how much to be bound by what she requested or demanded. But she had only one demand: to see her baby. She was willing to withhold important subjective clinical information in order to reach that goal. And on a less conscious level she had another goal: to cling to her belief that her baby was not going to die. In order to reach that goal, it was important for her not to believe what the doctors were telling her. And it was crucial that she not agree to stop life-sustaining treatment.

An interview with a different parent suggests a similar dynamic.

I: When did you first know that your baby was having medical problems?

M: He wasn't.

I: So you were having medical problems?

M: No. Not really. It was cervical incompetence. That's what they told me.

I: What did that mean to you?

M: I just couldn't hold the baby. I didn't understand because I had gone to all of my prenatal exams and everything was ok. The ultrasounds were good—showing a strong heartbeat. I was taking vitamins, I was doing all the right things. But I went into labor two weeks prior to delivering her. I didn't know it was labor then, but I was having pains, so I called the clinic. They told me that if I haven't had any bleeding or discharge, I was ok. I didn't know—I hadn't had a baby before. But I was dilating, and the pain got unbearable, so I came in on that Saturday. Dr. Martin said he would try to stop the contractions. But I was dilated already 5 cm, and he said there was no turning back, that I would be delivering the baby. He explained that my baby's chances were very slim. They asked if I wanted a pediatrician there. I did—just in case— so everyone was all there. But he was not viable, they told me. His lungs were not developed, and so we held him—I held him, my husband held him—I guess he died in our arms. I'm not sure how long he lived. They told me about an hour, but I was reading through my progress notes in my medical chart and I saw something about him living for half an hour, so I'm not so sure.

I: How far along were you in your pregnancy?

M: I was on my last day of the 22nd week.

I: Can we go to when he was born? What did you understand about his condition at that point? Did any doctor say anything to you?

M: After I gave birth to him, I had some hope. My husband was with me and he had seen him and was hopeful, because he saw him kicking and he thought he looked pretty big. So we were hoping he was developed and that there was some possibility. But I don't recall much—my blood pressure started dropping and I was getting kind of hazy and my vision was blurred. I know they took him from me . . . where they went with him . . . I'm not sure . . . I'm assuming they were trying to help him for a while, when the doctor came and said he was just not developed enough.

You know I do have a question about if DNRs [do-not-resuscitate orders, that is, orders to withhold cardiopulmonary resuscitation in the event of cardiac arrest] are automatic below a certain weight. One of my sisters said some doctor said something about that—that if a baby is below a certain weight it's an automatic DNR. But that doesn't sound right—otherwise, why would they ask me if I wanted a pediatrician there—the pediatrician was just going to weigh him and then if he didn't weigh enough, no one was going to do anything, no one would try to save him? Is that what happened? I wanted to ask someone about that, but up to now, I just haven't been up to calling yet. Do you know if there is a certain weight below which a DNR is automatic?

I: I don't know.

M: They asked about an autopsy. According to his age, they said he was developing fine. And if that was the case, that he was fine, except for this cervical incompetence, my husband and I decided there was no need to cut on him. I mean, what was the point . . .

I: Do you remember if the pediatrician spoke with you before Jimmy was born?

M: Only after, when they said that nothing could be done for him. That's about all I remember. I don't know, they may have talked more to my husband about—I just remember them telling us to expect him to move a bit and to be breathing. I don't know. Wait a minute— [*hollers to her husband in the next room*] John! John! [*he responds, "Yeah?"*] What did the doctors tell you about Jimmy? [*he replies, but I can't make out what he is saying, then she tells me*] Just to expect him to move and to breathe, but that he wasn't going to make it.

I: And so then they brought him to you?

M: I remember them telling me that I gave birth to a baby boy and then they asked if I wanted to hold him—I said yes—and they brought him in and laid him on my chest and they put up the bed, so my husband and I could sit and bond with the baby. This was still in the delivery room. Then they asked about the rest of the family seeing the baby. They rolled us back to the birthing room, I think it's called. And everyone got to see him and hold him. A lot of people were waiting for this baby, so they all wanted to see him.

For this mother, the events following the birth of her baby had a certain roller-coaster inevitability about them. She felt like a passive participant. Only now, and for the first time, does she raise questions about the DNR decision. She still wonders and worries about how that was made.

The mothers in these two interviews are recounting their perceptions of the actual events surrounding the birth and death of their babies. What does informed consent mean in cases like these? Did the parents give informed consent for discontinuation of treatment? They were certainly included, involved, and engaged, but they were not asked to make decisions or even really asked to participate in discussions about the decisions that were being made. By the strict standards of informed consent, the parents of these babies were treated negligently. Each could and perhaps should successfully sue their doctors for not obtaining informed consent. And yet, in interview after interview with both doctors and parents, we see that this is how the discussions generally go. This, then, is apparently the current "standard of care," if there is one, for discussions about discontinuation of life-sustaining treatment. Clearly, if Baby Boy Jones had died, as was expected, then Dr. Miller's treatment of the issues surrounding consent and parental involvement would have been well within the standard of care and would not have been scrutinized so carefully. Equally clearly, Dr. Miller did not meet a theoretical legal or philosophical standard of true parental involvement, true informed consent, or equally shared decision making.

The disparity between moral theory and professional practice raises a fundamental question. If sincere and well-motivated practitioners are not living by the theory, then either the theory needs to be reexamined and changed or the behavior of the practitioners needs to be altered. A number of factors suggest that the problem is with the theory.

In order to understand why this is so, and where to go next, it is necessary to be clear about how comprehensive some of the efforts have been and how dismal the failures in transforming the way patients, families, and doctors make end-of-life decisions. Twenty years ago high-tech medicine presented us with the new challenge of technology that could prolong lives in which there was no hope of recovery or survival. The conventional wisdom at the time was that doctors imposed this technology upon patients but that patients, if empowered, would make decisions to refuse meaningless prolongation of life in the ICU.[10] A series of court cases beginning with the 1977 New Jersey case *In re Karen Ann Quinlan,* in which the family of a comatose young woman sought and won the right to stop her ventilator, enshrined the right of patients to refuse life-sustaining treatment, and federal legislation ensured that patients would be informed of that right. A variety of legal mechanisms for making advance directives, including living wills and durable powers of attorney for health care, were created to help patients effectuate this right even if they were no longer competent.[11] These solutions have solved some of the problems but not others.

Americans seem to like and to accept advanced directives. Numerous studies show that with a little education and a little counseling, most people appreciate the value of an advance directive and many will even fill one out. However, even though people fill out advance directives and express their wishes, the documents themselves seem to have little effect on the actual care patients receive. Patients who have directives frequently don't tell their doctors about them, and even if they do tell them, the doctors don't change their treatment plans. Family members who are aware of the living wills are glad that they exist but don't feel bound by them. Thus, advance directives seem to have little effect on the end-of-life care that patients receive.[12]

Perhaps the largest study to show this is the so-called SUPPORT study. The SUPPORT investigators studied end-of-life care for 4,800 critically ill ICU patients. They found that only 569 patients (12%) had an advance directive of any sort. Only 90 of these documents (i.e., 16% of the documents, representing only 2% of the patients in the study population) went beyond naming a proxy or stating the preferences of a standard living will and provided additional specific instructions for medical care. Only 22 of these documents directed that life-sustaining treatment be forgone in the patient's current situation. For these, the treatment course was consistent with the instruction for only 9 patients. Thus, few patients have any kind of advance directive, and often they are vaguely worded or do not apply to the patient's situation. Often, even when patients do have advance directives that directly apply to their situation, the directives are not followed. A smaller study by Mark Goodman and colleagues leads to the same conclusion. They reviewed records of 401 elderly patients who died in an ICU. They compared the 19 (5%) patients who had advance directives of any type with 28 case-matched critically ill patients who did not have advance directives. They compared the cost per day; the number of surgical procedures; the number of radiographic studies; the number of central venous and pulmonary-artery catheter insertions; the number of lab tests; the number of days in the ICU or the hospital; and mortality rates. They could not find any differences between the treatments provided for those patients who had directives and the treatments provided for those who did not. They conclude, "Few critically ill seniors have advance directives. As assessed by objectively documented information, the level of care delivered to elderly ICU patients is not affected by the presence or absence of advance directive statements."[13]

These facts about care suggest a complicated reality. When care is inconsistent with what is specified in existing advance directives, it may not be that the directives are simply ignored. Instead, the directives may be interpreted less as binding prescriptions for a particular type of care and more as one of many sources of information that might help doctors and families reach a decision. Both doctors and family members *consider* the advance directive, but they are not *bound* by it. For better or for worse, decisions at the end of life seem to be made as communal decisions rather than individual ones, with the patient's voice just one among many. The goal in these discussions for both doctors and patients seems to be a little different from the goal initially imagined by lawyers and bioethicists. It is not simply to empower the dying patient against the doctor. Instead, it is to achieve some semblance of family moral harmony, some course of action that violates neither the values of the dying patient nor the values of the survivors, who must live with the memory of the action. In many cases, this reflects a more complex calculus than might be necessary if the only goal were to respect the patient's autonomy. Seen in this light, Dr. Miller did not ignore the parents, but he didn't specifically consult them either. Similarly, the mothers of babies in the NICU quoted above were included in discussions but, by their own accounts, were left with questions that they had never asked.

The disparity between theory and practice is quite basic and stark. Theory looks to individual autonomy as not just a good that might help us attain other goals but as a goal in itself. By this view, we want an individual to make decisions about his or her own care at the end of life. We don't simply accept, encourage, or eagerly seek these decisions. Instead, we insist upon them as the only valid moral barometer of the correctness of a decision. We get nervous about coercion if the individual appears to have been swayed by the opinions or sentiments of others. Furthermore, if we can be sure that the individual patient sincerely wanted something, we feel certain that that particular something must be a good thing. If we can't be sure that the patient's choices reflect his or her individually made and autonomous decisions, we worry that the choices are in some way morally tainted. And if we don't know what the patient wanted, then we feel helpless to make a moral judgment since the only reliable source of moral authority is absent.

Our actual practices are more nuanced and complex. They seem to incorporate ideas of interdependence and of responsibility for one another and to reflect concern about the hollowness of the theory that comes from its dichotomous simplicity. In practice, informed consent is not an either/or matter. Instead, it is a matter of more or less, better or worse. Our practices respond to the inextricably tangled web of moral obligations within families and among family members and to the complex negotiations that take place between doctors, patients, and family members. Perhaps because these areas of human experience are so complex and so difficult to describe in general terms or to regulate in rational ways, neither law nor bioethics has done a particularly good job in exploring them. Instead, they might be better understood through a domain of inquiry that focuses on the complexity of family decision making.

One of the greatest novels about life-and-death decisions, moral responsibility, guilt, and accountability is Dosteovsky's *The Brothers Karamazov*. Because the novel deals with families, death and dying, and accountability, it has insights that are particularly relevant to today's medical decisions. The novel opens with a discussion of why the father, Fyodor Karamazov, does not deserve to live. He is an evil, nasty man, a drunk, a child abuser, a rapist, and a cheat. He has four sons, one from his first marriage, two from his second, and one illegitimate son. Both of his wives have died. At the beginning of the novel we are told why and how deeply each of his sons hates him. Three of the four sons clearly wish he were dead. It is unclear whether any of them will actually murder him, but they are clearly considering the idea. They talk and bluster, testing their moral sentiments about whether Fyodor deserves to live or die. Each clearly knows that the others have thought about murdering their father.

At one point, Dimitri, the oldest son, and Fyodor are having a particularly heated argument. Dimitri thinks Fyodor owes him money, Fyodor says that the money is in the house, and Dimitri threatens to kill Fyodor in order to get the money he believes he is owed. At the time, Ivan, the middle son, is living in the house with Fyodor but is planning to take a trip to Moscow. Smerdyakov, the half-brother, suggests that if Ivan leaves and Fyodor is home alone, Dimitri might kill Fyodor. Nevertheless, he suggests that Ivan go anyway. Ivan is intrigued by Smerdyakov's suggestion and tries to understand exactly what his half-brother is telling him. The conversation that follows is interesting, subtle, and perhaps representative of the sorts of discussions family members have when the issue is taking responsibility for life-and-death decisions.

"Then why on earth do you advise me to go . . . ? If I go away, you see what will happen here." Ivan drew his breath with difficulty.

"Precisely so," said Smerdyakov, softly and reasonably, watching Ivan intently.

"What do you mean by 'precisely so'?" Ivan questioned him, restraining himself with difficulty.

"I spoke because I felt sorry for you. If I were in your place I would simply give it all up . . . ," answered Smerdyakov, with the most candid air looking at Ivan. . . .

"You seem to be a perfect idiot and what's more . . . an awful scoundrel." Ivan got up suddenly from the bench. He was about to pass through the gate but he stopped short and turned to Smerdyakov. He bit his lip, clenched his fists, and, in another minute, would have flung himself on him. But Smerdyakov shrank back. The moment passed without harm to Smerdyakov, and Ivan turned in silence toward the gate.

"I am going to Moscow tomorrow, if you care to know—early tomorrow morning. That's all!" he suddenly said aloud in anger. . . .

"That's the best thing you can do," Smerdyakov replied as though he had expected to hear it.[14]

Later in the novel it becomes clear that Smerdyakov understands this conversation to have been a clear agreement between the two of them that Fyodor should be killed. Smerdyakov thinks that by leaving after that conversation, Ivan clearly sanctioned Fyodor's murder. It is not clear what Ivan thinks or even whether he knows what he thinks. But Ivan goes on the trip to Moscow, leaving the house empty, and that night Fyodor is killed, just as Smerdyakov predicted. Dimitri is arrested and charged with the murder. The remaining two-thirds of the novel is an examination of guilt and accountability for the murder of Fyodor.

Dostoevsky's genius is to describe the motivations, the self-deceptions, the enigmatic conversations, the understandings, and the misunderstandings that flow in, around, and through the words and silences that characterize family decision making around life-and-death issues. No explicit discussion among the brothers led to a clearly articulated plan to kill Fyodor. In fact, the closer Ivan and Smerdyakov got to explicitness or honesty about their feelings, thoughts, and motivations, the angrier they became and the more difficult it was for either of them to say precisely what they meant or felt or wanted.

Clearly, whatever the brothers wanted, explicit conversation was not part of it. Throughout the novel Dostoevsky makes the point that although everybody wanted Fyodor to die, and many people even expressed a willingness to kill him, nobody wanted to take individual responsibility for the decision or the action. They were ambivalent. They had misgivings and moral qualms. Each son responds quite angrily to any implication that he should be the one to bring about the death or, after the murder, that he was the one who did.

Such sentiments, I believe, are similar to those of family members who are asked to make a decision to withhold or withdraw life-sustaining treatment. They may want the treatment to be withdrawn, but they often do not want to take individual moral responsibility for the decision. Alan Shapiro, a poet, recently wrote a book called *Vigil* about his sister's death. In the book, he makes the striking statement that "we were tired of seeing her languish, tired of the degradation that we were helpless to do anything about. We were tired of our helplessness and guilty for being tired. That we were all impatient to go home was our unspoken wish, our dirty secret."[15] In this passage Shapiro captures well the emotional challenges of caring for a dying family member and the shameful ambivalence that many must feel but few can articulate. This sort of ambivalence and shame is part of the complex psychic infrastructure that makes explicit conversation about the death of a loved one so difficult.

Sometimes family members act out this guilt by vigorous opposition to any suggestion that treatment be limited, just as Ivan vigorously rejected the suggestion that he was complicit in Fyodor's murder even though his actions suggested otherwise. In the study in which we interviewed doctors, nurses, and parents of babies who died in the NICU we sometimes came across situations like this. One doctor described the following scene,

I talked to the parents about [stopping the ventilator]. I told them we can't make their baby better and that we wanted to withdraw support. Dad said, "You can't. That's murder." And then he clenched both hands and started to come towards me. I thought he might hit me, but he walked past me and hit the wall. It was a strange moment. It's like time stood still. I watched him come towards me and I just stood there—I didn't want to flinch, because I didn't want him to think that I didn't trust him. And I wanted them to trust me. But I thought he might hit me. But fortunately he didn't and he didn't hurt anybody. He went out the door. A few minutes later, I saw him in the hall and he asked me if I had done it yet. I said I was on my way now. I turned off the oxygen and went up on the fentanyl to keep her comfortable. The father saw me and smiled. He was tearful and he left, smiling at me. It was a big turnaround for him.[16]

Both the Karamazovs and this father seem to arrive at their decisions without being willing to admit that they are arriving at a decision. Instead, they deny their moral sentiments and condemn those with whom they are collaborating. They evade the central moral issues and give contradictory messages. Alternatively, they test the emotional waters with ambiguous expressions of complicity or rage to see whether their feelings will be met with tolerance or condemnation. After such conversations, everybody is able to think that somebody else made the decision, that somebody else was morally accountable, that somebody else was to blame. Dostoevsky shows us as readers how difficult or impossible it is to judge who, in the end, was accountable and who, in the end, was to blame.

Similarly, in many clinical situations, doctors, patients, and family members arrive at a decision in a way that allows everybody to be absolved of responsibility for the decision. The goal of the process is not to assign accountability but to disguise it, not to promote individual autonomy but to submerge it.

There is, of course, a tremendous difference between appropriate end-of-life care in a modern hospital and parricide in a dysfunctional nineteenth-century Russian family. But there are also psychological similarities between Dostoevsky's portrayal of family decision making in the novel and the process of family decision making in the ICU. Many people in this situation describe the process as being asked to "kill" their loved one, a decision for which they want to avoid responsibility at all costs. The common theme in the two situations is a simultaneous desire to have someone die and a flight from accountability for those feelings. Neither family members nor doctors want to be the ones who "authorize" the death. Thus, in many hospital cases doctors, patients, and family members arrive at decisions in such a way that nobody feels individually responsible for the decision.

A brilliant and sensitive description of this process appears in another novel, *A Personal Matter,* written by the Nobel Prize winner Kenzaburo Oe. In real life Oe is the father of a son born with an encephalocele, or congenital brain malformation. In the novel he creates a character named Bird, who faces a similar situation. Bird's son is in the hospital, and the doctors have recommended surgery even though they believe that surgery will likely leave Bird's son with severe neurological deficits. One doctor describes the likely outcome as "a vegetable existence." Bird does not want to authorize the surgery but also does not want to appear to be authorizing his son's death. The conversation between Bird and the doctor has the same tone of both assigning and avoiding responsibility:

"Is this your first child?" the doctor said. "You must have been wild."

"Yes—"

"No developments worth mentioning today. We'll have somebody from brain surgery examine the child in the next four or five days."

"Then—there will be an operation?"

"If the infant gets strong enough to withstand the surgery, yes," the doctor said, misinterpreting Bird's hesitation.

"Is there any possibility that the baby will grow up normally even if he is operated on? At the hospital where he was born yesterday, they said the most we could hope for even with surgery was a kind of vegetable existence."

"A vegetable—I don't know if I'd put it that way . . . " The doctor, without a direct reply to Bird's question, lapsed into silence.

"You don't want the baby to have an operation and recover, partially recover anyway?"

"Even with surgery, if the chances are very slight . . . that he'll grow up to be a normal baby . . . "

"I suppose you realize that I can't take any direct steps to end the baby's life!"

"Of course not—"

"It's true that you're a young father—what, about my age." In a hushed voice that no one else on the ward could hear, he said, "Let's try regulating the baby's milk. We can even give him a sugar water substitute. We'll see how he does on that for a while . . . "

"Thank you," Bird said, with a dubious sigh.

"Don't mention it."[17]

This dialogue is laced with double entendres, misunderstandings, hints, and evasions. At certain points the author leaves it ambiguous which of the two characters is speaking. Nevertheless, they seem to reach a decision, but one that neither quite feels responsible for and one about which both are somewhat ashamed. Like Dostoevsky's novel, Oe's deals with questions of ultimate moral responsibility. The night after his conversation with the doctor, Bird has a nightmare in which "he has been subpoenaed by the tribunal beyond the darkness, and he is pondering a means of blinding them to his responsibility for the baby's death. Ultimately, he knows that he will not be able to dupe the jurors, but he feels at the same time that he would like to make an appeal—those people in the hospital did it! Is there nothing I can do to escape punishment" (77). Even in his dream he is both aware of his complicity and desperate to deny it. That situation does not lend itself to straightforward procedures designed to assign accountability.

In *The Brothers Karamazov*, questions about guilt and accountability lead to a narrative structure like that of a good detective story. Dostoevsky gradually reveals the circumstances of the crime, follows the extensive police investigation of Fyodor's murder, and gives a detailed account of the legal proceedings. In spite of these attempts to find the truth, the reader, like the jurors, is not sure who committed the murder until near the end of the novel. Even then, one can not be sure who is really responsible. More interestingly, the characters themselves are not sure either. They struggle to determine not only who actually committed the murder but who was morally accountable for it. Late in the novel, when Dimitri's trial is almost finished, Ivan and Smerdyakov talk again. Smerdyakov insinuates to Ivan that the two of them are complicit in Fyodor's death. Ivan is angry and demands,

"Do you believe I knew that my father was going to be murdered?"

"You were probably eager for your father's death," Smerdyakov answers.

Ivan jumped up and struck Smerdyakov with all his might.

"So you thought, you scoundrel, that together with Dimitri, I meant to kill my father?"

"I don't know what thoughts were in your mind," said Smerdyakov resentfully, "And so I stopped you then at the gate to sound you out on that point."

"To sound out what, what?"

"Why, whether you wanted your father murdered or not."

"What could I have done to put such a degrading suspicion into your mean mind? What grounds had I for wanting it?"

"What grounds had you? What about the inheritance?"

"So according to you I had fixed on Dimitri? I was counting on him?"

"How could you help counting on him? There's no doubt you counted on Dimitri."

"Listen, you wretch, if I counted on anyone, then it would have been you, not on Dimitri. And I swear I did expect something from you ... at the time ... I remember."

"I thought too at the time that you were counting on me as well. ... You are the real murderer. You are responsible for it all, since you suspected murder and wanted me to do it and went away knowing about it. You are the only real murderer, and I am not the murderer, though I did kill him."[18]

Dostoevsky and Oe both explore the different implications of legal, moral, and spiritual accountability. For Dostoevsky, the attempt to pinpoint legal accountability is a dramatic plot device. The trial is theatrical and has as its goal the handing down of a verdict. Whether the verdict is accurate is as irrelevant as whether the verdict in a malpractice case is just. The lawyers' focus on legal accountability is quite different from the moralists' focus on personal responsibility. Moral responsibility implies a more internal set of rules and standards by which we judge ourselves and our actions. The spiritual dimension is at once the most important and the most amorphous in modern discourse about these matters. It is not just about religion. In both the novels discussed above and in real life, the relationship between official religious figures and the spiritual longings of the characters is ambiguous. Through the spiritual struggle, characters define their views about the essential nature of human existence and human relationships, particularly the aspects that cannot be understood through public spectacle or public policy.

One important message of these works is that the goal of any moralist cannot be simply the practical task of resolving a particular moral conflict. Instead, it must be to put the conflict in a context that makes sense of it, to tell a coherent story about why the conflict is important and why a resolution will not simply be a moral compromise. To reach that goal, the language, narrative structure, tone, and mood are at least as important as the content. The implicit architecture of decision making carries messages that the explicit articulations cannot capture.

Over the last twenty years in America, both doctors and patients have tried to tell certain stories about end-of-life care in the language of bioethics and in the language of legal rights. Other stories have been told in the languages of clinical epidemiology and health services research. None of these stories captures the complexity of the drama that the people who are living their lives or dying their deaths are enacting in the same way that fiction or poetry does. Perhaps these other discourses are too idealistic. Perhaps they imagine too much possibility, too much freedom, too much responsibility. People may think they want unfettered autonomy, but they act as if they want community more. They may think they want individual accountability, but they act as if they really want personal absolution. They don't just want their decision to be legally or even morally correct. They want to be able to go on with their lives, to be characters in the next chapter of their own stories, to make things as right as possible with themselves, their loved ones, their God, and their community. These nonindividualistic needs are not recognized or acknowledged by today's institutional structures or moral frameworks. Perhaps that is why these frameworks have not been very effective.

To a certain extent the legal case and the current deposition were not putting Dr. Miller on trial: they were putting ambiguity on trial. The impulse behind the proceedings was anti-Dostoevsky, anti-Oe, anticollectivity. It was against the sort of murky, mushy, muddling through that seemed to be customary and at least acceptable, perhaps as the least unfavorable option, to most of the people most of the time. In its place there would be crystal clarity about responsibility and accountability. It seemed that that sort of clarity would only come at a very high price.

"Well, I believe that the parents in this case participated in the decision to withdraw life-support to the same degree that parents usually participate in such decisions."

"That's precisely the problem!" He was almost shouting. "They are routinely excluded from participation."

Aha, I thought. I've drawn him out of his shell. He's losing his cool. He's giving his opinions now instead of asking for mine. The deposition was as good as over. For better or worse, what I had probably just done was ensure that I would never be called to testify at the trial. This preliminary struggle, this test of ideas and wills, would be the only one. It would be "on record" somewhere, somehow, but would be totally irrelevant. A bittersweet sort of victory.

"I would describe what the doctor did a little differently," I replied. "Dr. Miller recognized that the parents were facing a terrible, tragic situation and that they were scared, vulnerable, and confused. He also knew, as most doctors know, that they would prefer a process of decision making that did not put them on the spot, that did not isolate them in the loneliness of accountability. I think he tried, as best he could, to share their grief and their sorrow and to help them understand that he had done all that seemed right and appropriate. He was also willing to share part of the terrible responsibility."

In *The Brothers Karamazov* Dimitri is found guilty though he did not commit any crime. I wondered whether Miller would fare any better.

SEVEN

Getting Paid

"Doctor, have you testified in malpractice cases before?"

One of the most maddening things about depositions is the way they set the pace and the tone and control the topics. Just when you think you're getting somewhere on something, they change the subject.

"Yes."

"How many malpractice cases have you been consulted about in the last year?"

"Oh, I get five or six calls per year. Sometimes, I just review the case but do not testify. Over the last ten years, I've probably testified ten times."

"Do you always testify for the doctors' side?"

"I'm happy to review cases for and give my opinion to anyone who asks."

"Doctor, are you getting paid for your testimony here today?"

"Well, I'm not getting paid for my testimony. I am getting paid for my time."

"And how much do you charge?"

"Three hundred dollars an hour."

"Is that similar to what you are paid for your time in your clinical work?"

"Yes it is." Well, sort of. I'm not really sure what I'm paid for my time in clinical work. I'm on a salary. Somebody else does the billing and collecting, and the reports I get of what they've charged and what they've collected are often inaccurate. Even when they are accurate, they make little or no sense. The "value" of my time seems to vary enormously with the context. Medical work is reimbursed according to an elaborately arcane code of "relative value units." The system was devised by Harvard researchers and is supposed to provide a metric by which payors can compare things as disparate as an hour of psychotherapy, a circumcision, and a coronary-artery bypass operation. I usually care for many poor and uninsured patients in the clinic, where I'm not paid at all for work that is difficult, stressful, and often thankless. For a while I worked with the child-abuse team; I would spend long hours in court trying to sort out impossible issues of who did what to whom beyond a reasonable doubt. There was no payment for that. Sometimes I get paid a lot for work that is far less taxing, like giving a lecture that I've given many times before, or being an expert witness.

The first time I was called to be an expert witness, I had no idea what to charge for my time. I asked some colleagues, and they all threw numbers around. One hundred and fifty, three hundred, five hundred, seven hundred and fifty dollars per hour. It seemed to have less to do with where the doctor had gone to medical school or his or her area of expertise and more to do with the doctor's chutzpah. They'd name a number, and some lawyers would pay. Of course, some got called more than others, some had particularly narrow, specialized areas of expertise, some were better in front of a jury, some made "witnessing" a significant and regular part of their life and earned more from malpractice cases than they earned in salary. And there were plenty of scholars at the university who were never involved in malpractice cases, so their expertise was never assigned a value on the open market. There was clearly some sort of "market" working here, but it was hard to tell whose needs, desires, tastes, or preferences were driving it.

"What percentage of your income do these cases provide?"

"Less than 10 percent." They always ask these questions, and they always make me feel uncomfortable. I always hate to calculate it out. It feels a little dirty to be participating in the malpractice system at all since I don't like the system, think the world would be better off without it, see the lawyers as parasites, and saw myself, then, as a parasite on a parasite. Even though I was often defending my colleagues, I still felt whorish, taking money for services in support of a system that I didn't like or want to support. I could remind myself that I was testifying on the side of right and good, but I'm sure everybody felt the same way about themselves. I couldn't figure out why this particular area of activity became the conduit for so much funny money. What about it was so worthy?

Money. Money. Money. I felt like asking the lawyer what percentage of his income came from these cases. I wanted to know why he had quit practicing medicine to do malpractice cases. I wondered how he decided just how much money to ask for, how he came up with a dollar value to quantify particular forms of pain and suffering. Did he feel like he is on the side of justice, the side of quality medicine? Or just that he has found a gimmick, an easier way to make a lot of money quickly than he ever could have made delivering babies in the middle of the night, worrying that he'd get sued if everything didn't come out just perfect? Malpractice cases seem to thrive in areas where there is already a lot of money at stake, where there are "deep pockets" capable of paying out large settlements. That was certainly true at the intersection of neonatal intensive care and moral judgment.

What was that money buying? In the world of malpractice litigation, it seemed to be buying a very peculiar sort of justice. Studies of the malpractice system show that most medical negligence is never noticed or punished.[1] In many cases juries are more moved by *bad outcomes* even if they did not result from negligence than by *bad practice* itself. The awards seem to be distributed in a way that appears almost random in terms of either the merits of the case or the harms suffered by the patients.[2] The arbitrariness is, to some degree, an inescapable feature of the jury system. Juries are, after all, designed and constituted specifically to be almost totally unaccountable to any particular authority, standard, or consistency.[3] Once they decide that the defendent is either innocent or guilty, that's the end of it. They don't have to give their reasons. And that particular jury will never have to make another such decision. The jury members disappear into the woodwork of society or make the rounds of the talk shows.

That seems to be the way Americans like it. Most countries do not rely on the jury system as extensively as America does. It is as if we acknowledge that the problem of coming up with truly consistent and enforceable standards of care, standards of negligence, and measures of quality is impossible. Instead, we have settled on this system of symbolic rewards and punishments, a system that functions more like a lottery in many ways than like a mechanism for justice or for quality assurance.

Perhaps that's not surprising. In many ways, we have become a lottery-driven society. The stock market goes up or down on a whim or a rumor. Companies make or lose money based less on the value of their products than on the "buzz" they create. "Hard work," whatever that might be, seldom pays off. The good are not rewarded, the bad are not punished. Actors who portray physicians on television are paid much more than physicians themselves. We seem to value spectacle more than we value actual events. The temptation to live the life that garners rewards in this crazy system is enormous. I get paid a lot more for reviewing malpractice cases, work that is not hard and that has no redeeming social value, than I get paid for work that seems truly important and valuable, such as teaching, caring for patients, or writing books. And even on the malpractice cases I get paid a lot less than the lawyers. At least the ones who win.

I don't know whether I am worth more or less than I get paid or even how to make sense of the question. I'm not sure whether the Jones family deserves some compensation for the suffering that they have endured or for the expenses that they have incurred or whether Dr. Miller deserves to be punished. I'm not even sure what the word *deserve* might mean in that context. Although I cannot answer these questions, they are not abstract or self-indulgent. The social organization of the markets that distribute the money in cases having to do with these issues is complex and bizarre but not random or meaningless. Instead, these markets reflect, in some strange way, the values, choices, and political commitments of those who participate. They clearly shape our behavior toward one another and the way we live together in a community. It would be nice to have a system of health care in which the Jones family did not have to play this lottery in order to try to get the resources they need to care for their son. It would be nice if they were simply guaranteed that his medical needs would be taken care of. I think they *deserve* that. Further, it seems likely that if they were guaranteed that, they would be far less likely to sue. But we, as a society, have chosen not to offer that guarantee. Instead, we offer them this strange malpractice lottery, where they put their future needs and their just deserts on a number and spin the big wheel. If my testimony is less compelling to the jury than that of the ethicist testifying for the other side, maybe their baby will get new shoes.

Instead of addressing questions of "good" or "bad," "deserving" or "undeserving," "just" or "unjust," it may make more sense to try to figure out just what sort of cultural work this peculiar system does. In itself, the malpractice lottery may seem to be irrational and arbitrary, but as part of a larger scheme of things in which the irrational and arbitrary are acknowledged and accorded a certain status, it makes symbolic sense. It is similar to other lotteries, especially the state-run lotteries, which seem to do the culturally important symbolic work of occasionally and randomly rewarding the powerless and the downtrodden. It offers the additional symbolic pleasure of punishing the rich and powerful.

The social order in the United States depends upon a political economy that institutionalizes inequality. Within this economy competitions are organized that allow a small but visible and important amount of social mobility. Faith in the fairness of these competitions helps to support our particular political ideology and to bolster the democratic political will that is necessary to oppose substantive redistributions of wealth and the amelioration of widespread poverty. In this system the winners win big and the losers lose badly. Faith in the procedural fairness of this system helps ameliorate our shame at the rampant inequality that is all around us.

After all, we Americans have chosen to live with a rampantly unequal distribution of resources, high levels of endemic poverty, large numbers of citizens without health insurance, and a regressive tax code, all in the midst of enormous wealth. And our society mirrors in a muted way the far larger inequalities that exist worldwide in the world order that our country has created and maintained. We convince ourselves that these inequalities are morally necessary and justifiable as parts of a larger system that is in fact fair and beneficial to all, or at least less unfair than any other system. Within that system, we tell ourselves, the inequalities do not signify any heartlessness or inhumanity on our part. Instead, they represent the difficult but necessary price we must pay as we strive toward ideals of independence, individuality, and liberty that are so necessary for the market-driven culture to deliver the goods that make us all better off than we would otherwise be.

Of course, it can be troubling that our poorest citizens, many of whom are members of racial or ethnic minority groups, have higher mortality rates, more years of life lost to medically preventable diseases, and shorter life expectancies than our middle-class or wealthy citizens do. On the other hand, it is comforting that our thriving market economy has led to materialistic wealth and technological improvements that allow all citizens, including the poor, to have lower rates of disease and infant mortality and longer life expectancies than they did a generation ago. Inequality is the fuel that powers the jealous competition that makes our economy hum. The question we seem constantly to face is how to find the balance between maximum market efficiency and imminent moral meltdown.

Clearly, in America today we don't "skimp" on health care. We spend more, much more, both per capita and as a percentage of our economy, than any other country in the world. Our massive inegalitarian health-care system is much more expensive to maintain than the egalitarian systems of most other countries. Ironically, part of the cost is earmarked specifically for the preservation of inequality. One of the primary purposes of our carefully and expensively maintained system of competition among insurance plans and hospital systems is to define different levels of benefits for different social classes and to stoke the flames of competitive envy. For this we spend at least 30 percent more per capita on health care than any other industrialized country in the world. And most of the industrialized countries manage to provide excellent health care to every one of their citizens at a far lower cost than we do. It is difficult, in a democracy, to see the extra cost and phenomenal inefficiency of our system as beyond our political control or as an unfortunate side effect. Instead, it seems to encode or reflect values that are so dear to us that we are willing to pay a premium of hundreds of billions of dollars (that is, the extra cost of running a health-care system as administratively complex and inefficient as ours) in order to uphold them. Other countries experiment with market-oriented approaches to health care but generally reject them.[4] By any theory of rational choice, by any view that imagines us to be politically free, democratically empowered, and personally accountable for our actions, we must conclude that for some reason many of us prefer it this way. When politicians suggest a change, we vote them out of office.[5]

At the same time, we are intermittently somewhat troubled by the injustices. When the economy is bad and working men and women lose their health insurance, we seek remedies. When the elderly, the poor, the widows, and the orphans are excluded, our religious sensibilities are offended. Though we officially endorse the heartlessness of the market, we are not heartless people. We want some mechanism within the system to reinstate balance, to redistribute wealth, to lift up the fallen, and to keep faith with those who sleep in the dust.[6]

The parents of Baby Boy Jones had clearly lost big in some vast cosmic lottery. A bad thing had happened to them even though they were good people. Our hearts went out to them. The bad thing seemed somehow related to the medical care their son had received. As a result of that care, he clearly needed much more medical care. Allowing them to petition for "justice," to make a claim upon us, as fellow citizens, would offer us not only the collective opportunity to help them but the opportunity to do so in a way that could symbolically lift up the fallen and punish the powerful. We would use the police power of the state to haul in the doctor, put him in the dock, and construct him for the jury and the world as heartless and reckless, cocky and insensitive, full of demonic hubris that must be punished. It wasn't a bad system, just a bad man! Who did he think he was, trying to play God, to make decisions about life and death, to toy with the lives of these poor parents? Didn't he see that by his reckless rush to judgment and his failure to communicate he had imposed upon these poor souls a lifetime burden of caring for a severely impaired infant? Ladies and gentlemen of the jury, it is in your hands. You can undo the double injustices here! You can reward the plaintiffs, who deserve their reward, and you can punish the defendant, who deserves to be punished, not just for his personal acts of medical negligence but also for his profession's overweening hubris. The doctor would be made to represent all that is bad about a medical system that is both unjust and imperfect, that sometimes does more harm than good, and that for better or for worse seems to be the one that we are stuck with.

The arbitrariness of the medical malpractice system has a Calvinist quality to it. Rewards and punishments need not be justified or justifiable. They should be random and arbitrary. Payments should not bear any necessary relationship to value, because value itself can only be determined through the admittedly inexplicable mechanisms of the marketplace, which has all the unaccountability of a distant and unknowable God. With similar arbitrariness, the state lotteries single someone out for absolutely no reason at all and reward him or her with undreamed of wealth. Both offer a gaudy spectacle of redress.

Of course, every bit of dramaturgy in the malpractice system seems designed to suggest that something less arbitrary is going on. The explicit narrative denies the very possibility of arbitrariness and suggests instead that there are standards of care that we can articulate and that we can then determine whether they were or were not followed. By this reading, the deposition and the trial had nothing to do with some vast, symbolic societal moral book balancing, some enactment of a theological-political drama. Instead, we were simply trying to determine whether not medical negligence had taken place. Dr. Miller was the only one on trial.

The inherent sleaze of the whole production belied this pretence. The lawyers' beautiful offices, my exorbitant fees, the ridiculous amounts of money being expended, and the even more ridiculous amounts that might change hands if the verdict were "guilty" all suggested that something larger was at stake, and we all acted with a kind of winking complicity in the charade. We all insisted that something quite normal was going on even though we all knew that it was in fact something very bizarre. Playing our roles, we all seemed quite pleased with ourselves, the plaintiff's attorney seeking justice, the defendant's attorney repeatedly reassuring me that Dr. Miller was an excellent doctor who was tormented by this whole process, me getting the accolade of "expert." This tentative line of questioning about money was the only subtle allusion to the problematic economics of it all. But the lawyer clearly wasn't crazy enough or imaginative enough to pursue it very far.

This intersection of economics and morality in the malpractice system creates some interesting patterns of motivation and meaning. Perhaps even more interesting, and more difficult to understand, is the nexus of meaning, money, and motives in the NICU. The money that flows through NICUs is, after all, the rushing river that feeds the little spring that nourishes the growth of the medical malpractice cases.

Neonatal intensive care is pretty big business although it's hard to tell precisely how big. Throughout the 1970s, as neonatology was being developed, it became apparent that to do it right was going to be expensive. The United States Congressional Office of Technology Assessment estimated that as a nation we spent about $3 billion per year on neonatal intensive care in the late 1970s. A more recent estimate, using data from 1988, stated that annual direct costs were closer to $6 billion. There haven't been any more precise estimates since then. Just adjusting for medical inflation, which has led to a doubling of national health expenditures over the last decade, would put the figure close to $12 billion today.

The annual expenditures are probably even higher than $12 billion today, however, since growth within neonatal intensive care has been greater than growth in other areas of medicine, for a number of reasons. First, neonatology has been the fastest-growing subspecialty within pediatrics. Board-certified neonatologists outnumber any other pediatric specialists. Second, the expenditures on neonatal intensive care are tightly correlated with the survival rates for extremely premature babies. That is because the extremely premature babies who survive have the longest hospital stays in NICUs and are thus the most expensive to care for. Finally, new technologies in neonatal intensive care have developed at a steady pace. All told, then, we probably spend at least $15 billion per year in this country on neonatal intensive care.

Expenditures on preemies don't end with neonatal intensive care. Preemies who survive continue to make disproportionate use of resources. One study reported that preemies used fifty-five times the health resources of full-term babies each year for the first eight years of life.[7] These costs included outpatient rehabilitation care, further inpatient stays for surgery, and home care for the treatment of chronic lung disease, short-gut syndrome, and seizures.

Expensiveness, of course, is relative. Building and running a NICU is more expensive than running a prenatal-care clinic or a pediatric outpatient clinic, more expensive than most of the things that pediatricians do. But it would be cheaper than building an aircraft carrier, running for the Senate in New York, or making a Hollywood blockbuster. Saving a tiny preemie is less expensive than many other sorts of medical interventions. Still, because the costs are so relatively high (and the patients so relatively small), many questions have been raised about whether NICU care is "worth it."[8]

Where there are truly free markets, there is no need to engage in abstract exercises to determine appropriate costs and benefits of goods or services. They are determined by what the market will bear. Medical markets are about as unfree as a market can be and still maintain even a modicum of capitalist respectability. Nobody purchases neonatal intensive care through market mechanisms. Nobody bargains over quality and price. Instead, it is collectively subsidized. As a result, valuation decisions must be made by nonmarket mechanisms. Economists must try to figure out what it might be "worth" and whether it is "cost-effective."

The problem with cost-effectiveness analysis of neonatal intensive care is that cost-effectiveness analysis is, by its very nature, comparative rather than absolute. Nothing can be cost-effective in and of itself. It can only be more or less cost-effective than something else. Different approaches to the organization of neonatal care services or different treatment regimens can be compared. We can decide whether neonatal nurse practitioners are more cost-effective than neonatologists, or whether regional care is more cost-effective than decentralized care, but the only alternative to providing some sort of neonatal intensive care is nontreatment and death. There doesn't seem to be a potentially cheaper alternative treatment for critically ill babies. Cost can be measured, effectiveness could be measured, and we can talk about how much effectiveness we think we can afford or are willing to buy.

One interesting economic phenomenon that follows recent changes in pediatrics and child health care in this country is that the total amount spent on neonatal care is high and keeps growing, but the proportion spent on neonatal intensive care compared with other aspects of pediatrics is growing even faster. If present trends continue, expenditures on neonatal intensive care will soon dwarf other pediatric inpatient expenditures. This is primarily because the number of inpatient hospital days for premature babies is increasing, while the number of inpatient days for children between the ages of 1 and 15 has been falling steadily and rapidly over the last twenty years. In 1980 these 1- to 15-year-old children accounted for nearly 9 million bed-days. By 1993 that number had fallen to fewer than 6 million.[9]

The large drop in hospital days for children is due largely to improvements in care. More diseases are preventable through effective immunization programs than were twenty years ago. Improved outpatient care of patients with asthma or diabetes and of those in need of minor surgery has led to more outpatient care, less inpatient care, and fewer and shorter hospital stays.[10] We also treat diseases more efficiently, so that the length of inpatient stays for many illnesses has decreased.[11]

At the same time, the number of inpatient days in the NICU has steadily risen. It is difficult to get precise values for the number of inpatient days accounted for by NICU babies, but we can make estimates. A recent study from two Boston hospitals reported on length of stay and cost of care for all babies with birthweights of less than 1,500 grams.[12] Overall, these 1,361 babies required 56,754 inpatient days of care. Survivors accounted for 94 percent of those inpatient days. In the study, the survival rate for these tiniest babies was 82 percent. One can calculate the number of bed-days allocated to such babies as a function of the survival rate. If the survival rate had been just 50 percent, as it was in the early 1980s, then the number of inpatient days would have only been 41,300, or 30 percent fewer.

Nationally, approximately 53,000 babies are born per year with a birthweight of less than 1,500 grams. Overall, at today's survival rate, these babies will account for 2.1 million bed-days. Just a decade ago, survival rates for such babies were 30–50 percent lower, requiring correspondingly fewer bed-days in the hospital, along with fewer associated expenses.

The trend toward shorter inpatient stays for most children and longer inpatient stays for premature babies has implications for the economic survival of children's hospitals. Counting both NICU and post-NICU hospitalizations, NICUs and care of chronically ill NICU survivors account for nearly half of the bed-days in tertiary-care children's hospitals in America today. The NICU has become the economic engine that keeps children's hospitals running. In a sense, the survival of hospital-based pediatrics as we know it is increasingly dependent upon the commitment to the technologies and the personnel that enable the survival of extremely premature babies.

This has been true, to a lesser extent, for decades. Rasa Gustaitis and Ernle Young, who studied the NICU at the Stanford University Medical Center in the early 1980s, noted that

for hospitals, the Intensive Care Nursery (ICN) constitutes one of the more lucrative sources of income. The proportion of revenue earned for a hospital through neonatology is consistently higher than the proportion of licensed beds devoted to newborn intensive care. At the Stanford University Medical Center, in 1984, the cost per day for an ICN bed was $1550. The hospital had 663 licensed beds, 25 of which, or 3.7 percent, were designated for newborn intensive care. In fiscal 1982–3, revenues from the ICN were $9.47 million, 4.4 percent of a total $217.57 million in hospital revenues. In 1983–4, the amount rose to $11.09 million, or 4.7% of total revenues of $236.44 million.[13]

In addition, they note that 82 percent of the faculty-generated income for patient care in pediatrics came through the ICN and was shared by the entire department (213).

These economic realities create the context in which we conceptualize the ethical dilemmas. This is not a Marxist claim. It simply recognizes the power of economic realities to shape our everyday moral and legal understandings. Our moral sensibilities both lead to and flow from the existing economic, political, and administrative arrangements in such a complex way that it is sometimes hard, from the inside, to see whether the moral sensibilities are shaping the institutions or vice versa.

The present financial dependence on NICUs in academic pediatrics creates an environment for doctors, hospital administrators, and financial officers of academic medical centers in which certain solutions to problems seem preferable to others. Economic circumstances have a reality to them that other moral considerations may not. It is a good thing to do what is right, and we all try, but it is a different sort of good than paying one's bills. Economic realities influence choices in subtle ways. Given the profitability of NICUs compared with most other areas of pediatrics today, certain choices are simply more rational.

Of course, to say that we simply "make choices" among different ways of caring for children is simplistic. The choice is never presented as an either/or decision. Instead, actions and programs reflect attempts to balance conflicting commitments, to achieve both good prevention and good crisis intervention. Given that, however, the implicit choices we have made in seeking a balance reflect an inexorable shift. Pediatrics was once the quintessentially preventive medical discipline. As an organized political force, pediatricians advocated for a public-health model that considered interventions in terms of what was good for *all* children. The American Academy of Pediatrics was founded in the late 1920s in part to oppose the American Medical Association over the issue of government support for universal access to preventive care for children. Some pediatricians seemed to have a sense of the relative unimportance of crisis intervention for a few children compared with preventive services for all children. As a societal program, comprehensive preventive services, through institutional arrangements called "infant welfare stations," led to decreases in infant mortality rates that were every bit as dramatic as those achieved by NICUs.

However, prevention is difficult to "cost-out" under prevailing economic arrangements. Preventive services don't behave well as profit-making commodities. They need to be provided to vast numbers of people, at low cost, often by unskilled personnel, in order to lead to cost savings. The cost savings accrue across society rather than to the particular providers of the preventive interventions. And returns on investment take time and are difficult to link directly to particular interventions. The critique, then as now, is that universal preventive services threaten the economic structure by implicitly undermining the individualistic view that we have of both providers and consumers of health care. It is easier and more lucrative, given current economic arrangements, to provide intensive care for a relatively few premature babies than it is to provide comprehensive family-planning services and excellent prenatal care to thousands of mothers.

In conceptualizing the moral dilemmas of neonatal intensive care, people often invoke "rights" of one sort or another. There is talk of a right to life in the political movements swirling around abortion. There is overlap between discussions of neonatal rights and the rights of disabled citizens.[14] There may or may not be a right to die.[15] A whole legal framework has evolved in this country to define the overlap between each of these generic rights and the situation of the newborn in the NICU.[16] In the discussions of rights it is seldom clear how the insistence that a particular baby has a particular right creates a set of political and economic obligations for others. But if babies have a "right" to neonatal intensive care, then somebody in society has an obligation to provide that care, and whomever that obligation falls upon can claim separate rights for whatever means are necessary to fulfill the obligation. The societal obligation can be made concrete in many ways. We can enact laws mandating insurance coverage for the care of critically ill newborns. We can support scientific studies to determine which NICU interventions are most beneficial. We can develop a legal surveillance system that will police both doctors and parents who act in any way that might be construed as violating those newborn rights. Within this nexus of laws, rights, programs, rules, supports, and punishments, certain types of actions will come to seem obligatory, while others will come to seem impermissible.

NICUs make a lot of money for the hospitals in which they are located and for the doctors who staff them. They make money not by competing in a free market but instead by making a moral claim upon society. The moral claim insists that we cannot, must not, should not turn our backs on these tiny, vulnerable babies. It constructs the NICUs as the epitome of our humanity, the measure of our devotion, the test of our will. The extraordinary individual child becomes a symbol of our moral commitment to all children. Our NICUs, then, "stand for" our moral commitment to children, our excellence in caring for them, and even our moral progress over time in recognizing that even the tiniest children have rights. In "allowing" each tiny preemie to make a moral claim upon us, we can see ourselves as altruistic, as concerned primarily with the best interests of children, as superior to other cultures in other eras that didn't recognize the common moral humanity of the newborn. It is ironic that we can lavishly fund such care when we do not adequately fund comprehensive follow-up care, rehabilitation, or schooling for children who survive with special needs. Many NICU survivors have hospital bills of more than a million dollars and cannot be discharged from the hospital because their parents cannot afford a telephone at home.

We like to think that we are working for the premature babies. However, it turns out that preemies, through their involuntary willingness to be treated, perform an important altruistic function for the other areas of our medical center. The rewards we claim for meeting the obligations that we've taken upon ourselves can support us quite nicely. NICUs can support many of the other clinical and academic activities in the academic medical centers. We depend upon the NICUs, and they depend upon the preemies.

One common response to this sort of sociopolitical critique is that we are not making value choices at all. Instead, we are simply acting pragmatically, doing what works. By this view, preventive care worked well in the 1920s and 1930s, when high infant mortality was caused primarily by inappropriate feeding practices. Immunizations worked best in the 1950s and 1960s, when infectious diseases were the leading killers of children. In the most recent decades, however, those interventions were already maximally used, and neonatal intensive care was the logical next step, the only intervention that can continue to lower infant mortality in postindustrial societies. Our commitment to neonatal intensive care thus becomes a measure of our commitment to saving the lives of our babies, and any opposition to the unfettered growth of NICUs becomes the moral equivalent of child neglect.

The problem with this scenario is that it is at least uncertain whether neonatal intensive care is the best, the only, or the most cost-effective way to lower infant mortality. Instead, the Scandinavian example, as well as some data from the United States, suggests that some combination of comprehensive social support, preventive health care for women, comprehensive prenatal care, and easy access to family-planning services may be far more cost-effective.[17]

In evaluating these studies of efforts to reduce the incidence of prematurity or to lower infant mortality, the interrelationships between what we "believe" and what we "know" become complex and subtle. The question can be seen as one about our frame of reference. If we want to know whether neonatal care is effective, we can imagine a number of ways to study it. One would be to examine the fate of all infants with a low birthweight. Within this frame, NICUs will clearly be quite effective. Or we might look not just at what happens to babies born at a given birthweight; we might look at the rate of low birthweight within a society. Over the last twenty years, as NICUs have proliferated throughout the industrialized world, rates of preterm labor and low birthweight have been rising both in the United States and abroad. In Sweden the low-birth-weight rate rose from 5.5 per 1,000 in 1973–84 to

6.7 per 1,000 in 1988, and in the United States the low-birth-weight rate in 1997 was 7.5 percent, equivalent to 75 per 1,000, the highest rate since 1974.[18] Overall, infant mortality rates are dropping in both the United States and Sweden, and this seems to reflect a delicate balance between the rising rates of premature birth and the effectiveness of neonatal intensive care in lowering birthweight-specific infant mortality. Still, it seems like a curious approach, almost as if society, by some mechanism, were working against health, and medicine were then working against the rest of society, desperately trying to patch the wounds caused by some nameless thing that forces babies from the womb too soon.

Or perhaps not so nameless. Premature birth is clearly associated with a number of social and economic factors, as well as a number of factors related to the availability of health-care services. In Scandinavian countries, which have consistently had the lowest infant mortality rates in the world, these factors are all considered in decisions about how to best target resources in order to maintain low rates of premature birth and low infant mortality.[19] In the United States, the effects of social factors are well studied and are even more dramatic. But here they are not seen as amenable to intervention. The political and economic arrangements that we endorse have as much effect, or more, on the health of children as do the particular clinical interventions we undertake.[20] To a certain extent, neonatal intensive care has become necessary because we have created a society that produces a lot of premature babies.

The moral dilemmas that are associated with neonatal care are linked to certain understandings of our collective commitments and obligations. In many legal and bioethical analyses these obligations are understood to be obligations to the individual child, the citizen, the tiny moral agent in the NICU Isolette. One theme of this book, however, is that our collective commitment is not only to a particular child but equally to a certain form of professional economic and political organization. The economic substructure of any society shapes the context of moral choices without directly forcing any particular decision. It is in this context, against this background, that certain decisions stand out as insoluble dilemmas. If the form of organization changes, subtle changes will appear in the type and the degree of moral commitments that the society is able to make.

One example of such a subtle change is the effect of today's rapidly changing health-care marketplace upon the organization of cooperative regionalized networks of NICUs. In the 1970s, as the power and the glory of neonatal intensive care became apparent, professional leaders advocated the development of regionalized networks of nurseries to care for critically ill babies.[21] In these networks, small community hospitals (designated level 1) or mid-size hospitals (level 2) were formally affiliated with larger referral centers (level 3). The level 1 and 2 nurseries would transfer the tiniest and the sickest babies to the designated referral centers. At the level 3 centers, professional expertise and technology promised better-quality care. It was understood that the level 3 centers would be more expensive, but overall cost savings were expected to accrue because the centers would also be more efficient and there would be less unnecessary duplication of services. These compelling arguments led to the rapid development of regionalized neonatal networks and transport systems in most parts of the country.[22]

Such regional care for any condition is unusual in the United States. Instead, every hospital competes with every other hospital in every profitable "market."[23] Thus, in spite of evidence that outcomes for patients who require invasive cardiology are better at referral centers, for example, each hospital tries to develop its own invasive-cardiology service. The same is true for cancer programs, transplant programs, and everything else. James Robinson, Deborah Garnick, and Stephen McPhee showed that the strongest predictor of whether a hospital would initiate such services was the presence of competitor hospitals in the local market area.[24] Duplication of services inevitably increases overall cost even though it may lower costs for particular patients or payors at particular hospitals. To the extent that it results in many hospitals doing relatively few procedures, it also generally lowers the quality of care and leads to mortality rates that exceed those we would expect if we extrapolate from those seen at the busiest neonatal centers.[25]

Regionalized perinatal networks survived in the 1980s and early 1990s, but many of those networks are now breaking down. The mid-level hospitals (level 2) now insist that they can safely keep the sicker babies that they once transferred. This is happening for two related economic reasons. First, since the level 3 hospitals are more expensive (at least in the short run), payors look for short-term cost savings. Second, the hospitals themselves see the potential for profits in the development of their own neonatal units.[26]

One response to this phenomenon is to regulate the proliferation of particular health-care technologies. Thus, many states require hospitals to obtain permits before they offer particular services. The results of this are not always straightforward, however. Steven Shortell and E. F. Hughes showed that hospital mortality rates might actually be inversely correlated with the degree of regulation, implying that regulation itself imposes costs or burdens on health-delivery systems that may decrease quality.[27]

Given the welter of statistics, studies, arguments, and counterarguments, it is hard to say what is right or wrong in this matter. As NICU technology gets simpler and better, and as the expertise to use it diffuses more broadly, the cost savings and the improvements in outcome that were originally associated with regional networks clearly decrease. It is difficult to predict, even from careful studies, which babies will do better at tertiary-care centers. Furthermore, what that means in this context is not unidimensional. Tertiary-care centers are expensive. We must ask not only whether they achieve better outcomes but what *better* means, both qualitatively and quantitatively, and who pays for each increment in quality.

But the existence of such choices and the need to evaluate the arguments leads to a certain moral anxiety. What if it turns out that the individual decisions we make about how to treat a particular baby in a particular situation do not reflect our deeply held moral values but instead are driven by large, socioeconomic forces over which we have no control? What if we realize that we live and work within a system that exists in the form that it does in order to serve political and economic interests that we oppose? Such situations challenge our self-image as moral beings with free will and sacred values. We need to oppose them somehow even if our opposition is largely symbolic.

Taken out of context, the case of *Miller v Jones* seems somewhat ludicrous. The doctor did his best. He tried to resuscitate the baby. The baby's chances of survival were minimal, and the likelihood was high that even if he did survive, he would survive with severe neurological damage. What happened was what had to happen, but it didn't seem like what should happen. It was hard not to look for a moral of some sort within this complex framework of costs and charges, valuations and controversies, active and passive participation in decisions and nondecisions made elsewhere by others. Through the malpractice case we could imagine a tale being told of individual moral responsibility for upholding the value that each life was priceless.

How much should I be charging for my time? Taken out of context, the whole process that we were going through, the lawyer questioning and I trying to answer, began to take on a surreal quality. I knew how inadequate each answer must be. I tried to respond in a doublespeak coded enough so that it would mean one thing for him today and, who knows, perhaps something altogether different for the imaginary jury that would someday hear my answers to similar questions. And perhaps I was also answering for some even vaguer tribunal beyond the darkness.

Is it a good or a bad thing for me to testify in a malpractice case such as this? I think Dr. Miller did the right thing. In my testimony I state that. Yet by participating in this drama I am implicitly validating both the procedure and, ultimately, the results. If my participation affects the outcome and helps shape the moral landscape in such a way as to lessen the likelihood that law-suits of this kind will be brought or will succeed, my moral gamble will have paid off.

"And I think it's fair to say," I said to the lawyer, "that I'm making less money through my involvement in the case than anybody else in this room."

"Doctor, please just try to stick to the questions."

I nodded disingenuously. My mind was beginning to wander. I realized that I could no longer just stick to the questions.

EIGHT

Home Births

After my residency I wanted to get as far from NICUs as I could. In medical school I had signed on with the National Health Service Corps. Through this idealistic experiment in distributive justice the federal government had paid my medical school tuition, and in return I had agreed to work for a few years in "a medically underserved area."

Each of the places on the underserved list—northern New Hampshire, southeastern Connecticut, the lowlands of eastern North Carolina, the mountains and hollers of Appalachia—was intriguing in its way. We selected the Appalachian Mountains, and after residency ended in 1984, my wife and I and our small baby moved to a small rural county on a rail line near a big river. The town we moved to was an unusual little place. It had thrived in the early twentieth century when the railroad was built along the river to bring the coal and timber out of the mountains. Then the bottom must have dropped out of the market, for nothing had been built there since about 1918 except a few fast-food restaurants near the highway. The downtown area looked almost freeze-dried. It could have been a stage set.

The mountains were beautiful, austere, remote. The people living there eked out a modest living from the land, raising goats, growing corn, or working on cars. Most of our friends were not natives. Many were veterans of the various social movements of the sixties—self-identified hippies, homesteaders, counterculturalists, and antiwar activists who had gone "back to the land" in the 1970s. They had bought old, rundown farms up in the hills cheap and tried to change the world by example rather than by confrontation, living simply and organically, heating with wood, and growing their own vegetables. It was a far more difficult sort of protest to sustain than a march on Washington. Many found the mountains congenial, and a community had taken root in that beautiful, rocky soil.

Many of our friends had somewhat unconventional health beliefs. They delivered their babies at home, sometimes in bed and sometimes underwater in the hot tub. Many didn't believe in giving their children unnatural things like immunizations. They grew their own St.-John's wort and echinacea long before Andrew Weil popularized these alternatives to traditional medical therapies. They practiced old-time healing techniques like cranial manipulation, therapeutic touch, yoga, and massage. They dabbled in witchcraft and pagan rituals and participated in harmonic convergences. Our neighbors had a cow that gave more milk than they needed, so they let us into the milking rotation. Sunday was our milking day. In principle, and as a matter of public policy, we favored pasteurization, but our cow looked pretty healthy. The unpastuerized milk was rich and sweet.

Periodically we argued about medical issues. The arguments were usually pretty friendly, conducted over dinners of homemade wine, fresh bread, and salad picked from the garden that afternoon. Some of our biggest arguments were about midwifery and home births. As a result of my months in the NICU, I had come to see every newborn as a tenuous, fragile creature hardly able to survive without sophisticated technology. The obstetricians with whom I had worked were enamored of intrauterine fetal monitoring to detect minute-to-minute changes in the heart rate of the fetus. Labor and delivery were managed like a space shuttle launch, with technicians, numbers, tubes, and wires. I didn't always like that way of doing things, but I wasn't afraid of it either. It seemed to have its place.

Jill, one of the midwives, was a flamboyant character. She always wore peasant dresses down to her ankles and flowers in her hair. She loved babies, loved to deliver babies, loved women and all the fecund forces of the earth and of nature that flowed through them and through her and nurtured us all. She had learned her craft from other "lay" midwives. They were unlicensed practitioners of an art that they didn't think of as medical or "professional," at least in the regulatory sense of the word, because they didn't think consider pregnancy, labor, and childbirth illnesses or diseases. Of course they also didn't think that physicians were necessary to care for pregnant women or to assist at the time of delivery.

The government disagreed. The state required that midwives be licensed in order to practice. To be licensed, a midwife needed a degree in nursing. Those midwives who rejected this medicalized approach had formed a semisecret organization. They thought of themselves as carrying on the Appalachian tradition of the "grannies," wise women who were midwives and much more, who knew which herbs helped make an easy delivery, cured asthma, or eased the pain and the passing of someone dying of cancer. The grannies were tough women who cut and split their own wood, drank moonshine with the men, birthed the calves, and castrated the bulls. What the lay midwives were doing was on the edge of the law, semi-officially tolerated, and not so clearly wrong.

Jill approached her midwifery with a fearless dedication that quickly brought her a loyal following and a steady stream of word-of-mouth referrals from satisfied clients. For her, childbirth was less like a shuttle launch and more like an organic garden. The forces of nature did the work. All we had to do was plant by the signs, clear the weeds, spread around a little manure, and get out of the way. She had enormous faith in the rightness and the reparative power of what would be.

There were no board-certified pediatricians in the town, but there were family practitioners who cared for the children, and there was a small hospital. It surprised me that the tiny town could sustain a hospital, but that little hospital was the pride of the community. It often ran a budget deficit, and the townspeople, who didn't have much to spare, would struggle to come up with donations to keep it going. Various for-profit hospital chains came through to look at it in the early 1980s, but even in those go-go days for purchases and acquisitions they were skeptical about the potential of this tiny facility. One wanted to buy it and convert it into a nursing home, but the board wouldn't allow it. The hospital had become a character with a personality all its own in the town's story.

From a health-policy perspective, keeping that little hospital open made no sense whatsoever. It was too small to provide any services efficiently, except, perhaps, emergency services. There were never many patients, so that the doctors and nurses didn't get enough experience to maintain skills and expertise in many of the areas in which they were called upon to provide treatment. The resources that were poured into that little hospital might have led to better health outcomes if they had been spent on better equipment for the football team, new guardrails for some of the more treacherous stretches of highway, supplemental food programs for some of the poorer families in town, or college scholarships. But those options were not available. The money that was spent on the hospital could only be spent on the hospital. It didn't exist until a billable service of some sort conjured it into an account receivable. And in the context of the economy of that little town it was a fair amount of money.

One reason why the town was so committed to the hospital was that it was the largest employer in the town. It was also the only source of outside revenue in a town with no industry, no manufacturing, and only a few locally owned retail stores. Ironically, as the largest employer in the town, the hospital was undeniably beneficial to the health of the citizens in a more tangible way than through its medical services. It improved health less by providing medical care than by providing jobs and a life-saving infusion of federal dollars.

The obstetrician on the hospital staff had a very busy practice. She had her own unique practice style, with the result that nearly 40 percent of her deliveries were by C-section, the highest rate in the entire state. A segment of the population seemed to like her practice style. They seemed to think that her willingness to do C-sections showed a real commitment to their health, just as others seemed to think that Jill's unwillingness to do C-sections showed a similar commitment. Many of the local women who were having babies had themselves been born at home, not because their mothers had chosen home delivery but because there had been no hospital at the time or because they couldn't afford a hospital delivery. For them, going to the hospital, getting anesthesia, and having an operation was a sign of progress, of modernity, just like the satellite dishes on the lawns of many of the mobile homes down by the river.

Interestingly, the obstetrician, whose high rate of C-sections made her practice seem somewhat shoddy by current professional standards, was societally sanctioned in her work. The hospital in town, though too small to achieve acceptable standards of quality or cost-effectiveness, was publicly subsidized through Medicaid, Medicare, and local charitable giving. The midwife received no societal sanction and served people who paid for her services entirely out of their own pockets. They seemed to think that they got good value for their money. Her measurable health outcomes were just as good or better than those of most obstetricians, and at much lower cost, but she was neither subsidized nor even legally permitted to work by the officials of society. Neither got sued. Both sometimes lost babies, of course, the obstetrician after perhaps doing too much, the midwife after perhaps doing too little.

It might be said that both women were doing excellent work because both had high rates of patient satisfaction. One way to evaluate their work would have been to bring some external criteria of excellence, competence, adequacy to bear upon their work and then decide whether, by these objective standards, they were doing good work. But that didn't happen. Because the town was so small, there were no professional societies that could review cases, and even if there had been, the two women would not have belonged to the same one. As the only pediatrician in that tiny mountain town, I worked with both.

One day Jill called to ask if I'd meet her to talk about a case. We met in a local coffee shop. I arrived first and ordered coffee for me and herbal tea for her. From the window I watched her battered, dust-covered pickup truck pull into the lot. As she walked across the parking lot, her long blonde hair blowing in the wind and her bright peasant skirt swirling around her calves, all eyes turned to follow her. She was a charismatic presence, strong, beautiful, and in her disregard for custom or convention a little dangerous. We hugged. She smiled, her eyes twinkling as they would when she was ready to start an argument. I smiled back. What the heck, I could argue. For a while neither of us spoke. We just looked at each other.

"How's business?" I finally asked.

"Wonderful," she said. "Ricardo and Marge just had a baby boy. They'd had a stillbirth before, so they were very nervous. And it was a long labor. But we sang, and prayed, did a lot of massage. Sometimes you just have to be patient. Babies come when they are ready."

Ricardo and Marge had actually lost their first two babies. One had been a fetal demise. The other, at the local hospital, had been born prematurely and couldn't be resuscitated. They had come to me for my opinion about this latest pregnancy, and I had suggested that they go over the mountain to a bigger hospital than the one in our town. But they didn't have much money or any health insurance, and after their last experience they didn't have much faith in hospitals.

"I'm glad it went well," I said. "I was worried about them."

"I know you were." Jill was staring right into my eyes, and I couldn't look away. Her smile had faded. She wasn't really frowning, but she had a sort of questioning look. "Do you ever think that your worry may cause some of the things that you worry about? I mean, parents who are anxious may need to be calmed, reassured. It seems like doctors do just the opposite. They're always imagining problems, even when there aren't any."

"Well, we see so many bad things, we can't help imagining the worst. It seems like the best way to avoid problems is to think about them, be aware of them, and that way be prepared to do something about them if they arise."

"Maybe. But for me, sometimes, thinking about all the problems that might happen makes me so anxious that I'm more likely to create problems. Instead, I try to visualize all the good things that will happen. That may be why midwifery works so well."

"What do you have coming up?" I shifted the subject. I was pretty sure she hadn't just asked me here to pick up the same argument we'd had twenty times before.

"Well, something I may need your help for. Twins. Low-risk twins. The mom has had three babies before, all doing well. The first was born in the hospital, and they hated that. I assisted with the last two at home, and they liked that much better. They called me to ask if I'd do twins at home. I don't see why not, although I'd like to have you be available, if possible, just in case there are any problems."

"Have you ever delivered twins at home before?"

"Oh, yeah." She paused. "Once."

"What does the association say about twins?" The lay midwives' association walked a fine line. Since they practiced illegally, they didn't want any disasters that might call persecutorial attention to their existence. Seeking legitimacy, they wanted to act like responsible professionals and to regulate themselves. But being fundamentally idealistic, they needed to be true to their own values and not to make too many value trade-offs in order to secure recognition. So, with all the chaotic acrimony and anarchy of any such idealistic organization, they had come up with very vague guidelines for appropriate and inappropriate practices.

"They say, you know, it's up to the parents, discuss the risks, consider referral, the usual stuff."

I was starting to see what all this was about. Jill was flouting even the vague rules of her fringe organization, apparently with the encouragement and complicity of the parents. So why not? Certainly the parents would consent. And given their experiences, they probably would be much better informed than most. Overall the risks were probably pretty low. Jill was a skilled midwife. The mother had had three previous babies without problems. People had been having babies at home for millennia, even twins. If things took a turn for the worse, she could always call an ambulance and go to the local hospital, where, if there were already medical problems, she might not be much better off. Jill had my number, all right. She was daring me to put my principles into practice, to take patient values and patient autonomy seriously. She was more committed to informed consent than any lawyer or bioethicist I'd met.

Unless, of course, the relevant consents here were not that of the mother and father but that of the babies. What would they want—the delivery that made their parents the happiest or the one that had the statistically lowest risk? Would it, or should it, matter at all to the babies that home deliveries cost much less than hospital deliveries or that if things worked out, the parents would feel better at home? Could we assume that the babies had the same values as the parents and so would want the same things? If not, was the only alternative to assume that the babies had the same values as the American Academy of Pediatrics, or the Association of Trial Lawyers, or the National Organization of Women, or the ACLU? Or should I impose my own values? Or should I support Jill's? Any of these options was available. The only option that wasn't available was to have no particular values. The babies made a claim on us. They needed to be cared for. We had to respond.

As a society we seem to want it both ways—to give the parents both freedom and responsibility for the choices they made but then to constrain those choices by a web of policies, subsidies, regulations, and restrictions that narrowed the choice down to something almost meaningless.

But why me? Why should I get involved? What did Jill really want of me? Was it really my expertise, or was it just a sort of complicity or cover? I was just out of residency, new in town, and inexperienced. I felt like I was being coerced and perhaps used in a gentle but uncomfortable way.

"Oh Jill, why do you come to me with these things? I can't help you out with these crazy projects. You know I don't approve of subjecting newborns to unnecessary risks. And even if I wanted to, I wouldn't be much help. I'm a technician, not a healer. I'm useless without a hospital around me. I need my tools, a laryngoscope, oxygen, suction equipment, IV lines."

"You can bring those things if you need them. And I think you like these 'crazy' projects. I've heard the way you talk about that hospital, those doctors. I've heard the way you talk about letting parents make choices, about respecting their autonomy. Come meet these parents, talk to them. They know what they want and they know what they're doing. We can work together to make something very beautiful. There is nothing like the moment of delivery at home, welcoming a new life into a loving, safe, familiar world with the whole family gathered around." Her eyes were really sparkling now. "The energy is incredible. It is beautiful, powerful stuff."

The mountains were beautiful too, especially before sunrise and at dusk, when the light began to change. In the mornings, the fog would settle in the valleys, and both sight and sound were muffled. The scuffling sounds of animals in the woods would mix with the sound of the trains' whistles as they announced their approach through the Big Bend Tunnel. Oddly, the train, which had once been the quintessential symbol of everything modern, technological, and unnatural, was now an emblem of the quaint old-fashionedness of the town rather than a threat to it. It no longer startled us the way it had startled Hawthorne in Sleepy Hollow or Thoreau at Walden Pond, representing for them the inexorably onrushing future. Now the long whistle and the rhythm of the wheels on the tracks had a reassuring pastoral, almost natural feel.

It had not always been so. The history of railroads in the area where we were living has been anything but serene. Our town was located at the confluence of two big rivers, which made it an important railroad junction. The railroads had first come to the area shortly after the Civil War in the exuberant robber-baron era of railroad building. The Appalachian Mountains were rich in timber and coal, waiting only on some form of transportation that could get it off the mountains and back to the Eastern cities. Given the existing technology, railroad building was extremely difficult and expensive in that rugged terrain, but the potential payoffs were enormous.

Because the area was so mountainous, the rail lines required numerous bridges and tunnels. Building both was dangerous work. One historian described the scene on a tunnel construction site as follows:

> Many tunnel workers died from tunnel sickness (also called miner's consumption or silicosis) inflicted by the horrible foul air and smothering heat encountered in the poorly ventilated underground. Thick stone dust, the noxious blasting fumes from the 833 pounds of nitroglycerin used daily, and the smoke from the lard and black-strap oil which fueled each day's 115 pounds of candles, were nearly intolerable. Workers also suffered frequent accidents from bungled blasting or crashing rocks. Most often the dead were simply buried in the big rock rill near the east portal, their deaths unreported.[1]

It was a time of rapid technological improvement in building tunnels. Between 1850 and 1875 Americans patented 110 different kinds of rock drills for building railroad tunnels.[2] Nobody knew which techniques worked best, and there were no organized technology-assessment projects. Nor were there unions, or a federal Occupational Safety and Health Administration, or a sense that companies had an obligation to protect the lives and the health of workers.

The Big Bend Tunnel, outside our town, was built in the 1870s. At that time it was the longest tunnel ever built. Hundreds of men died during the building. Many were recently freed slaves, hungry and desperate for work.[3] A couple of miles from our house there was a statue of the semilegendary black railroad worker John Henry. John Henry, according to the legend, was a natural man, devoted to work and to his family. But the work was disappearing. Men were being replaced by machines. He challenged the machine to a contest to see if he could pound stakes into the rock faster than the machine could. In some versions of the legend he won the race. In others he tied. In all of them he died at the end. The statue shows him holding a huge sledgehammer, his railroad cap cocked to one side, his arms rippling with strength, a challenging grin upon his face.

Scholars and historians disagree about whether John Henry was a real person, an amalgam of various people, or a fiction. As Brett Williams writes, "Ultimately, to believe that John Henry actually lived is an act of faith."[4] But perhaps veracity misses the point. Real or not, John Henry symbolizes the struggles and the choices that thousands of men made. Constrained by the social forces of the time, they had to choose how and where to take a stand, how to be and move in a world that no longer needed their strength or their skills. Born a slave, John Henry had lived through the war that set him free and then died fighting a war that was so much more amorphous that it is hard, even now, to see it clearly.

John Henry worked at a time when workers were more expendable than mules and when premature babies were carnival exhibits. Today we have different metrics for assigning value to the lives of both preemies and workers. We have a different sense of the proper balance between the needs of society and the rights of individuals. The moral climate of any particular time or place always seems intuitively correct to those who live in it—commonsensical, unquestioned, and unchangeable. Yet it does change over time, in ways that are hard to define and hard to direct. Today parents who choose to have babies at home face legal risk and social ostracism. The lay midwives who choose to help them must break the law to do so. Today doctors who stop resuscitation of tiny preemies without the parents' explicit consent, and sometimes even with it, are subject to punishing litigation. Today the CSX freight trains and the Amtrak southern route from Washington to Chicago still go through that Big Bend Tunnel, clickety-clacking and blowing their long whistles over the remains of the workers whose bodies were cast into the rock pit at the tunnel's east portal. Social forces shape our choices in ways that make it seem as if we are passive characters in larger moral dramas that have no author.

Sometimes individuals resist social forces and perhaps even change the world in which they live. Those who try are often seen as traitors, as outlaws. Sometimes it may be necessary to imagine them into a myth, a story, or a bigger-than-life character like John Henry who is more real and more true than any who really exist. Moments of individual moral choice are often quiet, private moments. They are always uncomfortable. We push against the edges of the seemingly irreconcilable contradictions until the discomfort makes it seem like the dangerous step outside the constraints of the prevailing narratives, understandings, and conventions of our time is the only relief. To make sense of that step we need to dramatize it. It refines itself into a story, takes shape as memory, legend, or folk song. Tentatively, partially, haltingly, apologetically, with fear and trembling, we sometimes learn to create within ourselves a new character, to write a different ending for a story.

I chose not to help Jill at the twins' delivery. As it turned out, it was a difficult delivery. The first baby did well, but the second was stuck for a while in the birth canal and may have been deprived of oxygen. He might have been better off if he'd been born in a hospital. But maybe not. Or he might have been better off if I'd been there with a portable oxygen tank. Perhaps he would have been born in a hospital if we had a system of universal access to health care and his parents hadn't had to figure the cost along with other factors in their decision about where and how to have their baby. But maybe not. Perhaps I would have been willing to help if I had not been afraid of being sued. Or if I'd been older, wiser, more self-confident. Or if I'd felt more like I belonged in that town, that its stories were mine to help author.

I saw the twins a couple of months later. Their parents brought them to my clinic for a checkup. I wasn't really sure why they had come. They didn't want immunizations for the babies. They thought the babies were doing fine and seemed to just be proudly showing them off. At first I thought they wanted to prove to me that I'd made the wrong decision, that home deliveries were OK. But then, toward the end of the visit, they asked some questions suggesting that they were just a little worried about the second twin. He seemed to them a little slower than the other. They wondered whether I thought the baby was having any problems. I examined him carefully, and I just wasn't sure. He seemed perhaps a little slow in his development. I told them I thought he'd probably be OK. I wanted to be his pediatrician, to keep an eye on him as he grew, but they did not ask me.

I thought of those twins as I came out of the deposition in the Miller case. Defending Dr. Miller made me wish that I had made a different decision myself. The late afternoon sun on Lake Michigan made the water sparkle and lit up the windows of the Sears Tower. It was one of those summer afternoons when the very blueness of the sky seems to swallow sound. Everything seems so visual and beautiful that it also seems quieter. The wispy clouds glowed golden, the airplanes on their approach path to O'Hare just floated over a city that looked as magical and shimmery as Oz.

I walked through Grant Park to the Buckingham Fountain, a glorious water sculpture given to the city to memorialize a boy who had died young. The city had put hundreds of sculpted cows of various colors all around the city—on street corners, in shop windows, resting in the park. Children crawled on them, tourists posed for pictures beside them. They evoked the history of the city—the cattle drives, the cruelty, the wealth of the stockyards—but in an oblique, amusing way. The brutal economic realities of the past become the conceptual artworks of the present. There are still stockyards somewhere, I suppose, but not in Chicago, not in sight of the restaurants where yuppies dine on veal. I bought a copy of the homeless people's newspaper *Streetwise* from a smiling black man who thanked me with a blessing. The lead story was about a little shanty village that homeless men had built under the expressways of Chicago that the city was now destroying. Thin young women in Lycra jogged and roller-bladed along the bike path by the harbor. A few old black guys sat still and silent along the retaining wall, fishing poles in hand. Some yachtsmen rowed dinghies out to their sailboats in the harbor.

. What would become of Dr. Miller? Would he win the case or lose it? Would he continue to practice? Might he take his life in despair? Perhaps he'd run off to Argentina with a nurse from Labor and Delivery . . .

What would become of me? My own career was at something of a dead end, or more charitably, a turning point. After West Virginia and my fellowship in medical ethics I'd floated on the periphery of academic medicine, doing the things that general pediatricians who don't want to go into private practice often find themselves doing. I got involved with the evaluation of child abuse, I cared for children with the sort of complex chronic diseases that impoverish their parents and make them unwelcome in private practices, I wrote about health policy and dabbled in health services research. I rarely saved lives, rarely got research grants. It was a clear sign of my directionless passage into middle age that I had begun to be offered the administrative jobs that nobody else in the medical school really wanted. In academic medicine, research is the most valuable activity. Patient care in the procedure-oriented subspecialties is the most lucrative. Those who can't do either very well try to teach others how to do them or take mid-level administrative jobs with moderate responsibility but minimal power. That was how I ended up being considered for the job of chief of the Division of General Pediatrics.

"Why the fuck would you want that job?" my neonatologist friend Bill asked. We were at the Midway Plaisance Park, a broad expanse of grass between the Hyde Park and Woodlawn neighborhoods on the South Side of Chicago. In Hyde Park, to the north, I could see the elaborate gargoyles on the pseudo-Gothic towers of the University of Chicago and the well-tended buildings and lawns of a middle-class urban residential community. Hyde Park is one of the few racially integrated communities in Chicago. It is not an entirely peaceful place. The crime rate remains high compared with that in the suburbs. Most of the houses have elaborate security-alarm systems. People think twice before walking around alone at night. But those are all features of the twenty-first-century urban lifestyle anywhere in America. We learn to live with a background level of inequality and paranoia. Within those parameters, Hyde Park is a model of urban serenity and multicultural tolerance.

In Woodlawn, to the south, by contrast, I could see mostly vacant lots and abandoned buildings. Woodlawn used to be an affluent, all-white residential community. Then, in the 1950s and 1960s, like many South Side communities, it became a battleground. The white folks eventually fled to the suburbs, the moneylenders redlined the area, credit dried up, property values plummeted, and the neighborhood underwent a long and slow decline. Today it is a typical bombed-out inner-city neighborhood, with boarded up buildings, vacant lots, and no new commercial development. There are many churches, a few liquor stores, a currency exchange, some fortresslike grocery stores, an office of the Women's, Infants', and Children's Supplemental Food Program, and a police station. Many of the vacant lots bear testimony to the deliberate abandonment of the neighborhood. In the 1970s many Woodlawn landlords decided that their only hope of getting any money out of the deteriorating neighborhood was to burn their own buildings down. The level of hopelessness and self-destructive despair even among people with some resources shocked even the longtime community organizer Saul Alinsky. It was the first time he had seen owners simply give up and turn their backs upon an entire community.

But there were signs that Woodlawn was starting to come back. The city had recently torn down the El tracks over 63rd Street, light and air were coming in, and new townhouses were being built for the first time in decades. There was a new YMCA. It seemed like a moment of partial, tentative hope.

The University of Chicago Hospitals serve both communities.

Bill and I, soccer dads both, were waiting for our ten-year-olds to arrive for soccer practice. It was a beautiful, sunny May afternoon. We were starting to prepare for the citywide Mayor's Cup soccer tournament. We thought we had a shot at the under-ten girls' division title. The boys' divisions were consistently dominated by the Hispanic teams, but the girls' divisions usually went to the groups designated by demographers as "non-Hispanic white." Our mostly non-Hispanic white girls usually ended up in the finals with a team of similar-looking blonde girls from the suburbs.

"You'll have less time for coaching, you know," he added.

"Yeah, maybe," I said. "I'll turn the coaching over to you."

Bill spends his working hours saving the lives of tiny, critically ill babies. One-pound patients come into his NICU looking like little washed-up water rats—blue, limp, and lifeless. He breathes for them and gives them nutrition, antibiotics, and warmth. They, for the most part, grow and thrive and go home with their parents healthy and cooing. He saves lives every day. Many of the lives he saves are the lives of patients whose critical illnesses might have been prevented if their moms had not gotten pregnant as teenagers, or if they had been better educated, or if they had received good prenatal care or been treated for their cocaine addiction. But those possibilities don't seem any more likely than a major economic revival in Woodlawn.

While Bill is saving lives, I and the general pediatricians are seeing patients with colds, ear infections, impetigo, ringworm, diaper rashes, and head lice. We talk to parents about immunizations, bicycle helmets, and school problems, we talk to teens about sexuality, and we counsel fourth graders who have had bellyaches since their parents divorced. We assess depressed teenagers who are starting to smoke pot or cut themselves with knives. We try to figure out which kids are really sick and which ones will get better by themselves. We then send the really sick ones to the hospital, to be cared for by the specialists. Consequently, we rarely actually save lives ourselves. At least not individual lives. We save statistical lives, whatever that might mean.

Bill and I are both members of the Department of Pediatrics, but nice as he is, he just doesn't get the point of the preventive, primary-care, general-pediatrics part of it. Bill plays to win, and the odds looked pretty bad for the incoming chief of general pediatrics. The night before, I'd had a dream: Bill and I were working in the NICU taking care of a baby who we thought might have overwhelming sepsis. I hadn't been in the NICU in years, and I wasn't at all sure what I was doing, but Bill seemed calm and self-assured. At one point he stuck a needle right into the baby's heart to draw blood. I was shocked. It seemed so needlessly and brutally invasive. Perhaps, I thought, things had changed since I'd been there, but I'd never seen anything like that. But he seemed so casual about it that I didn't say anything. I even felt an admiring awe at his mixture of bravado, danger, healing skill, and risk taking. The residents, bolder than I, raised their eyebrows. One of them said, "That baby doesn't even look septic." But I wanted to support Bill, so I calmly put the blood in a culture tube and asked him if he wanted me to start a line. He said, "Yeah, start fluids and antibiotics." Suddenly I realized that I was late for an important appointment, and I ran out to my car. The hospital lobby was crowded, so I had to push and shove my way to the parking lot. My car had been broken into and hot-wired, so I didn't even need the key to start it. I wondered why they had hot-wired it but not stolen it and looked to see what they'd taken. The radio was still there, and the phone, but it was a different phone, and when I tried to make a call to explain that I'd be late, it didn't work. The car didn't work, the phone didn't work, and I woke up in a panic of disorientation.

The dream suggested that I didn't know what I was good at, where I should be working, or even who I might call to help. Over the years since residency, when I'd worked many months in neonatal intensive care, I'd lost my competence at the sort of critical-care crisis intervention that was Bill's expertise. In the dream, I still wanted to help him even though what he was doing seemed barbaric, aimed right at the heart of the poor babies for whom he cared. But helping him do what he needed to do even though it didn't seem quite right was keeping me from some important appointment of my own. And when I left the NICU and tried to get where I had to go, the road was crowded, the environment hostile, and my phone was broken. I was going to be late, and I couldn't even call ahead!

I didn't know how to answer his question. Why the fuck *would* I want the job of managing the nonspecialty group with the least respect, the least reve-nue, and the least straightforward task of any in our medical center? Should I say to Bill that now, in my mid-forties, I realized that I'd taken a wrong turn somewhere on the road to tenure? That I'd had a vision? Dimly but power-fully, I saw a different model, a different purpose, a different mission for at least some of the pediatricians in our academic medical center. As a group we had perhaps become too oriented toward the critically ill children who found their way to our doors in the midst of a crisis of one sort or another— the preemies and the victims of motor-vehicle accidents and the children with rare forms of cancer. It was good to be there for them in those crises, but there was something a little strange in the way we focused on care for children whose treatment required us to cut them open, to stick needles into their hearts, to poison them with toxic drugs, children whose treatment was almost as bad as their disease. We seemed addicted to the adrenaline rush of critical care, the ambiguity of treatments so dangerous that they required every ounce of our concentration and even then were a therapeutic high-wire act, as likely to do harm as to do good. The best treatments were the most dangerous treatments. To obliterate the disease, we had to nearly oblit-erate the patient. Sometimes these terrible treatments went on for months or years. The "cutting edge" of medicine demanded that we focus our energy on making progress of this peculiar type.

I, like many others, looked out from our ivory tower at the children in our schools and our neighborhoods and saw a different set of health problems. These kids suffered from poor diet, the strange malnutrition of postindustrial society, obesity, and depression. They experienced high rates of homicide, suicide, child abuse, substance abuse, teen pregnancy and sexually transmitted diseases, lead toxicity. These are the problems that Alex Kotlowitz writes about in *There Are No Children Here* and that Jonathan Kozol describes in *Amazing Grace.*[5] Richard Powers's novel *Operation Wandering Soul,* set in a high-tech children's hospital in Los Angeles, captures the complex reality. Through the main character, a pediatric surgeon named Kraft, Powers witnesses and describes "the traffic of juvenile misery" and the sincere but paradoxical efforts the doctors and nurses make to patch up children ailing from life in a world that is toxic to them in spiritual, economic, and biochemical ways. Always, there is the hope that scientific and technical progress will lead to better cures in the future. "Cures are coming, just around the corner, all but here. Fantasy treatment, fictive fairy diagnostics, complete in-the-womb screenings, packets of substitute chromosome segments to replace the defective instructions." In the meantime, though, "doctors have only their blundering surgical corrections, bulling about with knives," while the statistics show a "tremendous spike in preemies, SIDS cases, placental substance dependence, inherited autoimmune deficiencies." Discouraged, he imagines an alternative: "What dying childhood needs—so obvious to anyone who's been paying attention—is not another swank kid-killer like Carver [Children's Hospital], perfunctory holding tank for prepping the virtually dead. It needs a larger-than-life tree-fort resort . . . an arcaded, terraced, gardened, courtyarded children's pavilion, with ceramic and brocade, half timber and gingerbread cupolas."[6] It needs more fantasy, more play, more room for children than currently exists in the child-hostile deserts of our inner cities.

Our biggest triumphs within the medical center were becoming more and more double-edged. Each life we saved took more and more effort, more and more money. While each life is inarguably precious and sacred, there seemed to be something crazily unsustainable about this approach of focusing on the rare case of a critically ill and individually identifiable child with a precisely diagnosable disease that could be cured only with a million dollars of neonatal intensive care, a heart transplant, or years of chemotherapy. In the midst of poverty we were sucking resources out of the poorest, most deprived communities in our city, often in order to morally impose upon them demands for even more complex medical care that would cost even more.

"Maybe I'm crazy, but I'd like to try to create a new kind of Section of General Pediatrics, to bring together innovative service programs, new types of inquiry into the causes of morbidity and mortality in childhood, to rethink the way we do pediatrics."

"You're crazy."

"I want to find the most creative thinkers around in this area, hire them, give them space and resources to work together, think together, develop programs, write papers, change the paradigms."

"They'll never give you the money for that," Bill said as he started his stretching exercises.

"Well, they've promised me a couple million dollars of development money. I'm going to be able to hire three new docs, a statistician, a grant writer. I'll be able to offer the docs some protected time for research. It's a modest beginning, but it's something."

"Well, you'll see what those promises are worth. They'll only let you finance the development stuff if the clinical revenue is there, and general peds will never bring in enough clinical revenue, so your development money will just disappear."

"Then I'll quit."

The girls were beginning to arrive. We started some dribbling drills. The sun was low on the horizon, and the clouds were changing to pink. It was a gorgeous dusk. We scrimmaged until the sky turned from pink to purple and then gray and we could barely see, until the girls were covered with mud and too exhausted to play (but not too exhausted to climb trees and hide while their parents impatiently shouted to them from the cars, or to squirt each other from their squeezable Nike and Gatorade water bottles).

Bill is convinced that since for the foreseeable future babies will be born prematurely, we may as well focus our intellectual and economic energies on saving as many as we possibly can. It is expensive, but it is doable. And it is satisfying. He loves working in the NICU. He loves teaching the residents about the complex physiology of the premature baby. He thinks pediatrics training programs should have more NICU time, rather than less, and less, rather than more, outpatient clinic time. I am convinced that we should be trying to find ways to eliminate NICUs, that they should go the way of the tuberculosis sanitarium or the iron lung. He is the realist. I am not.

A few years ago I went to hear a panel at the annual meeting of the American College of Surgeons. The topic was innovative surgical treatment. The doctors on the panel were famous surgeons who had developed some of the most exciting new operations of our time. Christophe Broelsch talked about liver transplants from live donors, Leonard Bailey talked about neonatal heart transplantation for hypoplastic left heart syndrome, and Michael Harrison talked about intrauterine fetal surgery. One of the doctors told how he routinely took time off from his regular work to do Christian mission work in developing nations. During the question-and-answer session somebody asked him if he wasn't troubled by the contrast he saw between the expenditure of millions of dollars to save the life of one baby in the United States and the enormous unmet needs that he saw in developing nations. No, he said, the developing nations look to us for inspiration. Their lives are enriched, as ours are, by attempts to develop new, dramatic cures for rare diseases. Even if we fail, he said, the symbolism of effort is ennobling.

Perhaps we are all engaged in that sort of metaphorical medicine. After all, if we just wanted to save lives, we'd close all American children's hospitals and use those resources to provide measles vaccine, malaria prophylaxis, or clean drinking water to children all over the world. Such facts reside on the edge of our consciousness, teasing us with the contradictions, taunting our moral self-conceptions. Though it sometimes seems impossible to change the patterns, it always seems essential to try.

Doctors all freely criticize the system or their colleagues, but they have trouble being hard upon themselves. The hardest belief to question is the belief in the inherently moral nature of the enterprise that, in the end, is available to each of us and can correct our personal failures and inadequacies. Perhaps medicine itself, like love or religion, depends upon an inherent mythologizing. We feel an urge to make the characters bigger than life, the work symbolic and transcendental. There has always been a strong religious theme to healing. The commitments go beyond ordinary, day-to-day caring for others. Healers have some special calling, some special commitment, not just to their profession and not just to their patients, but to some higher power as well. Even in modern, secular, pluralistic societies, with their capitalist ideologies and market economies, medicine and the health-care system retain some tenuously special spiritual status. It cannot be entirely shielded from the market, of course, but neither is it entirely abandoned to the market. Instead, we create complex layers of entitlements, tax shelters, programs supported by charities and their balls, biotech spin-offs started by university professors whose work was government financed. We see corporate-run, church-directed, not-for-profit hospitals and their health-care systems competing tooth and nail for market share and "covered lives" against venture-capital-financed corporate conglomerates that are one week the darlings of Wall Street and the next week torn by scandals for bilking the government.[7]

As citizens we all want certain things from the health-care system—universal access to high-quality, cost-effective care. As doctors we all want to work in a health-care system that delivers those goods. But we cannot seem to solve the administrative, political, regulatory, economic, philosophical, and bureaucratic problems that would allow such a system to flourish.

The chair of the Department of Pediatrics at a large midwestern state university recently wrote that "because of the close association between poverty and low birth weight, surviving premature infants are at increased risk for the new morbidities such as violence, homelessness, child abuse and neglect, and addictive drug use. A goal should be to reduce the risk of being born with a low birth weight, rather than having to treat the consequences of premature gestation."[8] He was talking of a familiar paradox of modern medical care: the more money we pump into high-tech care, the better we get at doing it. We can save ever sicker patients. The better we get, the more morally compelling it becomes to use such care for every patient who might possibly benefit. The more unlikely we are to succeed, the more success will cost, and the more energy and resources and dollars we need to keep our high-tech services humming. In small towns in Appalachia, the money that flows into the hospital system improves health in spite of the medical care that it finances. Tertiary-care hospitals rise from the ghettos like sacred temples, like shrines, great, awesome and terrible, morally ambiguous to the core, the focus of both generous federal funding and punitive federal investigations for fraud and abuse. Both types of hospitals embody an oddly unbalanced conception of health that cannot include either midwives like Jill or doctors like Miller. If, at some point, these hospitals shift from being a solution to being the problem, it seems incumbent upon us, as the people who create and maintain them, to figure out how to make them adapt. We mustn't give up neonatal intensive care. We're not quite ready to say that everybody should have their babies at home. But we should at least be honest about the strengths of alternative models and the weaknesses of our own. We should at least admit the possibility that we have made some big mistakes.

NINE

Mistakes in Context

"Doing everything possible" is a moral defense and not a
technical one. . . . When he claims that he did everything
possible, the professional claims that he acted in good
faith. Although results are open to debate, his conduct
is not.   —Charles Bosk, *Forgive and Remember*

A baby who should have died did not die.[1] The baby, who might have died,
survived instead with severe neurological problems. His parents loved him,
his doctors cared for him, his therapists worked with him. Would he thank
us for these efforts? Would he rather have just been left alone? He himself
would not testify in this case. Others would speak for him.

I have been called to testify under oath in a number of such cases. In each
I stated whether I thought what somebody else had done had been right or
wrong. The more I think about these cases, the less clear I am as to right or
wrong, good or bad, and the harder it is to understand why I am in any position to judge. I deeply believe that a doctor who acts as Dr. Miller acted
should not be punished even though he was perhaps mistaken in his judgment, in his motivation, or in his reasoning. I also believe that there is error
at the heart of the matter and that the error needs to be examined, understood, and corrected. Dr. Miller's only defense is that there was no right thing
to do, that any other course of action would have been equally wrong. The
parents should perhaps be compensated, not because they had been wronged
but simply because they were being asked to do more, pay more, and suffer
more than any parent should. Out of compassion, we as a society should help
them out. The rules should perhaps be changed to try to avoid such tragedies,
but the rules were not clear to start with, and nobody knows who made

them. *Post hoc,* we were looking for somebody who could accept responsibility and accountability for results that nobody desired. Clearly, however, nobody was individually and unambiguously accountable. Efforts to assign blame and punishment, to assess damages, and to rectify injustices seemed both crucially important and supremely irrelevant.

Perhaps, though, we tell ourselves, if we make our steady and regular offerings, if we take continuing medical-education courses, go to church, pay our insurance premiums, conduct more outcomes studies, develop new and better technologies, figure out more precise ways to talk to one another, perhaps if we just try hard enough, we can insure ourselves against tragedy.

Once, as a young doctor in the middle of the night, I saved the life of a tiny baby girl. Then the baby died. Without me she would have died within minutes of birth. Instead, through my efforts, she lived for two days. What kind of a life did I save? Other babies lived for months in the NICU and then died. I thought I'd come to understand the futility, the terrible wrongness. Then, just when I was sure that I could tell which babies would live and which would die, one whom I had written off as dead would surprise me, survive, grow up, go to high school, marry, have babies herself. Those days, those decisions, and the detachments that followed shaped me, shaped my life, shaped my career. I was drawn to the study of ethics. I wanted to try to understand the right and wrong of these matters, the "how ought we live," the rules, transgressions, punishments, and forgivenesses.

In the prosecution of this malpractice case the central task was to make some judgment about Dr. Miller and whether his behavior fell within or outside of some standard of professional practice. Everything else was either peripheral or transgressive. It would not be appropriate, within the context of the case, to discuss whether a case such as this one should even be considered in this sort of tribunal, whether the system of malpractice litigation that we have developed in the United States is itself good or bad. It was beyond the bounds of the deposition to ask what this all could possibly mean about the lawyers and me as individuals, about our notions of our professional responsibilities in situations like this, or about the way our culture encouraged and rewarded this peculiar type of conversation we found ourselves having in that luxurious room in that skyscraper, watching the shadows of the masts of the sailboats on Lake Michigan begin to grow long in the afternoon sun. The current complex rules of malpractice litigation make up the limiting grid against which a particular story, case, or action is defined and then evaluated.

Moral rules define both ideals and perfection, on the one hand, and deviation or negligence, on the other. The rules themselves vary from culture to culture and change over time even within a culture. What doesn't seem to change across cultures or centuries is the need for such rules. No matter how broad or narrow the notion of culture might be—whether it is taken to mean a continent, a country, a religion, a professional group, or a particular high-school class—the need for moral rules about social interactions is a constant. Each social, political, or cultural aggregation constructs its own specific moral categories. In each group there are rules about who can or cannot have sex with whom under what circumstances. We try to define rape, marriage, incest, and harassment in ways that are clear and consistent. But new circumstances, new events, challenge the old definitions. We try to define who can or cannot kill whom under what circumstances and to clarify the moral differences between abortion, capital punishment, euthanasia, and self-defense as different types of killing with different types of possible justification. There are rules about what can or cannot be eaten and how food should be cooked. Opinions vary about which virtues deserve to be rewarded, which vices should be punished, and what it means to exploit, be cruel to, or neglect one another. The general categories are broadly consistent, the need for categories universal, and the particulars widely variable.

Most of the time we comfortably and unconsciously accept our own system of rules. It is easy to lose the sense that *our* rules are simply *ours*. It is far easier, day to day, to see them as a universal, natural, or God-given set of moral absolutes against which our individual behaviors must be judged. Part of the grand project of moral philosophy has been to develop rules that might be understood and accepted as universal moral rules, systems, or metaphysics of ethics that might apply to all people everywhere and provide a nonrelativistic criterion for judgment.

The project is difficult, in part because the situations that call for judgments are of seemingly infinite variety. Murder may be wrong, but what if a policeman is shooting at an armed robber who is escaping arrest, or if a wife shoots a violently abusive husband? What does it mean for a husband to be abusive? What are the rules that define proper marital relationships? Adultery may be wrong, but what if there is no love left in a marriage, or if both partners agree, or if partners have been separated for years but not divorced? How should an employer treat an employee? What are the employer's obligations with respect to providing a safe working environment? Does safety mean just physical safety or protection from emotional insults as well? What are the rules for hiring, firing, promotion, or bonuses? How do we conceptualize parents' obligations to their children? What do those conceptions imply for our response to maternity leave, deadbeat dads, public subsidy for childcare, school vouchers, regionalized neonatal networks, or teenagers' access to confidential reproductive care?

The temptation to rely on well-understood local custom and tradition rather than on abstract and untested universals is based on practical considerations. If, in addition to judging a particular action, we also had to question or redesign the moral grid every time, we would become morally paralyzed. The risk of relying on local custom and tradition is equally clear. If we didn't sometimes question or redesign the grid, we would become morally complacent or simplistic.

Sometimes the grid does change. Our thinking about the legality of slavery, the ten-hour workday, or the conventions of sexual politics has changed. Most nondevout contemporary Americans believe in this sort of change, in this sort of moral relativity, to some extent. Belief in the appropriateness of such change is central to postmodern thinking. But in another, perhaps deeper part of our minds we remain resolutely premodern, as blind to and as unquestioningly dependent upon our mystifying, culture-specific rules, boundaries, conventions, and taboos as any Azande, Hopi, or Trobriand Islander. On that level, we live as if we believe that our particular system for making judgments somehow reaches the best possible truth. We think that our malpractice litigation system is preferable to the sacrifice of a pig or a ceremony to recall errant souls. Even if we have the feeling that Dr. Miller should have let the baby die, and even if we think it ludicrous to bring such a matter to litigation, we do not question the litigation system itself. Little matter if the judgments we reach by this mechanism are predictably random or idiosyncratic. The air of mysterious lottery seems to be an important part of the culture. We will live by the verdict that is handed down by the jury and give it all the ambivalent respect that we give to matters of law.

When we observe the rituals of other cultures, we may sometimes be surprised by the seeming gullibility of the natives. Do they really believe that when the witch doctor puts on a mask he becomes a god? Courtroom procedures in some cultures have a play-acting quality—the judges with their wigs—that seems almost humorous. And yet, when one of our juries renders a verdict that a doctor's action was a mistake that caused a patient's death, we grant that judgment authority and shape our own behavior to conform to its dictates. We are willing to punish people severely, even put innocent people to death or let guilty people go free, based on the pronouncements of juries. We suspend disbelief at the same time that we bring our sophisticated skepticism to bear on the process.

Our approach to these problems is unique in the particulars but not in a general sense. Clifford Geertz has shown that every culture's legal system has a set of rules for deciding who is a reliable witness, what facts will be admissible as evidence, and how such facts need to be presented. In his comparative study of the legal systems of different cultures he found that, though very different in particulars, all were similar in bringing to legal decision making an "imaginative, or reconstructive, or interpretive power, a power rooted in the collective resources of culture."[2] It is that power, according to Geertz, that forms the basis for a cross-cultural, anthropological understanding of what the law really does. The universality of such unique and particular conventions suggests a universal problem. In every culture judges render judgments about things they did not witness and may not understand, actions that nobody admires and everybody recognizes as problematic, and events that raise problems that are new, previously unimagined, and morally (as well as legally) unprecedented. Even as we acknowledge the fickleness of memory, the limitations of retrospective reporting, and the complexity of human motivations, we also recognize the necessity of agreeing upon a particular set of facts that will become the substrate upon which our judgments are rendered. Thus, we need rules for deciding which facts are going to be considered as we render our tenuous judgments.

These fact-finding rituals neither construct a truth out of whole cloth nor discover it in some far-off part of the universe like a distant comet or a tiny quark. Instead, they contextualize events into narrative truths so that as we go forward we can all at least agree upon the content of the story to which we are responding. Every detail matters. We take the raw material of human experience in the world, of actions that may or may not have happened in the way that some but not all of the people involved remember and recount them, and we refine it into plot, person, and dialogue. Once we've agreed upon the story, we can examine the events that are unsettling or disconcerting. We can perhaps rewrite the ending in such a way that it will seem that the baby did not die, or survive, in vain. Through such rewritings the events can suddenly make more sense than they did before, not so much in a particularly rational way as in an aesthetic way. Put another way, these dramatic retellings bring the conventional wisdom of the time and the culture to bear upon events that are new, troubling, and unlikely to go away, and they create a culture-specific harmony between these events and the context in which they take place. We are willing to act in the dramas, then, because we know how hard it is to live in disharmony. By creating these ritualistic roles for ourselves and acting them with stylized sincerity, we teach ourselves the rules by which we must live from day to day outside the rituals.

The moral drama of medical malpractice imagines an ideal world in which medical care can and should be perfect. This is crucial because the concept of mistake only makes sense against some context of nonmistake. In some cases this dynamic is straightforward. If the surgeon meant to amputate the right leg but amputated the left instead, or if the internist meant to prescribe morphine but gave digoxin instead, complex cultural interpretation is not necessary. But these are the easy ones. The tougher ones, such as whether a doctor should have told a painful and depressing truth to a sick and emotionally vulnerable patient, or whether whole classes of activities that are routine ought to be questioned, require a deeper analysis of the relationship between foreground events and background assumptions.

In order to address these questions it is necessary to develop ways for judging when the rules and rituals for identifying and judging error are themselves in error. Since our sense of what constitutes a mistake is itself contingent upon the mores and rituals that define the larger cultural story from which the concept of mistake derives meaning, we can recognize and begin to evaluate mistakes only if we can somehow tell the smaller story of the mistake and the larger story of the context in which it occurred at the same time. However, we cannot do this when the smaller story is told within a larger narrative that is viewed as fixed and immutable.

There are all sorts of ways to tell Dr. Miller's story, just as there are all sorts of ways to tell the story of the baby, the family, or the nurses. We may need to understand what it is about families and babies and reproduction in contemporary America that makes the death of a baby mean such different things to us today than it used to or than it does to people in other countries or in other subcultures within our own diverse polity. We need to understand what the medical-care system means, especially the high-tech medicine of intensive care units, in the stories that we tell one another about justice, salvation, and the meaning of life. As we turn the story inside out and upside down, new facets of the characters may emerge. We may even need to imagine characters who must have existed, just as astronomers imagine planets that must exist in order to explain why the known planets behave as they do or novelists, trying to piece together the past and understand why people behaved as they did, sometimes imagine characters who must have existed in order to make sense of the lives of the characters who are known to have existed. The "facts" themselves are mutable, as both a lawyer and a novelist might agree, and playing with them might help us get to the larger truths underlying them.

This approach to the relationship between "fact" and "truth" is more common in fiction than in law or philosophy. Certain works of fiction make moral arguments by seeking a multitrack appreciation of complex judgments about right and wrong. They contrast the intracultural judgments of characters situated in a specific time or place with the implicit and presumably superior judgments of the differently situated reader. Such moral narratives can play with the tension between the moral understandings of the characters within the narrative and those of the reader in many ways. In one common scenario, the protagonist defies the moral norms of his culture, and the author allows the reader to identify emotionally with the protagonist. The reader views the protagonist's opposition to his culture as courageous and correct. The culture may then be seen as corrupt or immoral. In another scenario, the protagonist adheres to the cultural norms of his or her time and place, but these are portrayed in a way to make the reader reject or critique the protagonist's choices. The inferences required of us as readers by this latter form of narrative reveal the character and thus, by analogy, the culture to be morally flawed. However much we may empathize with the protagonist's predicament, he or she becomes an example of what we should not be.

One of the best examples of the first sort of narrative, in which the protagonist defies the morality of the culture, is Mark Twain's *Adventures of Huckleberry Finn*. The naïve Huck has run away from home to avoid being beaten by his drunken, abusive father. He is a "bad" boy, never obeying his elders, skipping church, smoking, and otherwise getting into trouble. Running away from home, he meets up with Jim, a slave who is trying to escape from the South in order to reunite with his family. The two are both bad and good, fugitives from two different sorts of culturally sanctioned injustice. Each is desperate to get away and eager to help the other. But Huck is also part of the cultural narrative in which Jim is enslaved; as a white man raised in the South, he worries that it is wrong of him to help Jim. To his mind, he has an obligation to turn Jim in, and he is aware that he is committing a grievous sin by helping a slave escape to freedom. His "good heart," as Twain calls it, does battle with his "conscience": "The more I studied about this, the more my conscience went to grinding me, and the more wicked and low-down and ornery I got to feeling. And at last, when it hit me all of a sudden that here was the plain hand of Providence slapping me in the face and letting me know my wickedness was being watched all the time from up there in heaven, whilst I was stealing a poor old woman's nigger that hadn't ever done me no harm."[3]

Here Huck's "conscience" recognizes that turning Jim in would be the *right* thing to do, but at the critical moment he becomes aware of an opposing moral force, though he is not at all sure which moral force is for good and which for evil. "At last I struck the time I saved him and he was so grateful, and said I was the best friend old Jim ever had in the world, and the only one he's got now; and then I happened to look around, and see that paper [the letter offering to sell Jim]. It was a close place. I took it up, and held it in my hand. I was a trembling, because I'd got to decide, forever, betwixt two things. I studied a minute, sort of holding my breath, and then says to myself: 'All right, then, I'll go to hell'" (223).

In this passage Twain suggests to his antislavery readers just what it must have felt like for someone growing up within the culture of slavery to begin the process of questioning that might lead a conviction to crumble. It did not feel good or morally upright. Huck understands that, by the conventional morality that he has grown up learning, his choice will send him straight to hell. But he also intuitively understands that his deep and true friendship with Jim creates its own obligations. His crucial choice challenges accepted moral rules and yields the message that his heart provides a powerful and countervailing source of moral guidance.

By creating tension between the moral instincts of an individual and the moral dictates of a culture, Twain allows the reader to see the culture in a new way. This type of cultural critique is not linear or straightforward. It does not directly challenge. Instead, it creates a single situation and a single character who embodies larger abstractions. Huck himself disavows any philosophical generalizations or conclusions that might be drawn or any sense that he made a moral decision at all. In trying to figure out how he would decide such matters in the future, he declares, "So, I reckoned I wouldn't bother no more about it, but after this always do whichever come handiest at the time . . . what's the use you learning to do right when it's troublesome to do right and ain't no trouble to do wrong, and the wages is just the same" (224).

Examples of this sort of narrative critique abound in literature. Antigone's lone struggle against the dictates of her king when she decides that her obligation to bury her dead brother outweighs the prohibitions of her society allows us (and the chorus) to see the limitations of Creon's rigidity. In the same way, Hawthorne's Hester Prynne, in *The Scarlet Letter,* accepts her ostracism from Puritan society as a consequence of her transgression of its moral code. Her own self-banishment for her refusal to name the father of her child is far more severe than that inflicted by the community, but she is responding to a different set of moral dictates than they are. Her struggle emerges in the mind of the reader as a move toward integrity and some deeper reality that is both individually compelling and also powerfully critical of the prevailing moral norms. Such works all struggle with the same tension. We don't condone breaking laws, honoring traitors, or committing adultery, yet sometimes the particular rules or laws prevent us from meeting other, more crucial obligations. These heroes and heroines must, in some basic way, go wrong in order to be right. Sometimes they get away with it and are able to "light out for the territories." Sometimes they die for it. They and the authors who create them are the agents of a necessary moral questioning that stirs the prevailing moral sentiments and allows them to shift slowly over time.

Though not about medicine per se, these moral fictions have implications for a discussion of medical mistakes. Because the work that doctors do has moral urgency, doctors have a highly refined, professionally reinforced sense of right and wrong. Medicine as a social enterprise is a set of practices and standards that set criteria for both technical and moral excellence. These practices and standards allow certain types of relationships to develop between individuals who are sick and those who care for them. These standards enable both patients and doctors to know what is expected of themselves and each other as they try to face disease, disability, and death with a sense of moral rectitude. The challenges are enormous. The strong emotional temptation is to turn away from the anger, the sadness, the frightening helplessness, the pain, and the physical messiness of disease.

In our time the nature of these encounters is being transformed by the astounding successes of modern medicine. Since at least the early nineteenth century there has been an implicit message of progress and perfectionism in medical discourse, a sense that we are getting better at knowing and understanding what works and what doesn't, and why. Doctors today can often avoid the temptation to turn away not because of moral understanding and strength but because the technical tools at their disposal allow them to offer real and meaningful relief of suffering, cure of disease, or control of chronic illness. This can lead to a simplistic association of the moral goals of medicine with the physiological goals. We tend to think that "good" medical care leads reliably to "good" outcomes and "bad" medical care leads causally to "bad" outcomes. We derive our moral rectitude from our commitment to correcting mistakes both individually and collectively. Scientific inquiry allows us a measure of self-assurance. We think that we know better than ever before what works and how it works. The practices of science are supposed to make the practices of medicine self-correcting in that we scrutinize each intervention and are, in theory, always ready to discard those that have been scientifically discredited. Thus, because we see ourselves as somehow more scientific than doctors before us, we also see ourselves as more perfect. Doctors no longer have to be helpless with the sick; they can do something.

Sometimes, under the sway of this activist mindset, doctors develop treatments that seem to "work" but may not make patients healthier, happier, or better off. For example, new diagnostic tests for prostate cancer allow doctors to determine which patients have the disease. Once diagnosed, many patients choose interventions to treat the cancer. However, it is profoundly unclear whether such patients are made better or worse by the interventions.[4] Renal dialysis can perform the functions of failing kidneys, but if the patient cannot recover from other illnesses or ailments that either led to or are associated with the failing kidneys, we find ourselves supporting the renal function of patients in the absence of any hope for recovery from other ailments.[5] A whole program of medical innovation may be mistaken even though careful study and refinement within the program allows small but measurable improvements in the way certain things are done. For example, one critique of the technological innovations that allowed artificial cardiac support for patients awaiting heart transplantation was that although the devices worked technologically, they did not lead to any greater survival from cardiac transplantation. Because only a limited number of donor hearts were available, the technological "bridges" for patients awaiting transplants only increased the number of patients on the waiting list, not the number of patients who would ultimately receive a transplant and survive.[6]

Perhaps public policies that treat health care as a supreme political good are themselves mistaken.[7] It is clear that health care is only a small piece of the complex health puzzle.[8] Other factors, ranging from individual behavior to social environment to genetic endowment, seem to have a far more profound effect on health than the availability of bypass surgery or the latest cancer chemotherapy. Even if we are primarily committed to health improvement as a social and moral good, spending less on health care and more on other factors might be preferable.

Such concerns should force us to try to recognize or understand the historical story within which we situate our particular moral judgments—to see ourselves as we come to see Antigone or Huck or Hester Prynne in context—and then to ask whether that story might be told in a way that would make us consider acting differently. We could then develop a judgment of certain medical actions that derived not from the observation that other doctors would have done differently in similar circumstances but from a critique of the circumstances themselves. Circumstances are, after all, as artificial and malleable as any other human creation.

In *The House of God,* mentioned in chapter 3, Samuel Shem imagines a topsy-turvy medical world in which the accepted dogma about medical care, health, and disease is all wrong. In Shem's fictional account of an internship training program at a prestigious Boston teaching hospital, perfectly delivered medical care by the best and the brightest doctors does not cure disease, improve health, or relieve suffering. Instead, it increases suffering. The only patients who get better are those who get negligent care. The only patients who die are young and healthy. Older patients get sicker and sicker but don't die unless the medical-care system tries hard to cure them and consequently does them in. Recognizing this, the "best" doctors strive to deliver the most negligent care since that is really the best care. Tests are ordered but never carried out, medications are prescribed but not given, examinations that are not done are described in great detail. In Shem's satire, as in Twain's, everything that is supposed to be right turns out to be wrong. When the doctors do things "right," terrible things happen to the patients. When they do things "wrong," the patients improve.

A climactic conversation occurs after Roy Basch, one of the interns, cares for one of his patients, Dr. Saunders, who is dying of leukemia. Dr. Saunders's only wish is to die a painless death. Roy loves Dr. Saunders but is unable to fulfill the wish. Saunders's death is a horrible bloody mess, deeply disturbing to Roy both for what it says about medicine and for what it says about his ability to be the sort of doctor and friend that he would like to be.

Jo is Roy's senior resident. She is humorless, technocratic, and unemotional. Unlike Roy, who has come to understand the flaws of the prevailing medical model, Jo believes that the "best" medicine is the most technologically sophisticated medicine. Roy and his fellow interns have been deceiving her about what they are really doing on the wards, and she thinks the patients are getting better because of medical treatment rather than in spite of it. She views medical care as a dazzling scientific and technical achievement that has much to do with physiology and biochemistry and little to do with human interactions or human relationships. She wants Roy to get permission for an autopsy on Dr. Saunders. He refuses. Jo asks him why he won't ask Saunders's family for permission to do the autopsy.

"I didn't want to see his body ripped to shreds in the morgue."
   "That kind of talk has no place in modern medicine," Jo replies.
   "So don't listen."
   "The post-mortem is important. It is the flower of the science of medicine. . . . How do you think we're able to deliver such precise medical care to those entrusted

to us? This ward—my ward—is looked up to in the House for being the most efficient and having the most successes with placement and handling the toughies with
skill. My ward is a legend, Dammit."

"Jo, go fuck yourself. . . . Do you want to know why it's become a legend? You
don't want to hear."

"Of course I want to hear, even though I know already."

So I told her. I started by telling her about how Chuck and I had, after our origi-
nal empirical test on Anna O, become fanatics at doing nothing and had lied to Jo
about it, making up all forms of imaginary tests and buffing the charts. I told her how
in modified form we'd done the same thing with the dying young, who went ahead
and died, but died without the hassle, pain, and prolongation of suffering that their
care might otherwise have produced.[9]

Drawing on the same narrative dynamics that Twain used, Shem counts upon
the reader to negotiate the tension between Jo's conventional view of medicine as scientific, precise, and rational and Roy's subversive view that technical
competence must always be secondary to caring, compassion, loyalty, and human
relationships. The book is satirically delightful because we know that on one
level Shem and his mentor, the Fat Man, are "wrong," just as we know that Huck
was "wrong." They ignore the moral conventions of society, fail to follow the
rules, refuse to order the correct diagnostic tests, commit malpractice, and fail to
achieve the target goals of the Continuous Quality Improvement monitors.
Their superiors just don't get it. The chief of medicine says to Roy,

"I don't understand. The Fat Man taught you that to deliver no medical care is the
best thing you can do?"

"The Fat Man said that that was the delivery of medical care."

"To do nothing?"

"That's something."

"Ward 6-South is the best ward in the House. You mean to tell me it's from doing
nothing?"

"That's doing something. We do as much nothing as we can without Jo finding
out about it."

"But then why do doctors do anything at all?"

"The Fat Man says to produce complications."

"Why do doctors want to produce complications?"

"To make money." (181–82)

Shem's satire oversimplifies, for comic effect, the complexity of medicine's
confusions, inconsistencies, and mixed motives. Selfish characters do not act
for idealistic reasons, but at least they act for understandable, linear, alternative reasons.

A. B. Yehoshua's novel *Open Heart* focuses on the issues of mistakes and accountability in medicine in a way that suggests that these matters are not at all straightforward. It isn't a matter of suggesting alternative visions of medicine and choosing the better; instead it is one of finding a vision that acknowledges the inherent perils of any attempt to heal the sick or comfort the dying. The main character in *Open Heart,* Benjy Rubin, is an ambitious young surgical resident in a Tel Aviv teaching hospital. The CEO of his hospital is a powerful man named Lazar, whose 24-year-old daughter, Einat, developed severe hepatitis while she was backpacking around India. Worried, Lazar wants to bring Einat home, and he wants an Israeli physician to accompany him to India and help bring her safely home.

Two ambiguous medical events that may or may not have been mistakes frame the action of the book. One is a blood transfusion that Rubin decides to give Einat while they are traveling home from India. On the trip home Einat is very weak. She has recurrent nosebleeds. Her liver enzymes are elevated, her clotting factors depleted, and she is hypoglycemic. Rubin decides that she needs a pint of blood, but he doesn't trust the blood banks at the Indian hospital. He decides to give Einat a direct transfusion from her mother, Dorit, using techniques for emergency battlefield transfusions learned in the military.

The transfusion, done in a hotel room in New Delhi, goes smoothly and seems to help. Einat feels better afterwards. Rubin feels confident and heroic even though Lazar appears skeptical. "I knew that everything I did here was being registered down to the last detail, and that when we got home he would waste no time in asking Hishin and the rest of 'his' professors if it had really been necessary to perform the blood transfusion so urgently. But I was calm and sure of myself, ready not only to justify the urgent transfusion to all the professors in the hospital but also to demand the respect due to me for my diagnosis and ingenuity in a medical emergency."[10]

In one sense, then, the transfusion is "successful." But when Rubin gets home, people begin to question the appropriateness of this intervention. Levine, the chief of medicine and an expert in hepatitis, sharply criticizes Rubin's decision to perform the transfusion as "not only completely unnecessary but also irresponsible and perhaps even dangerous." Rubin defends himself by citing his understanding of the facts of the case: "If the transaminases rose to levels of a hundred and eighty and a hundred and fifty eight, it's clear that the clotting factors were also impaired . . . so why not strengthen the poor girl with some fresh, safe plasma, from someone as close as her mother, to help her overcome the bleeding? And the fact is, after my transfusion, the bleeding stopped." To which Levine replies disdainfully, "It stopped on its own, not because of you. The clotting factors, which you thought you were giving her in your transfusion, are enzymes, not blood cells, and they behave completely differently in a transfusion. They're absorbed and disappear—they're ineffective unless they're diluted in a special serum to bind them and prevent them from dissolving" (202). Levine has written an article about this that he suggests Rubin read.

The argument is heated and impossible to deconstruct. Who's right? Who's wrong? Hishin, the professor of surgery, isn't so sure and says to Rubin, "I'm behind your idea, especially from the psychological point of view, and as I've often told you, psychology is no less important than the knife in your hand" (150). Lazar was skeptical at the time but becomes convinced that the transfusion saved his daughter's life. One of Rubin's friends thinks it was a crazy and dangerous intervention that did little for Einat but inexcusably put the mother at risk for getting hepatitis herself. The reader doesn't know whether the transfusion was a mistake or a life-saving intervention. Was Rubin heroic, crazy, or lucky? Perhaps he was crazily heroic, or heroically lucky. Did he save a life or merely endanger one? Who really knows what works and what doesn't? Who has the authority to judge?

In a sense, Yehoshua is saying, you had to be there. You had to see how Einat looked. You had to feel India around you. The transfusion may have made no sense, objectively speaking. But in the context it worked in some strange way, perhaps by cementing a relationship between mother and daughter. And who knows? Perhaps the weakening of that bond may have been as much a cause of Einat's weakness as her liver infection, her low glucose, or her inadequate clotting factors. Earlier in the book Rubin speaks to family members of a patient who has just been operated upon and tells them that she has "been born again" (5). Einat's transfusion was, in a sense, a ritual of rebirth, taking lifeblood from her mother as she had in the womb.

The second ambiguous event occurs toward the end of the book. Lazar develops heart problems, and his doctors recommend open-heart surgery. The surgery goes well, but afterwards Lazar develops an irregular heart rhythm. Rubin notices this and points it out to Levine. Levine still dislikes Rubin as a result of what he considers to have been Rubin's "reckless and unjustifiable decision" to transfuse Einat in India, and he disdainfully ignores Rubin's concerns about Lazar's arrhythmia. Perhaps he is right to do so. After all, he seems to know more about cardiology than Rubin does, just as he seemed to know more about hepatitis. And after Rubin goes to the library to read about postoperative arrhythmia, he notes that "no clear conclusions emerged from my reading. It appeared that there were atrial beats that could look like ventricular beats" (358). Uneasy, he decides to be quiet.

But Rubin's concerns were prescient. Lazar dies. The death may have been a result of the arrhythmia. If so, it would have been preventable. But just as we couldn't tell whether the transfusion was necessary or dangerous, we also can't tell whether the arrhythmia caused Lazar's death. "Perhaps the immediate cause of death had been the arrhythmia," one doctor notes in reviewing the case, "but the deterioration in Lazar's condition stemmed from an infarct caused by an occlusion in one of the bypasses" (368). The department chiefs cover up for one another, and try as he might, Rubin is unable to find anybody who will support his contention that an avoidable mistake was made. The reader can't tell whether Rubin is just on a vendetta against Levine, whether the physicians at a leading Tel Aviv teaching hospital are incompetent or corrupt, or whether medicine itself is far less certain or scientific than it pretends to be.

Through these events Yehoshua asks what we find at the heart of medicine. No matter how piercing his gaze, the answer remains elusive. Things happen. People trust or do not trust one another. Doctors are by turns narcissistic, ambitious, irrational, well-meaning, brilliant, and compassionate. They have powerful tools and amorphous goals. We're left thinking that the quest for truth will never reach its goal, that the things we discover don't add to the total of our knowledge but instead drop out of the equations, leaving us no closer to solutions. Yehoshua highlights how difficult it is to know whether there is good medicine and shows how, in the end, all we can try to decide is what we have always tried to decide, namely, whether someone is or is not a good doctor. And that question, as Yehoshua elucidates it, is profoundly mysterious, qualitative rather than quantitative, mystical rather than scientific.[11]

The central tension of these novels is the central tension of medicine and of bioethics: how do we construct an argument or a belief system that will allow us to decide when knowledge or technical power might cause more harm than good? How do we direct our quest? How do we know whether we're on the right track?

For Shem or Yehoshua, the future of medicine will not depend upon the quality of our scientific discoveries. New drugs, new devices, new understanding of the human genome, and new methods of transporting information, of communicating with one another, will come with numbing, mind-boggling regularity. We will have more knowledge, information, and power than we know what to do with. Especially then, the kind of future we build with our powerful tools will depend upon our sophistication in developing the kind of medical education system or medical practices in which doctors will not only master the technicalities but also respect the ambiguities and the mysteries. They will need to work both with and against the latest scientific evidence. They will need the vision and the courage to order, perhaps just once in their lives, a dangerous but potentially salvational blood transfusion between a mother and daughter in a strange and mystical foreign country. It may or may not work. Sometimes they will need to do things that they don't fully understand, to acknowledge the limits of precision in medicine, the universes beyond knowability, and they will need to be empowered to make decisions.

Dr. Miller may have been trying to be such a doctor. When a baby like Baby Boy Jones is born, neonatal intensive care can be seen as a good thing or a bad thing. Perhaps no form of medical care has been subjected to the same sort of searching scrutiny as NICU care. Some authors, including some parents of NICU babies, have focused on the negative aspects of such care, even suggesting that it is a bizarre and unjustifiable form of torture.[12] Other parents have seen it as destructive to families and called for a shift to more family-centered care.[13] It can seem selfless and altruistic or heartless and mercenary. Given such a diversity of responses to the realities of NICU care, moral judgments about when and whether the doctors involved are making mistakes simply cannot be made by examining particular cases and determining whether they meet standards that are internal to the profession. They can be made only after examining both the cases and the contexts. Both actions and the accepted methods of evaluating actions must be examined. Dr. Miller's decision to stop resuscitation may be viewed as negligent. On the other hand, it may be viewed as heroic in ways that he may not even have understood. Intuitively, through his actions, he seemed to be rejecting a way of doing things in which some necessary things are impermissible. His actions suggest a new standard to which we might aspire in caring for one another.

TEN

Closing Argument

Doctors will have to learn to inhabit the complicated
world in which philosophers feel comfortable.
—Richard Smith, in the *British Medical Journal*

It is difficult to map a conclusion about Dr. Miller onto categories of "guilt"
or "innocence" or even onto categories of "exemplary" or "negligent." The
farther the lawyers got into the case, the more nervous they must have become about just how all this would play to a jury. After the deposition I never
heard from them again. The case never went to trial. Instead, there was an
out-of-court settlement. Part of the settlement was an agreement among the
parties that the terms not be disclosed. There was also, no doubt, a stipulation
that neither party would admit that it or the other had been right or wrong.
When a similar case went to trial in Wisconsin, the jury was sympathetic to
the doctors.[1]

No matter who wins or loses such cases, their implicit effect is clear. The
process of being sued is itself a sort of punishment for most doctors. The doctors who get sued have walked close to the censure line even if, in the end,
a jury cannot be convinced that they have crossed it. Doctors who have been
that close to the edge do not want to go back. By stopping resuscitation as
he did, Dr. Miller took a moral stand and a personal risk. In a sense, that was
what he was being punished for. I would guess that in the future he and other
doctors who hear about his case will provide neonatal intensive care for all
babies for as long as it is technologically feasible to do so unless the parents
explicitly ask them to stop. And very few parents will ask that such treatment
be stopped.

The parents' role in these matters is complex. Parents, it seems, are of two minds. On the one hand, they seem to be much more optimistic about the outcome for tiny premature babies than professionals. They clearly want the *right* to make the decision themselves and the *right* to refuse treatment for their baby even if they seldom exercise that right. They do not want to have decisions imposed upon them by doctors, ethics committees, or judges. Though they want such power, and though we are predisposed to give it to them, they generally do not anticipate just how disempowering the events themselves can be. Michael Hynan, a psychologist and father of a preemie, has written about his reactions during the first days after his premature baby was born. "Sometimes what is happening to high-risk parents is so horrible it must be blocked out. If something like this is happening to me, it may take all of my concentration to just walk or even look around. And if you're a peri-natal professional trying to explain something to me at the same time; it just doesn't register, even if I'm nodding my head."[2] Being a parent of a preemie in the NICU does strange things to one's sense of self. Hynan has shown that many parents of preemies, just like many ICU patients, suffer from symptoms of post-traumatic stress disorder.[3]

In NICUs, the option and the temptation of stopping treatment both dangle constantly in front of doctors, nurses, and parents. Some observers and policymakers worry that the option is too available and the temptation too strong. Others can't understand why the option is so often resisted.

The uncertainties, it seems to me, manifest themselves in the process by which individuals struggle with the decisions. Individuals question their own virtue and their own motivation when they feel the urge to discontinue treatment. They don't want to make the decision themselves, so they turn to others. Any indecision or lack of consensus about the value of continued treatment is taken as a sign that treatment should continue. Treatment is only discontinued when all the adults directly involved in the patient's care can agree that treatment is no longer indicated. The net result is that often treatment continues when many but not all of the people involved think that it is time to stop. As I have tried to show, even the terms and conditions under which one might say that agreement has been reached are themselves not at all straightforward.

This cautious approach may lead to the perception that doctors overtreat babies in the NICU.[4] One might ask, however, why or how one might decide that the amount of treatment being provided is excessive. Generally, a number of reasons are given for assuming that overtreatment is a bigger problem than undertreatment. The first, and most enduring, is the belief that parents don't want such aggressive treatment and that it is being foisted upon them. William Silverman has been the most persistent and articulate spokesperson for this view. In one paper, he tells of his early adventures with innovative neonatal care and his pride in his ability to keep a tiny preemie alive longer than any such preemie had ever been kept alive before. And then he notes, "I was very disappointed that the parents did not share my joyous feelings of high adventure." His disappointment led to curiosity and then to sensitivity to some of the concerns that parents secretly harbored. He writes, "I was impressed by the number of parents who feared disability more than death. They feared overtreatment."[5]

Such sentiments are not unique. Robert and Peggy Stinson wrote a book about their experiences as parents of a tiny preemie that describes in harrowing detail their desperate efforts to get the doctors to stop their aggressive interventions and let their son Andrew die.[6] Helen Harrison, a mother of a preemie, has started an organization and promulgated guidelines for what she calls "family-centered care."[7]

But it is not clear that such sentiments are particularly widespread. In many cases the parents seem to think very much like the doctors and to have a "bias" toward aggressive treatment. The authors of *Mixed Blessings* note that "parents' sheer determination coupled with their commitment to the survival of their infant also contributed to the aggressiveness of treatment in the NICU."[8] It would appear that these authors recognize that parents also "err" in their decisions, but the implications of this are not further explored. Shoo Lee, Pauline Penner, and Margaret Cox suggest the reason. They compared the attitudes of health-care professionals with those of parents regarding treatment of low-birthweight infants. They found that most parents, including parents of premature babies, wanted treatment to be offered even to babies who were so tiny that there was a good chance that they could survive only with severe disability. Pediatricians were evenly divided about whether treatment should be offered in those circumstances. Most NICU nurses objected to the provision of treatment in such cases. These authors also found that "pediatricians and nurses tended to overestimate the morbidity, mortality, and costs of care of VLBW [very-low-birthweight] infants. There was a direct correlation ($P < .05$) between a negative attitude toward saving VLBW infants and a negatively false perception of neonatal morbidity, mortality, and costs."[9] Norup found similar results in a survey of Danish adults: "There was strong consensus (more than 75% agreement) that life-prolonging treatment should be provided for an infant born after 24 weeks' gestation with respiratory distress and for an infant with myelomeningocele."[10] It seems that parents, as well as potential parents, do not want their infants to be denied the potential benefits of neonatal care. They believe in the promise. They hope.

My experience in counseling doctors and parents involved in ethics dilemmas in the NICU is that we don't often run into a situation in which parents request that treatment be discontinued and doctors insist that it continue. The opposite situation is far more common—doctors need to convince parents that further treatment is futile, while parents persist in believing in a miracle. This common situation was originally described by David Waller and his colleagues as "the Cassandra complex." They reported four cases "in which parents rejected their child's hopeless prognosis, counterprophesied miraculous cures, resolved to obtain exorcism, criticized the care, or accused nurses of neglect. This produced a painful breakdown in the usually harmonious relationships between doctors, nurses, and parents." These authors suggested that "the intensive-care pediatrician who prophesies to parents that their child's illness is irreversible may encounter denial and hostility. The physician may compare his plight to that of Cassandra—the mythical Greek prophetess of doom, who was cursed to see into the future and not be believed."[11] The frequency of such cases suggests that while the concerns of Silverman, the Stinsons, and Harrison are not irrelevant, they don't help focus the debate upon the most common problems.

Another common objection to "overtreatment" is that neonatal care is not "cost-effective."[12] Generally, proponents of this view compare neonatal intensive care as a program to reduce infant mortality with other types of programs, particularly preventive programs. While NICUs may be less cost-effective, they are certainly as cost-effective as most other hospital-based, high-tech interventions in medicine today.[13] Furthermore, as I have argued, given the current organization of our health-delivery system, they are also profitable for doctors and hospitals. So even if the general arguments about cost-effectiveness may make sense from a policy perspective, they make no sense at all from the standpoint of any rational actor within the system who is seeking to maximize his or her own utilities.

A final argument suggesting that we are overtreating arises from a concern that we are creating a disproportionate number of disabled babies. This argument looks at outcome studies for tiny preemies and suggests that there are many long-term sequelae of prematurity, including seizures, cerebral palsy, and learning disabilities.[14] The debate becomes one about whether the glass is half-empty or half-full. Clearly, tiny premature babies are at high risk for multiple developmental problems.[15] But there have always been babies with developmental problems. The question is whether, overall, neonatal intensive care increases the numbers of such babies or only shifts the risk factors and the subpopulations of babies likely to suffer neurological injury. Thirty years ago, before mechanical ventilation was an option, babies born a few weeks prematurely would routinely experience hypoxia, a lack of oxygen due to the immaturity of their lungs. If they survived, many had significant brain damage. Today, thanks to improvements in care, those babies survive without hypoxia or brain damage. Instead, today, it is the babies born three months prematurely who experience hypoxia and often survive with impairments.

It is extremely unclear whether the total number of babies who survive with impairments has increased or decreased. On the one hand, some epidemiologists note a rising prevalence of cerebral palsy and attribute that to the survival of tiny premature babies. V. Bushan, Nigel Paneth, and John Kiely have written that "most epidemiologic studies from industrialized countries show a rise in the childhood prevalence of cerebral palsy in recent decades, largely because of the increasing contribution of children of low and very low birth weight to its prevalence."[16] On the other hand, T. Michael O'Shea and his colleagues studied more than two thousand low-birthweight infants in North Carolina and noted that "the increasing survival of very low birth weight infants in the 1980s and 1990s has not resulted in an increased prevalence of cerebral palsy among survivors."[17] Instead, they reported that the incidence of cerebral palsy among the tiniest babies dropped from 11 percent in the 1980s to 5 percent in the 1990s.

Part of the problem lies in detection and reporting. Counting the number of babies with cerebral palsy didn't matter in the old days because there was nothing to be done about it. Today, the incidence of cerebral palsy is part of a larger argument about the benefits and burdens of neonatal intensive care, so there is motivation to count. In any case, predictions of the ultimate neurological outcome for any baby are more likely to be in error than predictions of survival. For better or worse, decisions about treatment will have to be made intuitively, with imperfect probabilistic information and a set of overriding moral presumptions.

More importantly, however, the whole argument against providing treatment based on the possibility of disabilities among survivors incorporates an implicit bias against the disabled. To have any power, such arguments must rely on a sense that life is not worth living if it is accompanied by certain disabilities. While many people believe that they would not want to continue living if they had irreversible cessation of all higher brain function, there are very few other physical states about which there is much agreement. In essence, then, the arguments about incidence of cerebral palsy can be reduced to arguments about prognostication in an area that is even more uncertain than prognostication about survival, namely, the prognosis for any baby to develop a particular pattern of neurological deficits. So while these concerns are theoretically appealing, they are practically irrelevant.

Every argument against "overtreatment" in neonatal intensive care contains its opposite. Are we causing or preventing cerebral palsy? Are we respecting parents' wishes or ignoring them? Are we wasting money or providing wise stewardship of our scarce resources? Was Dr. Miller a hero, or was he negligent? The general trend in both health law and pediatric ethics over the last fifteen years has been to answer these questions with policies that limit the discretion of both parents and doctors to discontinue treatment. Such responses show little tolerance for individual moral responses or personal moral struggles. Instead, they locate moral struggle in the realm of policy, law, or regulation and try to use these realms of analysis and response to protect doctors and parents from the difficulty of struggling with, articulating, and acting upon responses to these difficult dilemmas.

Oe's novel *A Personal Matter* suggests a different focus. Oe tries to understand why a parent would choose treatment or nontreatment for an imperiled newborn. He starts with the interesting presumption that it is important for his main character, Bird, to be empowered to make a decision about his newborn son. Bird may choose surgery and survival or nontreatment and death. Bird is not religious. For him, life is not "sacred" in any doctrinaire religious sense, so guidance about what to do will not come from above. He also quickly concludes that the baby's interests in such cases are essentially unimaginable, so that, try as we might, any attempt to convince ourselves that we know what the baby would have wanted are illusory and self-deceiving.

Instead, Oe suggests, it is the moral choices of the parents and their implications for the parents' life that must drive the decision. The father, Bird, is portrayed as a young man who is always trying to fly away from responsibilities, from the entrapments of difficult commitments. He is not a likable character. He drinks too much, gets in stupid fights with street thugs, is unfaithful and dishonest to his wife while she is lying in the hospital, and longs to let his baby die so that he will not be burdened by the responsibility of caring for a needy, dependent child. Instead, he imagines, he and his lusty girlfriend will escape to the beautiful wilds of Africa where he will be free. He almost makes the decision to fly away from the terrible implications of the decision he faces.

He wavers not because of moral arguments, legal fears, government regulations, or professional guidelines but because within himself another voice is struggling to be heard. During the day he convinces himself that it would be right to let the baby die, but at night he is haunted by dreams. "Sleep for Bird was like a funnel which he entered through the wide and easy entrance but had to leave by the narrow exit."[18] He dreams of himself ("subpoenaed by the tribunal beyond the darkness" [88]), of the baby ("It was a missile base on the moon, and the baby's bassinet was all alone on those fantastically desolate rocks" [120]), of death itself. Trembling, he realizes the terrifying contradictions of personal moral responsibility from which the book takes its name. He says to his girlfriend, Himiko, "You're right about this being limited to me, it's entirely a personal matter. But with some personal experiences that lead you way into a cave all by yourself, you must eventually come to a side tunnel or something that opens on a truth that concerns not just yourself but everyone" (120). Later, after he has taken the critically ill baby out of the hospital and is driving away, taking the baby to die, he swerves the car to avoid hitting a tiny bird in the road. "Bird saw a rain-soaked sparrow lying dead in the road just ahead of the car. Himiko saw it too. The car bore down on the dead bird, and, as it sank out of sight, sharply swerved and dropped one tire into a pothole which lay hidden under muddy yellow water" (150). He suddenly realizes how much of his own sense of self is tied up in the need to care for small, vulnerable creatures. If he will swerve to avoid crushing the body of a dead bird, how can he not swerve his life in order to care for his living child. He turns around and takes his baby back to the hospital for surgery, understanding full well that the decision is not so much about the baby as it is about himself and his own life.

The crucial process for Bird is the process of self-discovery that allows choices. For this process to take place, it is essential that Bird be free to choose. Thus, Oe implicitly places the domain of moral decisions in the personal struggles of individuals rather than in the more dramatic struggles of kingdoms, governments, or judicial tribunals. Even such huge issues as nuclear disarmament ultimately become primarily personal matters. In this, Oe and Dostoevsky come to similar conclusions. In *The Brothers Karamazov*, Dimitri's trial is a public spectacle that ultimately comes to a mistaken conclusion. The moral struggles of the protagonists are almost invisible and certainly irrelevant to the spectacular world of formal trials, with their dramatic scenes, grandstanding lawyers, and chattering socialites in the galleries. Oe and Dostoevsky both insist that the essential, crucial element of guilt, accountability, and ultimate moral responsibility must always be personal, rather than societal, bureaucratic, or legal, even as they acknowledge that societies, bureaucracies, and courts must do their jobs of making rules, punishing infractions, and passing judgments.

Oe is unusually courageous. When it comes to difficult decisions, especially those about life and death, many people may not want such individual responsibility and accountability. They certainly aren't used to it, and they may not be ready for it. When it is thrust upon them, they may use all the subtle psychological powers they possess to try to disguise accountability, to share it, to diffuse it, or to transfer it to someone or something other than themselves. In Dostoevsky's novel, what was Smerdyakov doing in that conversation at the gate? In a sense, he was trying to make himself Ivan's agent, to assure himself that if nothing else, Ivan would approve of what he did. What are doctors, patients, ethicists, and family members doing when they sit around the decision-making table in the family conference room of the ICU and the doctor suggests that further treatment is "futile" or asks what the patient would have wanted? The people in the group are not trying to exercise their own will. Instead, they are trying to play-act a scenario in which their own individual wills disappear and they become the passive agents of a larger, external, inexorable force.

Analogously, neonatologists, ethicists, lawyers, and administrators who create the regulatory and economic structures within which neonatal intensive care comes to seem morally and fiscally obligatory do a similar sort of shadow dance around individual choice and decision making. They create "obligations" out of the flimsiest scrim and then bind themselves to those obligations with a religious fervor.

Moral reflection begins with a particular type of personal suffering. Writing or reading about ethical dilemmas is an abstract exercise. Being there, in the night, was not. The babies and the parents were there with me. I truly did not know, and neither did they, whether I was a savior or a torturer of babies, whether I offered hope or hubris, whether it was good to use my technology and skills or better to acquiesce gracefully. Dr. Miller haunts my imagination because I stood where he stood. Even years later there is something unforgettably compelling about having actually been there, alone, at two in the morning, gloved, masked, and robed like a latex-covered priest, receiving into my hands a blue, bloody, and lifeless baby and having to decide. I existed in another zone where it was just my heart working to restore rhythm to the baby's heart, my breath coming fast as I tried to breathe life back into another human being.

In that moment I felt fear, power, and pain. I felt a tremendous sense of responsibility but also an equally strong sense of helplessness. I could make choices, but there seemed to be no choices to be made. I was free, but I was bound. I could only do the things I had been taught to do. I was at the end of a long tradition of scientific investigation, technologic development, and moral reflection. I had studied hard, prepared myself well, learned the rituals and responses and the ABCs. I was a technician, a healer, an instrument. I had shaped myself to an ideal. I was a vessel, a pathway, a conduit. What would happen simply flowed through me. There was something in the passivity of that role that was both reassuring and agonizing.

Later, years later, I would come to realize that it was not enough for me to be a passive vessel. Surprisingly, inexplicably, and perhaps incorrectly, I would come to believe that the sociologists, economists, communists, and other determinists don't tell the whole story. My actions and choices are not entirely shaped by my position in the social structure, my role in the professional hierarchy, or the rewards and punishments that society has structured to shape my behavior. Oddly, but compellingly, I can think, reflect, critique, choose, and act. As I gave the baby adrenaline, I felt my own adrenaline. Against the powerful social, cultural, economic, moral, religious, legal, and scientific forces pressing against me, squeezing me, shaping me, I can press back. There is pain for both of us, the baby and me, but the baby's pain is inexorable, whereas my pain is a choice. I can recognize and honor it or ignore and invalidate it. Such moments invite us to try to understand what happened—why we felt what we felt, thought what we thought, and did what we did.

We don't always recognize these moments right away. We can't always make sense of them as they happen. We try to forget them, to run away from them. And we're never prepared for them. When we're called, we wish somebody else were on call, that somebody else would arrive at the crucial moment and take over. We hear conflicting voices within ourselves and can't tell which is "conscience" and which is our "good heart," when to listen to distant voices and when to grasp the intuitions that are close at hand. We want to keep careful moral and fiscal accounts, to balance all the budgets, to end the year without a deficit.

End-of-life decision making in American hospitals today is, in many ways, more like a novel or a play than it is like the rest of life. It is set up as a drama of moral responsibility, choice, and accountability. We construct the choices that people are given to make, and the parameters within which they choose, in a way that makes them very much unlike any other choices they make in their lives. In the ICU even the most disempowered members of society are given absolute authority and autonomy. They are asked to make decisions that have enormous financial, institutional, and moral implications for many other people, and they are asked to do so in such a way as to be accountable only to their own individual consciences. It is ironic that ICU care was collectively developed, is collectively funded, and could not run except as a team of many players with many different professional, technical, and operational skills. Yet at the center we enshrine a degree of individuality that is almost hallucinatory. This dream of individual responsibility and accountability is every bit as fantastic and unreal as a novel or an opera.

Someday we will understand the physiology of premature labor and will developed a way to prevent it. Then there will be no more premature babies, and these moral dilemmas will seem as quaint and antiquated as Huck's struggles with his conscience as he floated down the Mississippi on a raft, as bizarre and exotic as a preemie exhibit at Coney Island, or just a piece of history, like the Chicago stockyards. Neonatal intensive care will perhaps seem as inexplicably barbaric as the tunnel-building projects on the C & O Railroad or as scientifically primitive as the iron lung. In the meantime, though, it seems strangely necessary to us, and because it does, we need to carefully consider the roles that each of us plays in order to keep it sacred. The story could still have a happy ending.

NOTES

One. Somebody Will Pay

1. Barbara Katz Rothman, "Ideology and Technology: The Social Context of Pro-creative Technology." *Mt. Sinai Journal of Medicine* 65 (May 1998): 201-9; S. Oliver, L. Rajan, H. Turner, A. Oakley, V. Entwistle, I. Watt, T. A. Sheldon, and J. Rosser, "In-formed Choice for Users of Health Services: Views on Ultrasonography Leaflets of Women in Early Pregnancy, Midwives, and Ultrasonographers," *British Medical Jour-nal* 313, no. 7067 (1996): 1251-53; S. Proctor, "What Determines Quality in Maternity Care? Comparing the Perceptions of Childbearing Women and Midwives," *Birth* 25 (1998): 85-93; Alice E. Adams, *Reproducing the Womb: Images of Childbirth in Science, Feminist Theory, and Literature* (Ithaca: Cornell University Press, 1994); John C. Hob-bins, Richard Freeman, and Julian T. Queenan, "The Fetal Monitoring Debate," *Ob-stetrics and Gynecology* 54 (1979): 103-9; Marshall H. Klaus, Phyllis Klaus, and John Kennell, *Mothering the Mother: How a Doula Can Help You Have a Shorter, Easier, and Healthier Birth* (London: Perseus, 1993).

2. James W. Smith, "Baby Incubators," *Strand Magazine* 12 (1896): 770-76.

3. William A. Silverman, "Mismatched Attitudes about Neonatal Death," *Hast-ings Center Report* 11, no. 6 (1981): 12-16.

4. William A. Silverman, "Incubator-Baby Side Shows (Dr. Martin A. Couney)," *Pediatrics* 64 (1979): 127-41.

5. Jeffrey P. Baker, "The Incubator Controversy: Pediatricians and the Origins of Premature Infant Technology in the United States, 1890 to 1910," *Pediatrics* 87 (1991): 654-62.

6. Thomas M. Adamson, "A Mechanical Ventilation in Newborn Infants with Respiratory Failure," *Lancet* 2, no. 7562 (1968): 227-31.

7. Robert W. Winters, "Total Parenteral Nutrition in Pediatrics: The Borden Award Address," *Pediatrics* 56 (1975): 17-23.

8. David K. Stevenson, Linda L. Wright, James A. Lemons, William Oh, Sheldon B. Korones, Lu-Ann Papile, Charles Bauer, Barbara J. Stoll, Jon E. Tyson, Seetha Shakaran, Avroy A. Fanaroff, Edward F. Donovan, Richard A. Ehrenkranz, and Joel Verter, "Very Low Birth Weight Outcomes of the National Institute of Child Health and Human Development Neonatal Research Network, January 1993 through De-cember 1994," *American Journal of Obstetrics and Gynecology* 179 (1998): 1632-39.

9. American Board of Pediatrics home page, <http://www.abp.org>, updated December 2000.

10. William A. Silverman, "Diagnosis and Treatment: Oxygen Therapy and Retrolental Fibroplasia. Report of a Conference," *Pediatrics* 43 (1969): 88-89; idem,

"The Windermere Lecture 1994. The Line between 'Knowing' and 'Doing': Medicine's Dilemma at the End of the Twentieth Century," *Archives of Disease in Childhood* 71 (1994): 261-65.

11. Raymond S. Duff and Arthur G. M. Campbell, "Moral and Ethical Dilemmas in the Special-Care Nursery," *New England Journal of Medicine* 289 (1979): 890-94.

12. John A. Robertson and Norman Fost, "Passive Euthanasia of Defective Newborn Infants: Legal Considerations," *Journal of Pediatrics* 88 (1976): 883-89.

13. James M. Gustafson, "Mongolism, Parental Desires, and the Right to Life," *Perspectives in Biology and Medicine* 16 (1973): 529-57.

14. Richard A. McCormick, "The Quality of Life, the Sanctity of Life," *Hastings Center Report* 6, no. 2 (1975): 22-26; idem, "To Save or Let Die: The Dilemma of Modern Medicine," *Journal of the American Medical Association* 229 (1974): 172-76.

15. John A. Robertson, "Dilemma in Danville," *Hastings Center Report* 11, no. 5 (1981): 5-8; Jeff Lyon, *Playing God in the Nursery* (New York: Norton, 1985), 199-200, describing "Baby Houle"; In re Philip B., 92 Cal App 3d 796, 156 Cal Reporter 48 (1979).

16. Al Jonsen, Roderick Phibbs, William H. Tooley, and Michale J. Garland, "Critical Issues in Newborn Intensive Care: A Conference Report and Policy Proposal," *Pediatrics* 55 (1975): 756-68.

17. I. David Todres, D. Krane, M. C. Howell, and D. C. Shannon, "Pediatricians' Attitudes Affecting Decision-Making in Defective Newborns," ibid. 60 (1977): 97-201; Anthony Shaw, Justin G. Randolph, and B. Manard, "Ethical Issues in Pediatric Surgery: A National Survey of Pediatricians and Pediatric Surgeons," ibid., 588-99.

18. I. David Todres, Jeanne Guillemin, Michael A. Grodin, and David Batten, "Life-saving Therapy for Newborns: A Questionnaire Survey in the State of Massachusetts," ibid. 81 (1988): 643-49.

19. I. David Todres, Jeanne Guillemin, and Anita Catlin, "Moral and Ethical Dilemmas in Critically Ill Newborns: A Twenty-year Follow-up Survey of Massachusetts Pediatricians," *Journal of Perinatology* 20 (2000): 6-12.

20. Steven B. Morse, James L. Haywood, Robert L. Goldenberg, Janet Bronstein, Kathleen Nelson, and Carlo A. Waldemar, "Estimation of Neonatal Outcome and Perinatal Therapy Use," *Pediatrics* 105 (2000): 1046-50.

21. Jeanne H. Guillemin and Lynda L. Holmstrom, *Mixed Blessings: Intensive Care for Newborns* (New York: Oxford University Press, 1986), 2, 17.

22. Renee Anspach, *Deciding Who Lives: Fateful Choices in the Intensive Care Nursery* (Berkeley and Los Angeles: University of California Press, 1993), 22, 58, 22.

23. Robert F. Weir, "Pediatric Ethics Committees: Ethical Advisers or Legal Watchdogs?" *Law, Medicine and Health Care* 15, no. 3 (1987): 99-109.

24. James M. Gustafson, "Moral Discourse about Medicine: A Variety of Forms," *Journal of Medicine and Philosophy* 15 (1990): 125-42; Renee C. Fox and Judith P. Swazey, "Leaving the Field," *Hastings Center Report* 22, no. 5 (1992): 9-15.

25. Leon R. Kass, "Practicing Ethics: Where's the Action?" *Hastings Center Report* 20, no. 1 (1990): 5–12; George J. Annas, "Ethics Committees: From Ethical Comfort to Ethical Cover." *Hastings Center Report* 21, no. 3 (1991): 18–21.

Two. Passing Out in the NICU

1. Emily Martin, *The Woman in the Body: A Cultural Analysis of Reproduction* (Boston: Beacon, 1992).
2. Annie Oakley, *Essays on Women, Medicine, and Health* (Edinburgh: Edinburgh University Press, 1993).

Three. Learning about Death and Dying

1. Rachel MacKenzie, *Risk* (New York: Viking, 1970).
2. Robert Pensack and Dwight Williams, *Raising Lazarus* (New York: Putnam, 1994).
3. Kenzaburo Oe, *A Personal Matter*, trans. John Nathan (New York: Grove, 1969), 17.
4. Lorrie Moore, *Birds of America* (New York: Knopf, 1998), 237–38.
5. Lakshmipathi Chelluri, Michael R. Pinsky, Michael P. Donahoe, and Ake Grenvik, "Long-Term Outcome of Critically Ill Elderly Patients Requiring Intensive Care," *Journal of the American Medical Association* 269 (1993): 3119–23.
6. Saroj Saigal, Barbara L. Stoskopf, David Feeny, William Furlong, Elizabeth Burrows, Peter L. Rosenbaum, and Lorraine Hoult, "Differences in Preferences for Neonatal Outcomes among Health Care Professionals, Parents, and Adolescents," ibid. 281 (1999): 1991–97.
7. D. K. Stevenson, L. L. Wright, J. A. Lemons, et al., "Very Low Birth Weight Outcomes of the National Institute of Child Health and Human Development Neonatal Research Network, January 1993 through December 1994," *American Journal of Obstetrics and Gynecology* 179 (1998): 1632–39.
8. Samuel Shem, *The House of God* (New York: Dell, 1978).

Four. Standards of Care

1. H. R. Arkes, R. L. Wortman, P. D. Saville, and A. R. Harkness, "Hindsight Bias among Physicians Weighting the Likelihood of Diagnosis," *Journal of Applied Psychology* 66 (1981): 252–54.
2. William L. Meadow, John Lantos, and R. R. Tanz, "Ought Standard Care Be the Standard of Care? A Study of the Time to Administration of Antibiotics in Children with Meningitis," *American Journal of Diseases in Childhood* 147 (1993): 40–44. Other literature on this question supplements our empirical findings. See, e.g., C. S. Bryan, K. L. Reynolds, and L. Crout, "Promptness of Antibiotic Therapy in Acute Bacterial Meningitis," *Annals of Emergency Medicine* 15 (1986): 544–57.
3. Christian F. Poets and Benjamin Sens, "Changes in Intubation Rates and Out-

come of Very Low Birth Weight Infants: A Population-Based Study," *Pediatrics* 98 (1996): 24-27; Jeffrey B. Gould, William Benitz, and Hao Liu, "Mortality and Time to Death in Very Low Birth Weight Infants: California, 1987 and 1993," ibid. 105 (2000): E37; Neil N. Finer, Jeffrey D. Horbar, and Joseph H. Carpenter, "Cardiopulmonary Resuscitation in the Very Low Birth Weight Infant: The Vermont Oxford Network Experience," ibid. 104 (1999): 428-34.

4. Guillemin and Holmstrom, *Mixed Blessings,* 114-15.

5. A. Neiberg, "Trends in American Medicine: Problems for the Defense Expert," *Medicine and Law* 15 (1996): 417-24.

6. Scott B. Ransom, Mitchell P. Dombrowski, Raenn Shephard, and Michael Leonardi, "The Economic Cost of the Medical-Legal Tort System," *American Journal of Obstetrics and Gynecology* 174 (1996): 1903-7.

7. Troyen A. Brennan, Colin M. Sox, and Helen R. Burstin, "Relation between Negligent Adverse Events and the Outcomes of Medical-Malpractice Litigation," *New England Journal of Medicine* 335 (1996): 1963-67; Anita Karcz, Robert Korn, Mary C. Burke, Richard Caggiano, Michael J. Doyle, Michael Erdos, Errol D. Green, and Kenneth Williams, "Malpractice Claims against Emergency Physicians in Massachusetts: 1975-1993," *American Journal of Emergency Medicine* 14 (1996): 341-45.

Five. Prognostication and Futility

1. Willard Gaylin, Leon Kass, Edward D. Pellegrino, and Mark Siegler, "Doctors Must Not Kill," *Journal of the American Medical Association* 259 (1989): 2139-40.

2. Arthur L. Herbst, "Diethylstilbestrol and Other Sex Hormones during Pregnancy," *Obstetrics and Gynecology* 58 (1981): 35S-40S; S. A. De Jong, J. G. Demeter, H. Jarosz, et al., "Thyroid Carcinoma and Hyperparathyroidism after Radiation Therapy for Adolescent Acne Vulgaris," *Surgery* 110 (1991): 691-95; C. G. Newman, "The Thalidomide Syndrome: Risks of Exposure and Spectrum of Malformations," *Clinical Perinatology* 13 (1986): 555-73; Silverman, "Diagnosis and Treatment."

3. Steven Neu and Carl M. Kjellstrand, "Stopping Long-Term Dialysis: An Empirical Study of Withdrawal of Life-Supporting Treatment," *New England Journal of Medicine* 314 (1986): 14-20.

4. Mark D. Silverstein, Carol B. Stocking, Jay P. Antel, and Mark Siegler, "Amyotrophic Lateral Sclerosis and Life-Sustaining Therapy: Patients' Desires for Information, Participation in Decision Making, and Life-Sustaining Therapy," *Mayo Clinic Proceedings* 66, no. 9 (1991): 906-13.

5. Lewis Thomas, *The Youngest Science: Notes of a Medicine Watcher* (New York: Penguin, 1995).

6. Renee Dubos, *The Mirage of Health: Utopias, Progress, and Biological Change* (New York: Harper & Row, 1959); Ivan Illych, *Medical Nemesis: The Expropriation of Health* (New York: Pantheon, 1976); Daniel Callahan, *False Hopes: Why America's Quest for Perfect Health Is a Recipe for Failure* (New York: Simon & Schuster, 1998).

7. Arnold S. Relman, "The Saikewicz Decision: Judges as Physicians," *New England Journal of Medicine* 298 (1978): 508-9.

8. Bernie Lo, "Behind Closed Doors: Promises and Pitfalls of Ethics Committees," ibid. 317 (1987): 46-50.

9. Pius XII, "Address to Those Taking Part in the Ninth Congress of the Italian Anesthesiological Society, 1957," *AAS* 49 (1957): 146-50.

10. Gabriel J. Escobar, Allen Fischer, David K. Li, Richard Kremers, and Mary Anne Armstrong, "Score for Neonatal Acute Physiology: Validation in Three Kaiser Permanente Neonatal Intensive Care Units," *Pediatrics* 96 (1995): 918-22; J. P. Sherck and C. H. Shatney, "ICU Scoring Systems Do Not Allow Prediction of Patient Outcomes or Comparison of ICU Performance," *Critical Care Clinics* 12 (July 1996): 515-23; Anthony A. Meyer, W. Joseph Messick, Peter Young, Christopher C. Baker, Samir Fakhry, Fuad Muakkassa, Edward J. Rutherford, Lean M. Napolitano, and Robert Rutledge, "Prospective Comparison of Clinical Judgment and APACHE II Score in Predicting the Outcome in Critically Ill Surgical Patients," *Journal of Trauma* 32, no. 6 (1992): 747-53.

11. T. Michael O'Shea, Kurt L. Klinepeter, and D. J. Goldstein, "Survival and Developmental Disability in Infants with Birth Weights of 501 to 800 Grams, Born between 1979 and 1994," *Pediatrics* 100 (1997): 982-86.

12. John E. Tyson, Neil Younes, Joel Verter, and Lynda L. Wright, "Viability, Morbidity, and Resource Use among Newborns of 501- to 800-G Birth Weight," *Journal of the American Medical Association* 276 (1996): 1645-51.

13. William Meadow, T. Reimshisel, and John Lantos, "Birth Weight–Specific Mortality for Extremely Low Birth Weight Infants Vanishes by Four Days of Life: Epidemiology and Ethics in the Neonatal Intensive Care Unit," *Pediatrics* 97 (1996): 636-43.

14. William Meadow, John D. Lantos, Mani Mokalla, and T. Reimschisel, "Distributive Justice across Generations: Epidemiology of ICU Care for the Very Young and the Very Old," *Clinical Perinatology* 23 (1996): 583-95.

15. John Kattwinkel, Susan Niermeyer, Vinay Nadkarni, and B. Phillips, "Resuscitation of the Newly Born Infant: An Advisory Statement from the Pediatric Working Group of the International Liaison Committee on Resuscitation," *Resuscitation* 40 (1999): 71-88, also in *European Journal of Pediatrics* 158 (1999): 345-58; Steven N. Wall and John C. Partridge, "Death in the Intensive Care Nursery: Physician Practice of Withdrawing and Withholding Life Support," *Pediatrics* 99 (1997): 64-70; John D. Lantos, William Meadow, Edem E. Kwo, Steven Miles, and Mark Siegler, "Providing and Foregoing Resuscitative Therapy for Babies of Very Low Birthweight," *Journal of Clinical Ethics* 3 (1992): 283-87.

16. Laura Frain, Yaya Ren, Alexander Meadow, John Lantos, and William Meadow, "Certainty, Uncertainty, and Accuracy of Daily Predictions of Non-Survival in the NICU: We're Often Wrong but Rarely in Doubt," *Pediatric Research* 43 (1998): 29A.

Six. Consent, Communication, Shared Decision Making

1. Mark Siegler, "Searching for Moral Certainty in Medicine: A Proposal for a New Model of the Doctor-Patient Encounter," *Bulletin of the New York Academy of Medicine* 57 (1981): 56–69.

2. Albert Camus, *The Stranger* (New York: Vintage, 1942), 121, 112.

3. Robert F. Johnson Jr., Teresa Baranowski-Birkmeier, and John B. O'Donnell, "Advance Directives in the Medical Intensive Care Unit of a Community Teaching Hospital," *Chest* 107 (1995): 752–56; M. A. Burg, C. McCarty, W. L. Allen, and D. Denslow, "Advance Directives: Population Prevalence and Demand in Florida," *Journal of the Florida Medical Association* 82, no. 12 (1995): 811–14; Jay A. Jacobson, Eric Kasworm, and Margaret P. Battin, "Advance Directives in Utah: Information from Death Certificates and Informants," *Archives of Internal Medicine* 156 (1996): 1862–68; Bernard J. Hammes and Brenda L. Rooney, "Death and End-Of-Life Planning in One Midwestern Community," ibid. 158 (1998): 383–90.

4. Linda Emanuel, "Structured Advance Planning: Is It Finally Time for Physician Action and Reimbursement?" *Journal of the American Medical Association* 274 (1995): 501–3.

5. Leslie J. Blackhall, "Must We Always Use CPR?" *New England Journal of Medicine* 317 (1987): 1281–85.

6. Amnon Halevy and Baruch A. Brody, "A Multi-Institution Collaborative Policy on Medical Futility," *Journal of the American Medical Association* 276 (1996): 571–74.

7. Marcia Angell, "The Case of Helga Wanglie: A New Kind of 'Right to Die' Case," *New England Journal of Medicine* 325 (1991): 511–12; John J. Paris, Robert K. Crone, and Frank Reardon, "Physicians' Refusal of Requested Treatment: The Case of Baby L," ibid. 322 (1990): 1012–15.

8. George J. Annas, "Baby Doe Redux: Doctors As Child Abusers," *Hastings Center Report* 13, no. 5 (1983): 26–27; N. K. Rhoden and J. D. Arras, "Withholding Treatment from Baby Doe: From Discrimination to Child Abuse," *Milbank Memorial Fund Quarterly of Health and Society* 63 (1985): 18–51.

9. John Lantos, Zaiga Robins, and William Meadow, "Negotiating Neonatal Deaths—Bioethical Dreams and Emotional Realities," *Pediatric Research* 45 (1999): 347.

10. Daniel Callahan, "Modernizing Mortality: Medical Progress and the Good Society," *Hastings Center Report* 20, no. 1 (1990): 28–32.

11. Larry O. Gostin, "Deciding Life and Death in the Courtroom. From Quinlan to Cruzan, Glucksberg, and Vacco—A Brief History and Analysis of Constitutional Protection of the 'Right to Die,'" *Journal of the American Medical Association* 278, no. 18 (1997): 1523–28; Deon M. Cox and Greg A. Sachs, "Advance Directives and the Patient Self-Determination Act," *Clinics in Geriatric Medicine* 10 (1994): 431–43; Steven H. Miles, R. Koepp, and E. P. Weber, "Advance End-of-Life Treatment Planning: A Research Review," *Archives of Internal Medicine* 156 (1996): 1062–68.

12. Joan M. Teno, K. J. Branco, V. Mor, C. D. Phillips, C. Hawes, J. Morris, and B. E. Fries, "Changes in Advance Care Planning in Nursing Homes Before and After

the Patient Self-Determination Act: Report of a Ten-State Survey," *Journal of the American Geriatrics Society* 45 (1997): 939-44; Jacobson, Kasworm, and Battin, "Advance Directives in Utah"; F. J. Landry, K. Kroenke, C. Lucas, and J. Reeder, "Increasing the Use of Advance Directives in Medical Outpatients," *Journal of General Internal Medicine* 12 (1997): 412-15; Paul R. Dexter, Frederick D. Wolinsky, Gregory P. Gramelspacher, Zhou Xiao-Hua, George J. Eckert, Marina Waisburd, and William M. Tierney, "Effectiveness of Computer-Generated Reminders for Increasing Discussions about Advance Directives and Completion of Advance Directive Forms: A Randomized, Controlled Trial," *Annals of Internal Medicine* 128 (1988): 102-10; John E. Heffner, Bonnie Fahy, Lana Hilling, and Celia Barbieri Celia, "Outcomes of Advance Directive Education of Pulmonary Rehabilitation Patients," *American Journal of Respiratory and Critical Care Medicine* 155, no. 3 (1997): 1055-59; Joan M. Teno, Sheila Licks, Joan Lynn, N. Wegner, and William Knaus, "Do Advance Directives Provide Instructions That Direct Care? SUPPORT Investigators Study to Understand Prognoses and Preferences for Outcomes and Risks of Treatment," *Journal of the American Geriatrics Society* 45 (1997): 508-12; "A Controlled Trial to Improve Care for Seriously Ill Hospitalized Patients: The Study to Understand Prognoses and Preferences for Outcomes and Risks of Treatments (SUPPORT)," *Journal of the American Medical Association* 274 (1995): 1591-98; Johnson, Baranowski-Birkmeier, and O'Donnell, "Advance Directives in the Medical Intensive Care Unit."

13. Mark Goodman, Michael Tarnoff, and George Slotman, "Effect of Advance Directives on the Management of Elderly Critically Ill Patients," *Critical Care Medicine* 26 (1998): 701-4.

14. Fyodor Dostoevsky, *The Brothers Karamazov*, trans. Constance Garnett (New York: Signet, 1957), 251-52.

15. Alan Shapiro, *Vigil* (Chicago: University Of Chicago Press, 1997).

16. Unpublished interview conducted as part of an ongoing study. For an abstract of the study, see Lantos, Robins, and Meadow, "Negotiating Neonatal Deaths."

17. Oe, *A Personal Matter*, 74-76.

18. Dostoevsky, *Brothers Karamazov*, 556-57.

Seven. Getting Paid

1. T. A. Brennan, C. M. Sox, and H. R. Burstin, "Relation between Negligent Adverse Events and the Outcomes of Medical-Malpractice Litigation." *New England Journal of Medicine* 335 (1996): 1963-67.

2. Stephen J. Spurr and Walter O. Simmons, "Medical Malpractice in Michigan: An Economic Analysis," *Journal of Health Politics, Policy and Law* 21 (1996): 315-46.

3. Guido Calabresi and Philip Bobbit, *Tragic Choices* (New Haven: Yale University Press, 1976).

4. M. I. Harrison and J. Calltorp, "The Reorientation of Market-Oriented Reforms in Swedish Health-Care," *Health Policy* 50 (2000): 219-40.

5. Jacob S. Hacker, "National Health Care Reform: An Idea Whose Time Came

and Went," *Journal of Health Politics, Policy and Law* 21 (1996): 647-96; R. J. Blendon, D. E. Altman, J. Benson, M. Brodie, M. James, and G. Chervinsky, "Health Care Policy Implications of the 1994 Congressional Elections," *Journal of the American Medical Association* 273 (1995): 671-74.

6. Larry R. Churchill, "The United States Health Care System under Managed Care: How the Commodification of Health Care Distorts Ethics and Threatens Equity," *Health Care Analysis* 7 (1999): 393-411.

7. R. C. Stevenson, C. J. McCabe, P. O. Pharoah, and R. W. Cooke, "Cost of Care for a Geographically Determined Population of Low Birthweight Infants to Age 8-9 Years. I. Children without Disability," *Archives of Diseases of Childhood, Fetal and Neonatal Edition* 74, no. 2 (1996): F114-17.

8. Michael H. Boyle, George W. Torrance, John C. Sinclair, and Sargent P. Horwood, "Economic Evaluation of Neonatal Intensive Care of Very-Low-Birth-Weight Infants," *New England Journal of Medicine* 308 (1983): 1330-37.

9. U.S. Department of Health and Human Services, *Health United States 1995,* PHS 96-1232 (Hyattsville, Md., May 1996), 203.

10. Daniel M. Hughes, Marjorie McLeod, Barry Garner, and Richard B. Goldbloom, "Controlled Trial of a Home and Ambulatory Program for Asthmatic Children," *Pediatrics* 87 (1991): 54-61; Barbara Morray and Gregory Redding, "Factors Associated with Prolonged Hospitalization of Children with Asthma," *Archives of Pediatrics and Adolescent Medicine* 149 (1995): 276-79; Remy A. Hirasing, H. Marten Reeser, Regina de Groot, Dirk Ruwaard, Stef Van Buren, and S. Paulina Vervloove-Vanhorick, "Trends in Hospital Admissions among Children Aged 0-19 Years with Type I Diabetes in the Netherlands," *Diabetes Care* 19 (1996): 431-34; J. P. Pestian, C. S. Derkay, and C. Ritter, "Outpatient Tonsillectomy and Adenoidectomy Clinical Pathways: An Evaluative Study," *American Journal of Otolaryngology* 19 (1998): 45-49; N. C. Saenz, K. C. Conlon, D. C. Aronson, and M. P. Laquaglia, "The Application of Minimal Access Procedures in Infants, Children, and Young Adults with Pediatric Malignancies," *Journal of Laparoscopy and Advanced Surgical Techniques* 7 (1997): 289-94.

11. Pierre Wacker, Daniel S. Halperin, Marinette Wyss, and James Humbert, "Early Hospital Discharge of Children with Fever and Neutropenia: A Prospective Study," *Journal of Pediatric Hematology/Oncology* 19 (1997): 208-11.

12. Jeffrey W. Stoltz and Marie C. McCormick, "Restricting Access to Neonatal Intensive Care: Effect on Mortality and Economic Savings," *Pediatrics* 101 (1998): 344-48.

13. Rasa Gustaitis and Ernle Young, *A Time to Be Born, a Time to Die: Conflicts and Ethics in an Intensive Care Nursery* (Reading, Mass.: Addison-Wesley, 1986), 212.

14. John D. Lantos, "Baby Doe Five Years Later: Implications for Child Health," *New England Journal of Medicine* 317 (1987): 444-47.

15. David L. Sloss, "The Right to Choose How to Die: A Constitutional Analysis of State Laws Prohibiting Physician-Assisted Suicide," *Stanford Law Review* 48 (1996): 937-73; Amnon Goldworth, "Human Rights and the Omission or Cessation of Treatment for Infants," *Journal of Perinatology* 9 (1989): 79-82.

16. John A. Robertson, "Legal Aspects of Withholding Treatment from Handicapped Newborns: Substantive Issues," *Journal of Health, Political Policy and Law* 11 (1986): 215–30.

17. T. Joyce et al., "A Cost-Effectiveness Analysis of Strategies to Reduce Infant Mortality," *Medical Care* 26 (1988): 348–60.

18. Anders Ericson, Jan Gunnarskog, Bengt Kallen, and Petra O. Olausson, "A Registry Study of Very Low Birthweight Liveborn Infants in Sweden, 1973–1988," *Acta Obstetrics and Gynecology of Scandinavia* 71, no. 2 (1992): 104–11; Bernard Guyer, Marian F. MacDorman, Joyce A. Martin, Kimberly Peters, and Donna Strobino, "Annual Summary of Vital Statistics—1997," *Pediatrics* 102 (1998): 1333–49.

19. S. Cnattingius and B. Haglund, "Socio-Economic Factors and Feto-Infant Mortality," *Scandinavian Journal of Social Medicine* 20 (1992): 11–13.

20. Peter A. Gorski, "Perinatal Outcome and the Social Contract—Interrelationships between Health and Humanity," *Journal of Perinatology* 18 (1998): 297–301.

21. Paul R. Dwyer, "The Regional Organization of Special Care for the Neonate," *Pediatric Clinics of North America* 17 (1970): 761–76.

22. Jerold F. Lucey, "Why We Should Regionalize Perinatal Care," *Pediatrics* 52 (1973): 488–91; H. S. Chiu, J. F. Vogt, L. S. Chan, and C. E. Rother, "Regionalization of Infant Transports: The Southern California Experience and Its Implications. I: Referral Pattern," *Journal of Perinatology* 13 (1993): 288–96.

23. R. B. Thomson, "Competition among Hospitals in the United States," *Health Policy* 27 (1994): 205–31.

24. James C. Robinson, Deborah W. Garnick, and Stephen J. McPhee, "Market and Regulatory Influences on the Availability of Coronary Angioplasty and Bypass Surgery in U.S. Hospitals," *New England Journal of Medicine* 317 (1987): 85–90.

25. David R. Thiemann, Josef Coresh, William J. Oetgen, and Neil R. Powe, "The Association between Hospital Volume and Survival after Acute Myocardial Infarction in Elderly Patients," ibid. 340 (1999): 1640–48.

26. Marie C. McCormick and David K. Richardson, "Access to Neonatal Intensive Care," *Future of Children* 5 (1995): 162–75; S. A. Cooke, R. M. Schwartz, and D. E. Gagnon, *The Perinatal Partnership: An Approach to Organizing Care in the 1990s. Project #12129* (Providence, R.I.: National Perinatal Information Center, 1988); David K. Richardson, K. Reed, J. C. Cutler, et al., "Perinatal Regionalization versus Hospital Competition: The Hartford Example," *Pediatrics* 96 (1995): 417–23.

27. Steven M. Shortell and E. F. Hughes, "The Effects of Regulation, Competition, and Ownership on Mortality Rates among Hospital Inpatients," *New England Journal of Medicine* 318 (1988): 1100–1107.

Eight. Home Births

1. Brett Williams, *John Henry: A Bio-Bibliography* (Westport, Conn.: Greenwood, 1983), 3–6.

2. Gosta Sandstrom, *Tunnels* (New York: Holt, Reinhardt, Winston, 1963), 55.

3. L. Chappel, *John Henry: A Folk-Lore Study* (reprint, Port Washington, N.Y.: Kennikat, 1968), 61–70.

4. Williams, *John Henry,* 3.

5. Alex Kotlowitz, *There Are No Children Here* (New York: Doubleday, 1991); Jonathan Kozol, *Amazing Grace: The Lives of Children and The Conscience of a Nation* (New York: Crown, 1995).

6. Richard Powers, *Operation Wandering Soul* (New York: Harper Perennial, 1994), 283.

7. Charles J. Dougherty, "Tradition, Mission, and the Market: Faith in Ultimate Purposefulness Makes Catholic Healthcare Different," *Health Progress* 78, no. 4 (1997): 44–51; Bruce C. Vladeck, "Market Realities Meet Balanced Government: Another Look at Columbia/HCA," *Health Affairs* 17, no. 2 (1998): 37–39.

8. Robert M. Kliegman, "Neonatal Technology, Perinatal Survival, Social Consequences, and the Perinatal Paradox," *American Journal of Public Health* 85 (1995): 909–13.

Nine. Mistakes in Context

1. Some of the ideas in this chapter were developed in John D. Lantos and Martha Montello, "Mistakes in Context," in *Margin of Error: The Ethics of Mistakes in the Practice of Medicine,* ed. Susan B. Rubin and Lauri Zoloth (Hagerstown, Md.: University Publishing Group, 2000), 73–84.

2. Clifford Geertz, "Fact and Law in Comparative Perspective," in *Local Knowledge* (Princeton: Princeton University Press, 1985), 12.

3. Mark Twain, *The Adventures of Huckleberry Finn* (New York: Modern Library, 1948), 191.

4. Steven H. Woolf, "Screening for Prostate Cancer with Prostate-Specific Antigen: An Examination of the Evidence," *New England Journal of Medicine* 333 (1995): 1401–5.

5. Arnold R. Eiser and Dena J. Seiden, "Discontinuing Dialysis in Persistent Vegetative State: The Roles of Autonomy, Community, and Professional Moral Agency," *American Journal of Kidney Disease* 30 (1997): 291–96.

6. George J. Annas, "Temporary Use of the Artificial Heart before Transplantation," *New England Journal of Medicine* 317 (1987): 314–15.

7. P. Musgrove, "Public Spending on Health Care: How Are Different Criteria Related?" *Health Policy* 47 (1999): 207–23.

8. M. G. Marmot, G. M. Kogevinas, and M. A. Elston, "Social/Economic Status and Disease," *Annual Review of Public Health* 8 (1987): 111–35.

9. Shem, *House of God,* 238.

10. A. B. Yehoshua, *Open Heart* (New York: Doubleday, 1996), 116.

11. For further discussion of these themes, see John D. Lantos, "Open Heart (Shiva M'Hodu)," *Annals of the New York Academy of Sciences* 913 (2000): 41–51.

12. Robert Stinson and Peggy Stinson, *The Long Dying of Baby Andrew* (Boston: Little, Brown, 1983).

13. Helen Harrison, "The Principles for Family-Centered Neonatal Care," *Pediatrics* 92 (1993): 643–50.

Ten. Closing Argument

Epigraph: Richard Smith, "Informed Consent: Edging Forwards (and Backwards)," *British Medical Journal* 316 (1998): 949–51.

1. John J. Paris, J. P. Goldsmith, and M. Cimperman, "Resuscitation of a Micro-preemie: The Case of Macdonald v. Milleville," *Journal of Perinatology* 18 (1998): 302–5.

2. Michael T. Hynan, "Helping Parents Cope with a High-Risk Birth: Terror, Grief, Impotence, and Anger," <http://www.uwm.edu:80/people/hynan/minnaep.html>.

3. R. Demie, M. T. Hynan, H. Harris, and R. Manniello, "Perinatal Stressors as Predictors of Symptoms of Post-Traumatic Stress in Mothers of Infants at High-Risk," *Journal of Perinatology* 16 (1996): 276–80.

4. William A. Silverman, "Overtreatment of Neonates? A Personal Retrospective," *Pediatrics* 90 (1992): 971–76. See also comments on Silverman in ibid. 91 (1993): 169–71 and 92 (1993): 187–88, 509.

5. Silverman, "Overtreatment of Neonates?"

6. Stinson and Stinson, *The Long Dying of Baby Andrew.*

7. Harrison, "Principles for Family-Centered Neonatal Care."

8. Guillemin and Holmstrom, *Mixed Blessings,* 139.

9. Shoo K. Lee, Pauline L. Penner, and Margaret Cox, "Comparison of the Attitudes of Health Care Professionals and Parents toward Active Treatment of Very Low Birth Weight Infants," *Pediatrics* 99 (1991): 110–14, quotation on 112.

10. M. Norup, "Limits of Neonatal Treatment: A Survey of Attitudes in the Danish Population," *Journal of Medical Ethics* 24 (1998): 200–206.

11. David A. Waller, I. David Todres, Ned H. Cassem, and Ande Anderten, "Coping with Poor Prognosis in the Pediatric Intensive Care Unit: The Cassandra Prophecy," *American Journal of Diseases in Childhood* 133 (1979): 1121–25, quotations on 1122.

12. J. Rogowski, "Cost-Effectiveness of Care for Very Low Birth Weight Infants," *Pediatrics* 102 (1998): 35–43.

13. G. W. Chance, "Neonatal Intensive Care and Cost Effectiveness," *Canadian Medical Association Journal* 139 (1988): 943–46.

14. Marie C. McCormick, "The Contribution of Low Birth Weight to Infant Mortality and Childhood Morbidity," *New England Journal of Medicine* 312 (1985): 82–90; Maureen Hack and Avroy A. Fanaroff, "Outcomes of Children of Extremely Low Birthweight and Gestational Age in the 1990's," *Early Human Development* 53 (1999): 193–218.

15. Betty R. Vohr, Linda L. Wright, Anna M. Dusick, Lisa Mele, Neal P. Simon, Dee C. Wilson, Sue Broyles, Charles R. Bauer, Virginia Delaney-Black, Kimberly A. Yolton, Barry E. Fleisher, Lu-Ann Papile, and Michael D. Kaplan, "Neurodevel-

opmental and Functional Outcomes of Extremely Low Birth Weight Infants in the National Institute of Child Health and Human Development Neonatal Research Network, 1993–1994," *Pediatrics* 105 (2000): 1216-26.

16. V. Bhushan, Nigel Paneth, and John L. Kiely, "Impact of Improved Survival of Very Low Birth Weight Infants on Recent Secular Trends in the Prevalence of Cerebral Palsy," ibid. 91 (1993): 1094-1100.

17. T. Michael O'Shea, John S. Preisser, K. L. Klinepeter, and R. G. Dillard, "Trends in Mortality and Cerebral Palsy in a Geographically Based Cohort of Very Low Birth Weight Neonates Born between 1982 to 1994," ibid. 101 (1998): 642-47.

18. Oe, *A Personal Matter,* 88.

INDEX

182   *Index*

Parents/family (continued)
3, 45; doctors' communication with,
87–95; fear of overtreatment by, 159;
guilt and responsibility of, 100–105,
162–64; individual implications of treatment choice of, 162–64; informed consent of, 82, 84, 86–88; post-traumatic
stress disorder among, 158; refusal of
treatment by, xii–xiii, 16–18, 29, 89
Penner, Pauline, 159
Pensack, Robert, 42–43
"Playing God," 17, 111
Pope Pius XII, 72
Post-traumatic stress disorder, 158
Poverty, 140; Appalachian health care and,
123–32
Premature infants, xi, 6–7; futile treatment
for, 78, 80, 89–90; historical management of, 12–15; illness severity scores of,
75–76; length of hospital stay of, 114;
long-term complications in, 9–10, 14,
47–48, 75, 160–62; moral claims of, 117;
in NICU, 25–28, 40, 44–45; specialist
care for, 13–14, 19–20, 26, 29; survival
of, xii, 9, 19, 33, 46–47, 76–80. *See also*
Low-birthweight infants
Preventive pediatric care, 116–18, 135
Profitability of NICUs, 115–17, 160
Prognostication, 9, 10, 64–81; for adult
ICU patients, 77; birthweight and,
46–47, 76–77; Cassandra complex and,
160; illness severity scores for, 75–76;
length of survival and, 77; of neurological deficits, 162; race, gender and, 76–77;
response to therapy and, 77–78

Quality of life, 17, 54

Racial effects on survival, 76–77
Raising Lazarus, 42–43
Referral centers, 5, 13, 14
Refusal of treatment, xii–xiii, 16–18, 29,
65, 89
Regionalized perinatal networks, 119–21
Respiratory distress syndrome, 14, 15, 159

Risk, 41–42
Robertson, John, 16

Saigal, Saroj, 45
Sandberg, Carl, 10
Sarah Morris Hospital, 13, 19
Scarlet Letter, The, 148–49
Schiedermayer, David, 45
Shapiro, Alan, 100
Shaw, Anthony, 18
Shem, Samuel, 51, 151–52, 155
Shortell, Steven, 120
Silverman, William, 12, 15, 159, 160
Smith, Richard, 157
Social inequalities, 109–10
Spiritual resources, 72–73
Standards of care, 54–63; actual practice
and, 59–60, 62, 63; authorities for,
56–57; for discussions about discontinu-
ing life-sustaining treatment, 95; mal-
practice litigation and, 57–63; negli-
gence and, 1, 58, 59, 62; process of
defining, 57
Stinson, Peggy, 159, 160
Stinson, Robert, 159, 160
Stranger, The, 86
Suicide, 65
SUPPORT Study, 96
Survival of premature infants, 33, 76–80,
115, 141; ambiguity about chances for,
56; birthweight and, 46–47, 76–77; after
discontinuation of treatment, xiii, 9, 64,
87; doctors' estimates of, 19; length of,
77; long-term complications and, 9–10,
14, 47–48, 75, 160–62; negative value of
suffering and, 81; prognostication of,
75–80; race, gender and, 76–77; response
to therapy and, 77–78

Tarnier, Etienne Stephane, 12, 13
Technological interventions, 26, 29, 34, 39,
61, 67–71, 74; advance directives and, 65;
88–89, 96–97; cost of, 113; "half-way
technologies," 70–71
Thalidomide, 69